Tobias Scheunchen

Cosmology, Law, and Elites in Late Antiquity: Marriage and Slavery in Zoroastrianism, Eastern Christianity, and Islam

ARBEITSMATERIALIEN ZUM ORIENT

herausgegeben von

Jens Peter Laut, Ulrich Rebstock,
Tilman Seidensticker

Band 32

ERGON VERLAG

Tobias Scheunchen

Cosmology, Law, and Elites in Late Antiquity: Marriage and Slavery in Zoroastrianism, Eastern Christianity, and Islam

ERGON VERLAG

Cover illustration:

Abū Muḥammad al-Qāsim b. ʿAlī b. Muḥammad b. ʿAlī al-Ḥarīrī al-Baṣrī, *Les Makamat de Hariri (Al-Maqāmāt li-l-Ḥarīrī)*, with illustrations by Yaḥyā b. Maḥmūd al-Wāsiṭī (1236–1237), Bibliothèque nationale de France, Ms. Arabe 5847, folio 21r (accessed February 22, 2019, https://gallica.bnf.fr/ark:/12148/btv1b8422965p/f51.item.r=makamat%20de%20hariri#).

The scene depicts a married couple accusing each other before a judge from the *Maqāmāt* of al-Ḥarīrī.

Bibliografische Information der Deutschen Nationalbibliothek
Die Deutsche Nationalbibliothek verzeichnet diese Publikation in der Deutschen Nationalbibliografie; detaillierte bibliografische Daten sind im Internet über http://dnb.d-nb.de abrufbar.

Gedruckt auf alterungsbeständigem Papier.
Satz: Thomas Breier
Umschlaggestaltung: Jan von Hugo

www.ergon-verlag.de

ISSN 1436-8072
ISBN 978-3-95650-467-9 (Print)
ISBN 978-3-95650-468-6 (ePDF)

Acknowledgements

I feel deeply honored and grateful that this thesis, which was written and submitted as a master's thesis at the American University of Beirut (AUB) in 2017, has been selected for publication in Ergon's *Arbeitsmaterialien zum Orient.* Without the relentless and enduring intellectual, personal, and emotional support of Ulrich Rebstock, it would have probably never appeared as a published monograph and most likely been buried in the archives of Jafet Library. Ulrich Rebstock has arguably been my most prolonged and persistent intellectual advisor. Our relationship began in 2011 when I signed up for his famous lecture *Geschichte und Geographie der islamischen Welt.* Since then, our correspondences, admittedly, most often digital, have traveled between the vast landscapes of Germany, Turkey, Lebanon, and most recently the United States. Ulrich Rebstock has not only been an advisor to me but a constant intellectual and personal role model. I am deeply indebted to his inspiration, encouragement, and patience.

I am grateful to the Center for Arab and Middle Eastern Studies (CAMES) at AUB. The tireless support I received from its academic and non-academic staff is unmatched. Mario Kozah, Nader El-Bizri, Dahlia Gubara, Aliya Saidi, and Rima Kanawati need to be specially mentioned. The Islamic Studies' program at CAMES has challenged my scholarly and personal capacities in ways I could not anticipate when I first came to Beirut in 2015. Everybody who has had the joy of studying at AUB for an extended period knows about the unique, critical, and rigorous intellectual environment the university provides for academic and personal growth. It is in that very environment–the Jafet and Saab Medical Libraries and several coffee shops in Beirut–in which this thesis was thought and written.

Without the financial support I received from AUB, I would not have been able to study in its beautiful and stimulating environment.

My admiration and personal gratitude go to Mario Kozah. When I first entered his class *Christian-Muslim Encounters* in 2015, I did not foresee what journeys we would embark on together. He has been a constant source of encouragement and inspiration and accompanied my every step in graduate school–from the first Syriac scribbles up to the last em-dash of this thesis. His unequivocal criticism and honesty have always pushed me to my personal and scholarly limits.

At this point, I would also like to thank my committee members, Lyall Richard Armstrong and John Lash Meloy, for their comments, critical feedback, and support in the process of writing this thesis. I also want to thank Fred Donner and Ahmed El Shamsy for their critical feedback on an earlier version of this thesis.

None of this could have been achieved without meaningful friendships that blossomed during my two years at AUB. I am especially thankful to Janina Santer, Camilla Garder, Jan Altaner, Rabeeh Abou Ismail, Huria Ibrahim, Saleh Moheidly, and Haytham. Their cheerfulness, comfort, warmth, laughter and support always helped to stray off my mind from academic matters and take refuge in the mundane pleasures in and outside of Beirut.

I would also like to thank my parents Silke and Ulrich, my sister Ann-Marie, my grandparents Gerda and Karl-Heinz, and my great-grandmother Gerda who passed away in the initial stages this thesis was written. Their encouragement over all these years of studies has given me the strength to persevere with and achieve my goals. Their uncompromising trust in something they cannot fully appreciate is admirable. My love and profound gratitude are with them.

I also want to thank the friends I have made more recently during my doctoral studies at the University of Chicago. Shehzad Arifeen, Sarah Shaer, Joseph Hermiz, Elon Harvey, Murat Bozluolcay, and Cecilia Palombo have created so many memorable moments and helped me cope with everyday life in the United States. Lastly, I want to thank my partner Samin Rashidbeigi who has been supportive and inspirational during the last two years and with whom I have had the honor and pleasure of traveling the geographical, intellectual, and familial scapes of the United States, Europe, and the Middle East.

I take full responsibility for all errors and incomplete presentations in this thesis. I admit that turning this thesis into a monograph was challenging, given the new and unexpected intellectual avenues I have more recently been familiarized with, in the context of my doctoral studies. While this thesis was admittedly written in ignorance of studies in the fields of anthropology and gender studies, I nevertheless hope that it provides some useful material for more thorough theoretical inquiries into the marital and slavery practices of the Sasanian and Islamic Empires. I also hope that it may contribute to rethinking the place of philology and textual analysis in the study of Islamic law and Late Antiquity and to exposing how reproducing of the same conclusions the uncritical use of specific methodologies may be.

Contents

Illustrations

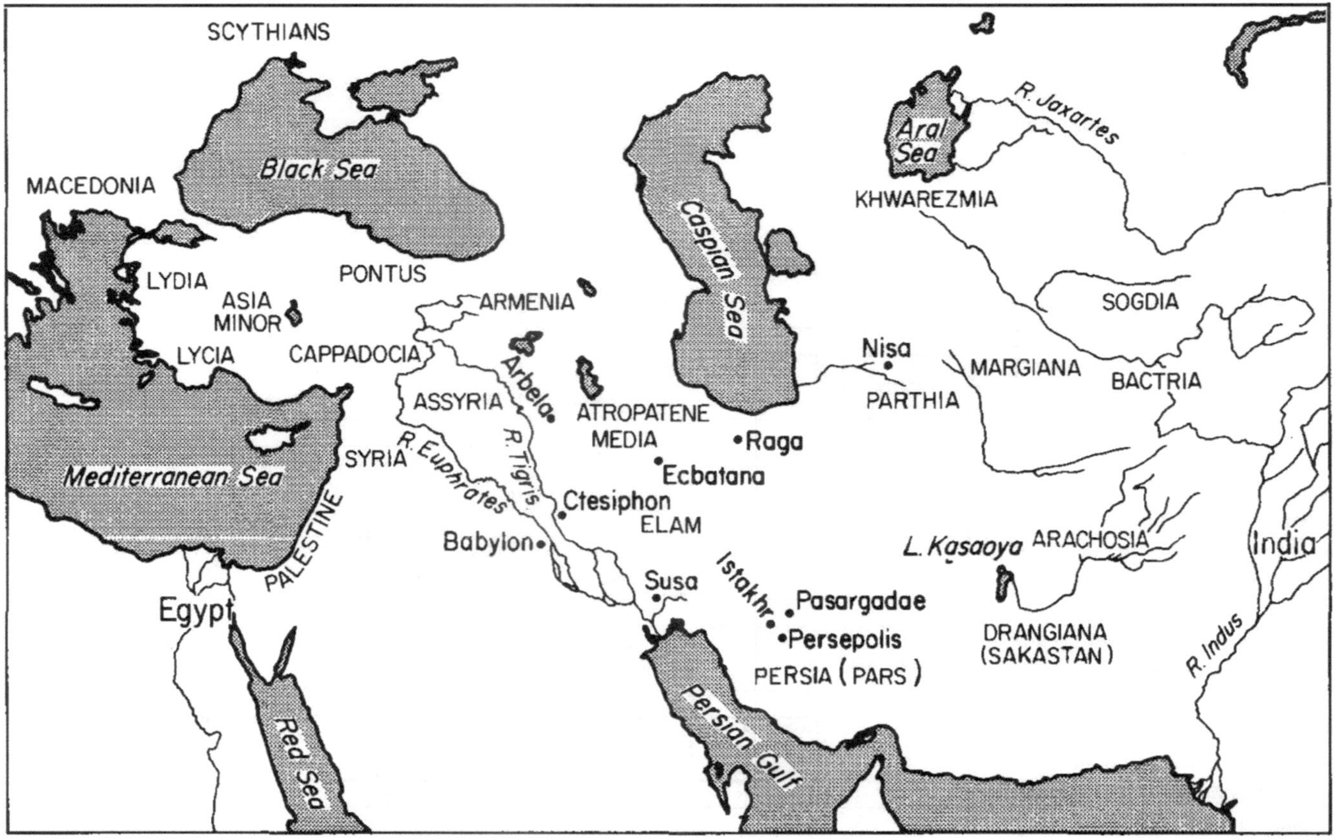

Figure 1: Map of Imperial Iran

From: Mary Boyce, *Zoroastrians. Their Religious Beliefs and Practices* (London, Boston and Henley: Routledge & Kegan Paul, 1979), xx.
[I would like to thank Taylor and Francis for kindly granting me permission to reproduce the above map.]

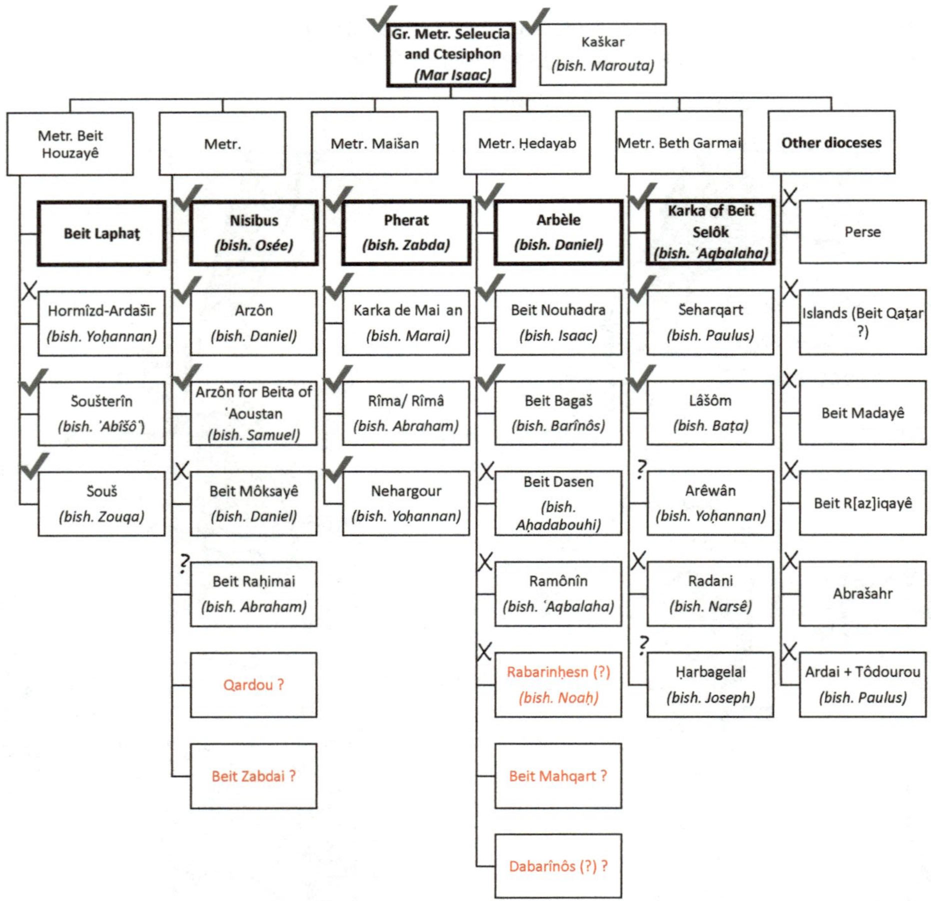

Figure 2: Organization and authority in the Church of the East

General Note:

The scheme has been prepared according to the description of the structure of the (proto-) Church of the East in the Synod of Mar Îsḥaq (410).
Please note that the rules of transliteration for Syriac applied throughout the remainder of this thesis have not been applied here. Rather, the names of cities, regions, and persons are in accordance with the French translation by J.B. Chabot.

Description of the scheme:

Bold lines indicate metropolitans.
Place names highlighted in red indicate textual disagreements leaving uncertainty on whether or not these constituted episcopal seats.
A tick indicates that the bishop mentioned was present at the respective synod, a cross that he was not, a question mark that we do not know exactly.

List of abbreviations

HazDP	*Hazār Dādestān* (Anahit Perikhanian)
HazDM	*Hazār Dādestān* (Maria Macuch)
SynO	*Synodicon Orientale*
CorJ	*Corpus Juris des persischen Erzbischofs Jesubocht*
EheM	*Eherecht des Patriarchen Mâr Abhâ*
MudK	*al-Mudawwana al-Kubrā*
RisF	*al-Risāla fī Uṣūl al-Fiqh*

Note on transliteration

Middle Persian (Pahlavi)

For the transliteration of Middle Persian (Pahlavi), I adhere to the "Transliterationsindex juristischer Termini" and "Transkriptionsindex juristischer Termini" which can be found in Farroḫmard i Wahrāmān, *Rechtskasuistik und Gerichtspraxis zu Beginn des siebenten Jahrhunderts in Iran. Die Rechtssammlung des Farroḫmard i Wahrāmān*, ed., tr., and ct. Maria Macuch (Wiesbaden: Harrassowitz Verlag, 1993), 663–740.

Syriac

The Syriac transliteration corresponds to the rules for East Syriac used in *Gorgias Encyclopedic Dictionary of The Syriac Heritage*, eds. Sebastian P. Brock, Aaron M. Butts, George A. Kiraz and Lucas Van Rompay (Piscataway: Gorgias Press, 2011), x:

Consonants			
ܐ	ʾ	ܠ	l
ܒ	b	ܡ	m
ܓ	g	ܢ	n
ܕ	d	ܣ	s
ܗ	h	ܥ	ʿ
ܘ	w	ܦ	p
ܙ	z	ܨ	ṣ
ܚ	ḥ	ܩ	q
ܛ	ṭ	ܪ	r
ܝ	y	ܫ	š
ܟ	k	ܬ	t

Vowels	
ܒܲ	a
ܒܵ	ā
ܒܸ	e
ܒܹ	ē
ܒܝܼ	i
ܘܿ	o
ܘܼ	u

Diphthongs	
ܒܵܘ	bāw
ܒܵܝ	bāy
ܒܝܼܘ	biw

Arabic

The transliteration for Arabic is in accordance with the *IJMES Transliteration System for Arabic, Persian and Turkish:*

Consonants				
ء	ʾ	ط	ṭ	
ب	b	ظ	ẓ	
ت	t	ع	ʿ	
ث	th	غ	gh	
ج	j	ف	f	
ح	ḥ	ق	q	
خ	kh	ك	k	
د	d	ل	l	
ذ	dh	م	m	
ر	r	ن	n	
ز	z	ه	h	
س	s	و	w	
ش	sh	ي	y	
ص	ṣ	ة	a	*or* at (in constructs)
ض	ḍ	ال	al	*and* -l-

Vowels				
Long	ا or	ى	ā	
		و	ū	
		ي	ī	
Doubled	-ِيّ	iyy	(final form ī)	
	-ُوّ	uww	(final form ū)	
Diphthongs	وَ	au	*or* aw	
	ىَ	ai	*or* ay	
Short	-َ	a		
	-ُ	u		
	-ِ	i		

Chapter I
Introduction

Historians interested in studying the various landscapes and places, empires and dynasties, religions and religious movements, societies and peoples of Late Antiquity may quickly feel perplexed by the seemingly endless imaginative possibilities its spatial and temporal dimensions offer to creative minds. Those ambitious enough to fathom its complex dynamics will have to indulge in the extant Late Antique material culture and a significant number of writings ranging from inscriptions to chronicles, histories, letters, disputations, apologies, refutations, grammars, encyclopedias, manuals, legal texts, and minutes.

Those seeking to turn away from Romanocentric conceptions of Late Antiquity may be intrigued by the domains East and Southeast of the Roman Empire. This region, referred to as the Near or the Middle East, is circumscribed by Asia Minor in the West and the Caucasian highlands in the North. Its Eastern frontier stretches down the Iranian plateau all the way to the Indian Ocean. The Southern coastline of the Arabian Peninsula forms a natural boundary in the South, while Ethiopia and Egypt demarcate its southern and western limits. To begin with, lumping together these territories and localities is neither conditioned naturally by a cohesive topography nor does it accurately reflect the political realities of Late Antiquity. The boundaries delimiting the Near East in Late Antiquity are, except for a few, artificial creations. Those that are not, and operated as actual frontiers, did not resemble the borders of modern nation-states; rather they were porous structures constantly renegotiated and redefined, which accounted for the movement and trade of a vast number of people, animals, and goods.

For those interested in the field a significant number of languages are worthwhile studying. The most important languages of the Late Antique Near East are Hebrew, Aramaic, Arabic, Middle Persian, Armenian, and Ethiopian, not to mention the various dialects, spoken varieties, and scripts used throughout different periods. The critical role of Aramaic until the seventh or eighth century and its replacement by Arabic as the *lingua franca* of the region have led to extensive libraries in these and the Hebrew language.

The study of the Near East in Late Antiquity is complicated by the reality of disciplinary boundaries which have curtailed scholarly efforts to either an epoch, a language, empire, dynasty, religion, or society. An enthusiast of Sasanian history is likely to work in the field of Iranian Studies, whereas someone with interest in the Arabic language and literature is not unlikely to find herself in Islamic Studies. Semitic Studies often subsume the Near Eastern varieties of Christianity. Other disciplines with no generic interest in the Near East have had their significant share in producing the most formidable scholars and research literature and have significantly enriched the study of Late Antiquity with their takes on methodology. History, archeology, sociology, and more recently anthropology and ethnography are cases in point. Despite the obvious possibilities for research, the reality is such that conflating these disciplines and fields is occasionally perceived as "out of touch" and threatening their academic rigor, expertise, and internal mechanisms. Efforts that attempt to bridge the disciplinary divide were made during the last four decades, and collaborative projects to study Late Antiquity are steadily increasing. The endeavors of Patricia Crone, Michael Cook, Jany János, and Uriel Simonsohn attest to this development.

In this thesis, I seek to move beyond the conventional boundaries of Islamic Studies. Thematically focusing on matrimony and slavery, I inquire into the legal writings of Zoroastrians, Eastern Christians, and Muslims from the fifth to the ninth centuries. The law on matrimony regulates relations of kinship for property to be bequeathed and inherited in the case of a person's death. It delimits the boundaries of the family as the basic unit of living and normalizes sexual reproduction by forbidding, tolerating, or demanding sexual relationships between members of society. Slave law restricts the legal capacity of certain individuals as opposed to other members of society who are granted freedom. The legal status of slaves frequently constitutes an intermediary stage before a legal subject is bestowed with the privileges of a free person.

Why focus on the laws of matrimony and slavery while excluding other relevant fields of law such as property, obligations, and inheritance? Apart from the historian's convenience, the selected fields are narrowly related in the sense that, in the main, their concern is with the delimitation and organization of authority over an individual. Whereas marriage laws, in these Late Antique societies, mostly focus on demarcating the boundaries of authority of a husband over his wife and specify the spouses' mutual legal capacity, the laws on slavery typically center on defining and delineating relationships of power between masters and slaves. The mere fact of selecting these two realms of jurisprudence arguably affects the outcome of this thesis in the sense that the validity of its main arguments may not necessarily be extended to other fields.

This thesis seeks to answer three questions. First, what legal forms do the laws of matrimony and slavery cultivate? Speaking about legal forms, I mean the assemblage of legal opinions and configurations suggested by jurists, the concepts through and the rationales alongside which they understood and described legal problems. Secondly, I seek to understand how these legal forms are related to cosmology and the practical interests of the community/empire in which they originated. The notion of cosmology encompasses the cosmological imagery inscribed in the belief systems in which these legal writings emerged. More specifically, I try to understand how matrimony and slavery are imagined in the scriptural writings of Zoroastrians, Christians, and Muslims and what significance they have within the broader worldview of their respective belief systems. What I mean by practical interests are the elite's sociopolitical and ethical rationales and their ambitions to shape distinct notions of community or empire. Lastly, I seek to ascertain whether there were and, if so, through what patterns the interactions between the legal forms in Sasanian, East Syrian, and Islamic law can be described.

My first question necessitates a descriptive approach. Through a close reading of relevant passages in the legal writings of Zoroastrians, East Syrians, and Muslims, I conceptually outline the types of matrimony and the ways in which jurisprudence imagined contractual relationships with slaves in the Sasanian and the early Islamic Empires. For my second question, I mobilize some of the insights gained from legal scholarship on "legal culture." The interpretative framework of legal culture constitutes a way of imagining legal texts as situated in a reciprocal relationship with society. That is, legal forms should not be misconceived as always dictating a certain way of life, but instead they themselves are reevaluated, reshaped, and adjusted continuously according to the needs of society. My research shows that the types of marriage and the legal configuration of slaves, as discussed in the primary sources, are notably tied to cosmological imagery. Such cosmological arguments are, in turn, commissioned for sociopolitical purposes, more often than not, to mobilize and sustain certain notions of community or empire, while obliterating others. I, therefore, develop my thesis which is that the legal forms in Sasanian, East Syrian, and Islamic law are negotiated in the triangle of cosmology, lawmaking, and the sociopolitical needs of community/empire. To be more precise, I argue that the taxonomy of marriage and the legal configurations of slavery are significantly informed by cosmological imagery and the sociopolitical and ethical concerns of their respective communities.

To respond to my third question, I employ the theory of legal pluralism. Legal pluralism assumes that individuals in society, instead of relating only to a single overarching power, may navigate between multiple centers of authority. Each center may be tantamount to a legal system. In the context of Near Eastern law, a similar approach was recently taken by Uriel Simonsohn in his *A Common Justice.*[1] Most importantly, legal pluralism provides

[1] Uriel Simonsohn, *A Common Justice* (Philadelphia: University of Pennsylvania Press, 2011).

the general framework for understanding through what patterns the legal forms in Sasanian, East Syrian, and early Islamic law may have interacted with one another. The argument I develop in this section is that the relationship of Sasanian, East Syrian, and Islamic law is marked by a variety of patterns, which is not, as so often argued, restricted to influence.

Through the combined approach of legal culture and legal pluralism, I seek to move away from the overstretched and controversial 'influence'-paradigm which has significantly dominated comparative studies of Near Eastern law. That is, while a multitude of studies addresses the relationship of Islamic law to adjacent systems of jurisprudence, their methodological approach is often problematic. By identifying legal forms in Islamic law which resemble those in adjacent legal systems, such studies usually ascribe foreign origins to Islamic institutions and legal concepts, relying mainly on Roman-Byzantine and Judaic law. I seek to theoretically contribute to the field by proposing the combination of legal culture and legal pluralism as an alternative methodology to proceed with in the comparative study of Near Eastern law.

This thesis is divided into eight chapters. The historical, social, and religious contexts in which the laws on matrimony and slaves in Sasanian, East Syrian, and Islamic jurisprudence unfolded are discussed in the second chapter. To support my arguments, I lay out some of the cosmological doctrines in Zoroastrianism, Eastern Christianity, and Islam and the specific notions of identity drawn on by the Sasanians, the East Syrians, and the Arabs. I limit my inquiry to the period between the fifth and the ninth centuries.

In the third chapter, I review the secondary literature relevant to this thesis. To situate my research, I map and discuss the state of the field and point out the most salient research gaps. This prepares the ground for the fourth chapter, in which I develop my method of inquiry which interlocks the theoretical insights gained from legal culture and legal pluralism.

The fifth chapter is dedicated to theorizing jurisprudence, legal practices, and different modes of lawmaking in the legal traditions covered here. Towards the end of this chapter, I discuss the primary sources I use in this thesis.

The sixth chapter deals with matrimony. Its subchapters are arranged chronologically–proceeding from the Sasanians to the Church of the East, to Islam. Within these chronological units, I follow a three-fold division: the cosmological imagery, the legal forms of marriage, and their implications and significance for society. This combined structure is adopted to increase comparability between the different legal systems and hopefully, makes it easier for the reader to move back and forth between the chapters to see similarities and differences. As for Sasanian law, I am particularly concerned with shedding light on the practice of next-of-kin marriage (*ẖwēdōdah*) and the institutions of the intermediary (*ayōkēn*) and substitute-successor (*stūr*). For East

Syrian law, I highlight the reforms the law of matrimony underwent beginning in the late fifth century. As for Islamic law, I bring into focus the bridal dower (*mahr/ṣadāq*) underlining the high importance associated with it in matrimonial agreements. I end this chapter with a preliminary conclusion, in which I converse the findings from the chronological sections.

The seventh chapter deals with slavery and is structured in accordance with the former. Again proceeding chronologically, I examine the concepts and particular justifications through which the legal status of slaves was understood; secondly, I bring these in conversation with the needs of the respective societies; thirdly, I make comparisons between the legal systems. In this chapter, I mainly focus on transactions involving slaves and the various legal problems arising from such. As is known at least for Islamic law, the restricted capacity of the slave with respect to owning property proved to be contentious among legal specialists (*fuqahāʾ*). We will see that similar debates existed in Sasanian and East Syrian law. This chapter ends with a preliminary conclusion, before I summarize and conclude my findings in the eighth chapter.

Chapter II
Historical, social, and religious context

In this chapter, I shed light on the cosmological imagery in Mazdaism, Christianity and Islam as well as the notions of "community" of the Sasanians, East Syrians and the Arabs which burgeoned between the fifth and the ninth century. This will provide the necessary background for the main arguments of this thesis.

A. Zoroastrianism and the Sasanians

Martin Haug's *Essays on the Sacred Language, Writings, and Religion of the Parsis*[1] from 1907 discuss the nature of Zoroastrianism (Mazdaism), its divine beings, liturgical rites, customs, and observances. Haug emphasizes the close relationship of Zoroastrian beliefs and practices with Brahmanical religions, manifested in the dogmatic and linguistic overlaps of the *Old Avesta*–a collection of the earliest Zoroastrian hymns written in Old Avestan language–with the *Rig Vedas*. It is thought that the Iranians and Indo-Aryans used to be a united people until around 2000–1800 BC after which their linguistic evolution continued separately.[2] The linguistic and religious resemblances found in Mazdaism and Vedic religions are attributed to this shared historical legacy.

The unmistakable hallmark of Mazdaism is its intrinsic dualism between Good and Evil reflected in the cosmic struggle between Ohrmazd (Ahura Mazdā) and Ahriman. Ohrmazd, the Beneficient God, initially brought the creations into being in a spiritual state (*mēnōg*). They then remained in this immaterial condition for 3,000 years. Meanwhile, Ahriman, dwelling in darkness, attacked the world of light. Ohrmazd offered peace, Ahriman rejected and the two spirits settled on a treaty (*paymānag*) stipulating that they would wage war for about 9,000 or 12,000 years in the material world (*gētīg*). With the treaty, the cosmic drama unfolds in three stages of 3,000 years each: the material creation (*bundahišn*), followed by the mixture of

1 Martin Haug, *Essays on the Sacred Language, Writings, and Religion of the Parsis* (London: Kegan Paul, Trench, Trübner & Co. Ltd., 1907), 267–314.

2 Mary Boyce, "The Origins of Zoroastrian Philosophy," in *Companion Encyclopedia to Asian Philosophy*, eds. Brian Carr and Indira Mahalingam (London and New York: Routledge, 1997), 5.

good and evil (*gumēzišn*), and a final period in which evil again separates from good (*wizārišn*).[3]

Ohrmazd, the Beneficent God, created the world of living beings (*gētīg*), and, with it, humanity, to assist Him in the struggle against the lie (*drug*) represented by Ahriman. The struggle is present on all levels including the world of thought (*mēnōg*).[4] To expand the truth (*asha*) and reestablish order, man is required to support Ohrmazd on three levels: the mental, verbal, and physical. One must think, speak, and act beneficiently. Therefore, the purpose of Mazdaean rituals and liturgical practices is not simply to worship Ohrmazd but, more importantly, to create direct benefit in the cosmic order.[5] The *telos* of human existence is, other than in Christian and Muslim belief, to assist Ohrmazd in His battle against Ahriman to reestablish the cosmos.

As a living faith, Mazdaean belief is ubiquitous. Its ontology is intimately tied to the notion of exemplification (as opposed to symbolism). All mundane realities are not symbols but rather samples or instantaneous reifications of the macrocosm. For instance, the sacred fire used in worship is not a symbol of the divine spirit but immediately partakes in the divine light. That is to say, the fire hypostasizes the divine–it is Ohrmazd Himself.[6] This similarly applies to acts of worship and rituals bringing about an awe-inspiring universal reality: through every thought, word, and action, the worshipper creates direct benefit or damage in the cosmos.

The dualistic nature of Mazdaean cosmology has been the subject of much controversy. At its center is the question of whether or not Mazdaism typifies a form of monotheism.[7] The dilemma is that Ohrmazd and Ahriman are thought of as originating from the same seed. This has cast doubts on the nature of Zoroastrianism as a strictly monotheistic religion. As Herrenschmidt notes, "[t]he most widespread thesis was certainly that of a monotheistic reform [...]"[8] at the hands of the Prophet Zarathustra. The

---

3 Philip G. Kreyenbroek, "Cosmogony and Cosmology i. In Zoroastrianism/Mazdaism," in *Encyclopedia Iranica* (1993). For a useful introduction to eschatology see Shaul Shaked, "Eschatology i. In Zoroastrianism and Zoroastrian Influence," in *Encyclopedia Iranica* (1998).

4 Prods O. Skjærvø, *The Spirit of Zoroastrianism* (New Haven and London: Yale University Press, 2012), 8.

5 Prods O. Skjærvø, "The Literature of the Most Ancient Iranians," in *Proceedings of the Second North American Gatha Conference*, eds. Sarosh J.H. Manekshaw and Pallan R. Ichaporia (Houston, TX: Federation of Zoroastrian Associations of North America, 1996), 229–230.

6 Dastur F. M Kotwal and James W. Boyd, *A Persian Offering. The Yasna: A Zoroastrian High Liturgy* (Paris: Association pour l'Avancement des Études Iraniennes, 1991), 7.

7 For an overview of this debate from the 17th till the 20th centuries; cf. Clarisse Herrenschmidt, "Once Upon a Time, Zoroaster," in *History and Anthropology* 3 (1987), 209–237.

8 Clarisse Herrenschmidt, "Once Upon a Time, Zoroaster," 217.

prophet, who may have lived between 1700 and 1500 BC,[9] supposedly acted as a reformer of ancient Iranian religion elevating Ohrmazd over the various other deities in pre-Zoroastrian belief. How, then, can one account for the problem of Ohrmazd and Ahriman supposedly being twin brothers? The Zurvanites, occasionally condemned as heretics, settled on the existence of Zurvan (Infinite Time), a divine being that is superior and prior to Ohrmazd and Ahriman.[10] On the contrary, modern scholarship has widely accepted the resolution presented by Haug:

> The leading idea of his [Zarathustra's] theology was Monotheism, i.e., that there are not many gods, but only one; and the principle of his speculative philosophy was Dualism, i.e., the supposition of two primeval causes of the real world and of the intellectual; while his moral philosophy was moving in the Triad of thought, word, and deed. [11]

Alternatively, Mazdaism can perhaps be described as a henotheistic religion, a term coined by Friedrich Max Müller to capture the belief in a supreme god without precluding the existence of other deities.[12]

The message Zarathustra proclaimed was genuinely revolutionary. Apart from his exaltation of Ohrmazd to the apex of the Iranian pantheon–a quasi-monotheism–Zarathustra promised his fellow citizens individual judgment and salvation after death. His vision, therefore, differed profoundly from traditional Iranian religions in which happiness in the hereafter was declared a privilege granted only to leaders of the community.[13] The promise of an afterlife in heaven or hell, depending on the thoughts, words, and deeds achieved in the worldly sphere, had radical consequences. Most significantly, the believer was now entirely responsible for her own and the shared fate of her community in the afterlife.[14]

The world of the Sasanians (224–651) was deeply imbued with Zoroastrianism (Mazdaism).[15] Yet, it is difficult to make an argument for the ortho-

---

9 Mary Boyce, *Zoroastrians,* 18.

10 Robert C. Zaehner, *Zurvan: a Zoroastrian Dilemma* (Oxford: Clarendon Press, 1955), 5.

11 Martin Haug, *Essays,* 300.

12 Friedrich Max Müller, *Vorlesungen über den Ursprung und die Entwickelung der Religion. Mit besonderer Rücksicht auf die Religionen des Alten Indiens* (Strassburg: Verlag von Karl J. Trübner, 1881), 323–324.

13 Mary Boyce, *Zoroastrians,* 16.

14 Ibid., 29.

15 *Grundzüge der Geschichte des Sasanidischen Reiches* is a useful introduction to Sasanian history and contains additional chapters on the Empire's structure, economy, religions, and art; cf. Klaus Schippmann, *Grundzüge der Geschichte des Sasanidischen Reiches* (Darmstadt: Wissenschaftliche Buchgesellschaft, 1990). Also, cf. the English introduction by Touraj Daryaee, *Sasanian Persia. The Rise and Fall of an Empire* (London: I.B. Tauris, 2009).

doxy of Mazdaism. The Zurvanites, Manichaeans (third century), and Mazdakites (sixth century) are cases in point. Khodadad Rezakhani recently argued that their common designation as Mazdaean heterodoxies is *de facto* the product of early and medieval Muslim historiography. Those accounts chiefly derive from post-Sasanian efforts that purposefully aimed at manufacturing the notion of orthodoxy.[16] The Iranian socio-religious movements can best be distinguished from one another, as Shaked suggests, with regard to how they deal with the problem of evil: as a separate principle, entirely detached from the deity (e.g. Manichaeism); as on par with it (e.g. Zurvanism); or, as secondary, derivative to the good deity (e.g. Zoroastrianism/Mazdaism).[17] Regardless of where we situate these movements, as heterodoxies or within Mazdaean orthodoxy, they were invariably suppressed and obliterated by the Sasanian authorities.

For our purposes, it is worth looking at Mazdakism more closely. Following the reign of the Sasanian King Kavad I (488–531), who had initiated cadastral surveys and sweeping tax reforms, a certain Mazdak was able to rally support for his surprisingly egalitarian vision of society. He was convinced that worldly discord is the result of quarrels involving women or property. Attempting to tackle evil at its root, he advocated communal access to women and joint property.[18] His egalitarianism must have not only fallen on deaf ears with the Zoroastrian priesthood (*āsrōnān*) but seriously unsettled them. After all, Iranian jurisprudence, particularly the law on matrimony, aimed at restricting access to women of elite households to elite males, while the complex institutions and laws of inheritance ensured that status, wealth, and nobility were maintained within the lineages of the ruling class.[19] This is most evident in the principle of next-of-kin matrimony (*ẖwēdōdāh*) which was practiced and promoted among the Sasanian elite. Besides indicating the formalistic way of thinking of the Mazdaean priesthood which enforced these regulations, it, moreover, illustrates that sexual

16 Khodadad Rezakhani, "Mazdakism, Manichaeism and Zoroastrianism: In Search of Orthodoxy and Heterodoxy in Late Antique Iran," in *Iranian Studies* 48/1, 55–70. Al-Ṭabarī (d. 310/923), al-Hamadhānī (d. 1025), al-Bīrūnī (d. ca. 442/1050), Ibn Ḥazm (d. 456/1064), and al-Shahrastānī (d. 548/1153) are among the most important sources for reconstructing Sasanian history; Shaul Shaked, "Islam," in *The Wiley Blackwell Companion to Zoroastrianism*, eds. Michael Strausberg Yuhan S.-D. Vevaina, (Chichester: Wiley Blackwell, 2015), 492.

17 Shaul Shaked, *Dualism in Transformation. Varieties of Religion in Sasanian Iran* (London: School of Oriental and African Studies, 1994), 21–22.

18 Patricia Crone, "Zoroastrian Communism," in *Comparative Studies in Society and History* 36/3 (Jul. 1994), 452. On the social movements in Late Antique Iran; cf. Patricia Crone, *The Nativist Prophets of Early Islamic Iran. Rural Revolt and Local Zoroastrianism* (New York: Cambridge University Press, 2012).

19 Richard Payne, "Sex, Death, and Aristocratic Empire: Iranian Jurisprudence in Late Antiquity," in *Comparative Studies in Society and History* 58/2 (2016), 521.

relations were tried to be harmonized and tied to the precepts of Mazdaean religion.[20] Mazdak's proposition for communal access to women was diametrically opposed to this thinking and threatened to dissolve the supposedly "pure" lineages of the Sasanian elite, and hence their foundation of power.

B. Christianity and the Church of the East

The political and social history of the Church of the East in the Sasanian and Muslim Empire must be situated against the broader developments in and outside the Christian community. To begin with, we probably cannot talk about the Church of the East as an independent church before 431. In the Council of Ephesus, convened by Theodosius II wishing to gain unanimous consent of the Church, the Christological controversy surrounding the nature(s) of Christ reached a pinnacle.[21] The egregious theological position of Theodore of Mopsuestia (d. 428) had given rise to this debate:

> If I was asked: Mary, is she the mother of man or the mother of God, *anthropotokos* or *theotokos*? I would answer that I admit both terms. The Virgin is *anthropotokos* by nature of her parturition; she is *theotokos* in virtue of relation. She is *anthropotokos* by nature due to him who was in her bosom and who was human when he came forth; she is *theotokos* because God was engendered as a man without being constrained by him.[22]

The Patriarch of Constantinople, Nestorius (d. ca. 450), had built on the explications of Theodore advocating a strict dyophysitism, or two distinct natures of Christ. Martin Jugie puts his position in a nutshell:

> The disciple of Theodore [Nestorius] recognized in Christ two subjects, two hypostases and persons: on the one hand, the Word, eternal Son of God to whom the divine qualities must be attributed, on the other, man, the son of Mary, subject of human qualities.[23]

Referring to the Virgin Mary by the title *Christotokos* (Χριστοτόκος: Christ-bearer, "Mother of Christ"), Nestorius thought he could appease all sides in the storm that Theodore had raised.[24] However, his doctrine was opposed;

---

20 Maria Macuch, "Inzest im vorislamischen Iran," in *Archäologische Mitteilungen aus Iran* 24 (1991), 153.

21 Peter Brown, *The Rise of Western Christendom. Triumph and Diversity, A.D. 200–1000* (Oxford: Wiley-Blackwell, 2013), 116–117.

22 [Theodore of Mopsuestia] *Fragmenta. Dogmatica*, P.G. t. LXVI, col. 992 BC, quoted and translated in Martin Jugie, *Nestorius et la Controverse Nestorienne* (Paris: Gabriel Beauchesne, 1912), 29, my translation into English from French.

23 Martin Jugie, *Nestorius et la Controverse Nestorienne*, 31, my translation into English from French.

24 Ibid., 31.

most fiercely by his adversary Cyril of Alexandria (d. 444) whose opposition is perhaps symbolic of the internecine rivalry between the cities of Alexandria and Constantinople.[25] At any rate, the bishops at Ephesus anathematized Nestorius and his supporters, proclaimed the Virgin Mary *Theotokos* (Θεοτόκος: God-bearer, "Mother of God"), and reconfirmed the Nicene Creed (325).[26] The consequences of Ephesus were momentous. It brought about the schism of the Church of the East with the rest of the Church and reinforced a discrete development of the Christian communities in the East which was perhaps adumbrated in the autocephalous status their bishops had already achieved in 424.[27] Moreover, the controversy on Christology would continue for decades to come.[28]

The official severing of ties with Constantinople was probably a relief for the Sasanian authorities. The fear of divided loyalties of Christians living in their dominions was one reason. Sebastian Brock tells us that before the mid-fifth century

> [...] the fate of the Christian population in Persia was intimately linked with the course of political relationships between 'two shoulders of the world' [...]: times of war were times when persecution was apt to break out, while political peace meant peace for the church.[29]

In other words, international relations, to varying degrees, had influenced the attitude of the Sasanian authorities towards their Christian subjects.[30] The schism undoubtedly put Persian Christians in a less precarious position, even if it did not vanquish the fears of the Sasanians.

---

25 John A. McGuckin, *St. Cyril of Alexandria. The Christological Controversy. Its History, Theology, and Texts* (Leiden, New York and Köln: E.J. Brill, 1994), 12.

26 Steven A. McKinion, "Ephesus, Council of," in *Cambridge Dictionary of Christian Theology*, eds. Ian A. McFarland et al. (Cambridge: Cambridge University Press, 2011).

27 In 424, the Synod of Dadishoʿ had stipulated that bishops in the jurisdiction of the 'oriental' church must not bring their grievances before 'occidental' patriarchs, *SynO*, 51, ll. 16–18 (*Syr.*)/296 (*Fre.*):

ܘܗܢܐ ܕܡܬܚܙܐ ܕܠܗܘܐ ܗܫܐ: ܕܢܦܩܘܢ ܩܕܡ ܦܛܪܝܪܟܐ ܡܥܪܒܝܐ ܥܠ ܐܚܝܗܘܢ ܒܢܝ ܡܕܢܚܐ
ܠܡܩܒܠܘ ܥܠ ܦܛܪܝܪܟܐ ܕܠܗܘܢ..

28 The Council of Chalcedon in 451 reanimated the dispute: does Christ maintain two separate natures, human and divine (dyophysite); or merely one, a hypostatic synthesis of human and divine (miaphysite)? The negotiations at Chalcedon resulted in another schism between the Roman-Byzantine, Melkite, and Maronite Churches on the one hand, and the Syriac Orthodox, Armenian, Coptic, and Ethiopian Churches on the other.

29 Sebastian Brock, "Christians in the Sasanian Empire: A Case of Divided Loyalties," in *Religion and National Identity*, ed. Stuart Mews (Studies in Church History, 18, Oxford: Basil Blackwell, 1982), 7.

30 Ibid.

To understand identity concepts of the Church of the East, we need to penetrate more deeply into how Sasanian subjects related to the notion of empire. The semantic language of Iranianness (*ērīh*) as opposed to non-Iranianness (*anērīh*) was at the heart of Sasanian identity. Sasanian nobles perceived and represented themselves capitalizing on the imperial ideology of *ērānšahr* ('territory of the *ēr*'). This notion, according to Richard Payne, dovetails Iranianness (*ērīh*) with belonging to the Good Religion (*wehdēn*).[31] Christians, by definition, did not partake in this identity; rather they were, together with other minorities, pigeonholed in the "Bad Religion" (*agdēnīh*). As non-Mazdaeans, they were considered a threat to the Zoroastrian social order because, with their different purity rites, they could potentially disrupt it and, in turn, facilitate the presence of Ahriman in the material world (*gētīg*).[32] Their lack of Iranianness (*ērīh*), however, did not prevent them from collaborating in the imperial project of *ērānšahr*.[33] To legitimize itself, the Church of the East had to produce a distinct notion of identity:

> Indeed, by drawing on literary sources and landscapes to reinvent the past, the [Christian] hagiographers communicated claims to civic and noble status in novel ways to equip Christian elites with narrative arguments with which to position themselves in late Sasanian society.[34]

By mobilizing the written culture of the past, the Church elite could firmly place itself within Sasanian society. Indeed, its strategy of defining identity appears to have been entrenched in consciously marking its tradition as written and opposed to the oral culture of Zoroastrians which it probably looked at with condescension.[35]

C. Islam and the Arabs

The conquests of the Arab Muslims (*futūḥ*), who took over many parts of the ancient Near East in less than thirty years, are overwhelming even from a modern viewpoint. Indeed, many speculations have been made with re-

---

31 Richard E. Payne, "Avoiding Ethnicity: Uses of the Ancient Past in Late Sasanian Northern Mesopotamia," in *Visions of Community in the Post-Roman World. The West, Byzantium and the Islamic World, 300-1100*, eds. Walter Pohl, Clemens Gantner and Richard Payne (Farnham: Ashgate, 2012), 212–213.

32 Richard E. Payne, *A State of Mixture: Christians, Zoroastrians, and Iranian Political Culture in Late Antiquity* (Transformation of the Classical Heritage, 56, Oakland: University of California Press, 2015), 31.

33 Richard E. Payne, "Avoiding Ethnicity," 212.

34 Ibid., 220.

35 Reuven Kiperwassser and Serge Ruzer, "To Convert a Persian and Teach Him the Holy Scriptures: A Zoroastrian Proselyte in Rabbinic and Syriac Christian Narratives," in *Jews, Christians and Zoroastrians: Religious Dynamics in a Sasanian Context*, ed. Geoffrey Herman (Piscataway, NJ: Gorgias Press, 2014), 116.

gard to what led to the success of the Arabs who had pushed forward as far as Nihāwand in 640/1 and Khurāsān in 650/1.[36] Theologically, the prophecy of Muḥammad–his radical demand for submission to the One God (*Allāh*), his promulgation of the resurrection (*qiyāma*) of the bodies and individual judgement by God, and his claims of an afterlife (*ākhira*) in the lofty gardens (*jinān*) or the abominable hellfires (*jahannam*)–was sweeping, but not entirely unfamiliar to the people of Late Antiquity.[37] Historically, Muḥammad is usually deemed to have had remarkable leadership skills and a charismatic personality.[38] Politically, the fatigue of the Byzantine and Sasanian Empires which had for centuries engaged in intermittent warfare, the close acquaintance the Arabs had made with them providing regiments on either side in times of war, and the perpetuation of the administrative and organizational fabric of the Sasanians and Byzantines in the conquered areas probably contributed to the success of the conquests.[39] It is definitely outside the scope of this thesis to address the sweeping takeover of the Arab Muslims in more detail; however, it is important to note that Islam did not simply wipe out the centuries-old traditions of the Late Antique Near East but rather set the stage for renegotiating established practices and creating new meaningfulness.

The death of Muḥammad in 9/632[40] ushered in a pervasive identity crisis of the Muslim community (*umma*) marked by contestations of and negotiations over the entitlement to political and religious authority. In addition, as the *umma* progressively transformed into an imperial polity, it was paramount for it to define its identity against the backdrop of the vast number of non-Muslims and new converts to Islam. As concerns claims to leadership, these were, at least initially, based on the preeminence of Arab Muslims reflected and epitomized in the caliphal prerequisites such as kinship (*qarāba/ṣihr*), genealogical descent (*nasab*), companionship with the Prophet

36 Abū al-Ḥasan Aḥmad b. Yaḥyā b. Jābir al-Balādhūrī, *Futūḥ al-Buldān* (Bayrūt: Dār al-Kutub al-ʿIlmīya, 1971), 184 (Nihāwand), 241 (Khurāsān). For the Arab conquests of the Iranian provinces in more detail, cf. ibid., 182–281. In fact, the last Sasanian king Yazdegird III was forced to escape the Arab armies, first to Merv and then Balkh. He was supposedly killed in 651/2; Klaus Schippmann, *Grundzüge*, 77.

37 Müller shows that monotheistic motives can even be found in Arabic poetry from the pre-Islamic period such as the *qaṣāʾid* of Labīd b. Rabīʿa; Gottfried Müller, *Ich bin Labīd und das ist mein Ziel: zum Problem der Selbstbehauptung in der altarabischen Qaside* (Wiesbaden: Steiner, 1981), 143.

38 Frants Buhl, Alford T. Welch, Annemarie Schimmel et al., "Muḥammad," in *EI²*.

39 Robert G. Hoyland, *In God's Path. The Arab Conquests and the Creation of an Islamic Empire* (Oxford: Oxford University Press, 2015), 93–95, 98–99.

40 In this thesis, I provide most dates from the Islamic era by first mentioning the *hijrī* (AH) and then the common era (CE) date.

(*ṣaḥāba*), excellency in faith (*sābiqa*), and personal preeminence (*faḍl*).[41] Put differently, to substantiate their claims to power, the early caliphs mobilized notions of legitimacy resting on propinquity to the tribe of the Prophet and their personal, meritorious achievements for the early Muslim community (*umma*). Naturally, the more generations came to be in between caliphal authority and the Prophet himself, the more arduous it became to mobilize notions of acquaintance with the Prophet as claims to caliphal legitimacy.[42] Therefore, as Crone and Hinds rightly state, political authority slowly transformed into a system in which "the caliphs are central to the faith here and now."[43] This is perhaps most evident in the substitution of the caliphal title *khalīfat rasūl Allāh* with *khalīfat Allāh* by the Umayyads, and the more boastful *as-sulṭān ẓill Allāh fī l-arḍ* with the ascension of the ʿAbbāsids.[44] The increased centering on caliphs in the authority claims and the self-representation of the ruling class does not mean that claims of genealogical descent from the Prophet were obliterated; however, such claims became simply more difficult to make and increasingly had to rest on evidence that was doubtful at best.[45]

The reconfiguration of the cultural landscape, initially dominated by a Syro-Arabian elite, was possible because Islam provided an idiom that was attractive to diverse religious communities especially due to its linkage to power and the elite.[46] More specifically, the ʿAbbāsid Revolution opened the stage for renegotiating the relationship between conquerors and conquered. This relationship had been strained due to the increasing number

41 Cf. Gernot Rotter, *Die Umayyaden und der Zweite Bürgerkrieg (680-692)* (Wiesbaden: Deutsche Morgenländische Gesellschaft, 1982), 1–36.

42 Ibid., 248.

43 Patricia Crone and Martin Hinds, *God's Caliph. Religious Authority in the First Centuries of Islam* (Cambridge: Cambridge University Press, 1986), 33.

44 Ignaz Goldziher, "Du Sens Propre des Expressions Ombre de Dieu, Khalife de Dieu: Pour Désigner les Chefs dans l'Islam," in *Revue de l'Histoire des Religions* 35 (1897), 332. For the development of the notion *khalīfat Allāh*, cf. W. Montgomery Watt, "God's Caliph. Qur'ānic Interpretations and Umayyad Claims," in *Iran and Islam. In Memory of the late Vladimir Minorsky*, ed. C.E. Bosworth (Edinburgh: Edinburgh University Press, 1971), 565–574 and Rudi Paret, "Ḫalīfat Allāh – Vicarius Dei. Ein differenzierender Vergleich," in *Mélanges d'Islamologie. Volume dédié à la Mémoire de Armand Abel par ses collègues, ses élèves et ses amis*, ed. Salmon Pierre Salmon (Leiden: E. J. Brill, 1974), 224–232.

45 To illustrate, the ʿAbbāsids staged the Prophet in a narrative which claims that he entrusted ʿAlī with the mysteries who then handed them over to his son al-Ḥanafiya who once more passed them on to a representative of the Banū ʿAbbās; David S. Margoliouth, "The Sense of the Title Khalīfah," in *A Volume of Oriental Studies. Presented to Edward G. Browne, M.A., M.B., F.B.A., F.R.C.P. Sir Thomas Adams's Professor of Arabic in the University of Cambridge on his 60th Birthday (7 February 1922)*, eds. T. W. Arnold and Reynold A. Nicholson (Cambridge: Cambridge University Press, 1922), 326.

46 Robert G. Hoyland, *In God's Path*, 207–208.

of new converts to Islam who by affiliation to Arab Muslims as clients (*mawālī*) were kept aloof from the society of the conquerors.[47] Daniel Pipes puts this in a nutshell:

> A non-Arabian who converted to Islam was, in effect, petitioning to join the society of the conquerors. To prevent this from happening in large numbers, the conquerors had to exclude non-Arabians, whether Muslim or not, from the Register [*Dīwān*] and the fruits of victory. Herein lay the usefulness of the mawla-convert status; it provided an Islamic mechanism whereby the Arabians restricted to themselves the benefits of victory.[48]

What the revolution did, was to challenge the *status quo* with the conquerors and pave the way for a thorough transformation of the ruling class of the Islamic polity. This, in fact, becomes evident when taking into consideration that the majority of ʿAbbāsid caliphs was not of 'pure' Arab origin but born of mothers (*umm walad*) who had been foreign concubines.[49] More importantly, with the ʿAbbāsid dynasty, the Islamic polity witnessed an increasing inflow of the large Persian heritage into the cultural domains of Islam.[50]

This contextualization is not intended to be exhaustive. Instead, I attempted to sketch the historical, social, and religious dimensions which I perceive as relevant to and constitutive of the burgeoning of the laws on matrimony and slavery in Sasanian, East Syrian, and Islamic jurisprudence. Laying out the cosmological imagery and notions of identity promulgated helps us understand the evolution of marital and slavery laws in these communities. I now continue with the literature review.

---

47 Patricia Crone, *Slaves on Horses. The Evolution of the Islamic Polity* (Cambridge: Cambridge University Press, 1980), 49–50.

48 Daniel Pipes, "Mawlas: Freed Slaves and Converts in Early Islam," in *Slavery and Abolition* 1/2 (1980), 144–145. Also, cf. the argument by Elizabeth Urban of the political ascension of the "concubines" (*umm walad*) towards the end of the Umayyad period which provides an important perspective on the rise of the *mawālī* and the ʿAbbāsids, Elizabeth Urban, "The early Islamic mawālī: a window onto processes of identity construction and social change" (PhD diss., University of Chicago, 2012), 156–7, accessed August 18, 2017, https://search.proquest.com/docview/1027764937?accountid= 8555.

49 Bernard Lewis, *Race and Slavery in the Middle East. An Historical Enquiry* (New York and Oxford: Oxford University Press, 1990), 39.

50 Robert G. Hoyland, *In God's Path*, 221.

Chapter III
Literature review

The concern of this chapter is to outline and discuss the literature on matrimony and slavery in Mazdaean, East Syrian, and Islamic jurisprudence. I have compiled here for the reader the most pivotal studies in order to introduce these legal systems and the socio-political milieus that produced them effectively. At the end of this chapter, I state how, based on this review, I am building on previous studies while developing a distinctive methodological approach. In support of my first main argument–the types of matrimony and the legal configuration of slaves being negotiated between the cosmological imagery and the sociopolitical needs of the community's elite–I discuss the literature that draws connections between law, cosmology, and the elite's sociopolitical concerns. To theoretically situate my second argument–the relationship of Sasanian, East Syrian, and Islamic law being marked by varying patterns–I evaluate the methodological approaches that scholars have employed for similar arguments.

The field of Sasanian history has recently seen significant contributions which challenge us to rethink the way we hitherto interpreted Sasanian relations with the Church of the East. The traditional narrative, derived from the ideological *topos* of the Christian hagiographies, has prioritized recurring persecutions of Christians at the hands of the Sasanian authorities. We currently have an increasing number of studies emerging which have put this narrative into perspective. Antonio Panaino has argued that the presence of the Christian martyrs, in particular, their frequent mention outside hagiographical literature, in secular and even non-Christian sources, more broadly indicates that persecutions were not the norm, but rather that Christians were not as a rule of thumb excluded from influential positions.[1] He furthermore points out that the decision to locate the patriarchal see of the Church of the East in Seleucia-Ctesiphon was possibly influenced by the desire to facilitate communication with the Persian emperors who resided close-by.[2] In the same vein, Brock reminds us of the dramatic expansion of church structures under the Sasanians; whereas in 410 there were merely six metropolitan sees and about 30 bishoprics, by the collapse of the Sasanian Empire in the seventh century, there were as many as ten metropolitan

1 Antonio C.D. Panaino, "The 'Persian' Identity in Religious Controversies. Again on the Case of the 'Divided Loyalty' in Sasanian Iran," in *Iranian Identity in the Course of History*, ed. Carlo G. Cereti (Rome, 2010), 228.

2 Ibid., 230.

sees and 96 dioceses.[3] Having said that, the argument that Sasanian Iran would have witnessed a Christian conquest from within if it had not been for the Arabs is not persuasive.[4] Nevertheless, the Church of the East, in fact, appears to have married into and maintained its supporters in the families of the Sasanian authorities.[5] This resonates with its increasing wealth and power towards the end of the Sasanian dynasty.[6] Richard Payne claims, more generally, that the Sasanian rulers patronized church institutions and, moreover, integrated them into the imperial structures of the Sasanian Empire.[7] This seems to turn the narrative of recurring persecutions of Christians on its head. On that note, he points out that the martyr accounts were mostly written at the hands of East Syrian authors with the intent of polemicizing and using the misdeeds of their adversaries to shape a notion of community, based on the experience of violence.[8] Moreover, "differentiated, hierarchical inclusion"[9] on the part of Zoroastrian authorities could indicate an almost *millet*-like structure of the Sasanian Empire. This could point to a legally pluralistic society in which individuals navigated between multiple centers of power.

As to Sasanian jurisprudence, we are still far from a comprehensive legal theory. However, thanks to Maria Macuch–author of more than four dozen articles on Sasanian law–we do have a solid idea of its nature, institutions, principles, and regulations. Macuch has also significantly contributed to our understanding of the various types of matrimony found in Iranian jurisprudence. To begin with, she argues that the Sasanian laws on marriage and kinship more broadly indicate that:

> Almost none of these complex institutions determining the structure of kinship in Sasanian Iran would have been possible in a society confessing Manichaeism or Christianity [...]. The Zoroastrian concept of life and fertility, its encouragement of endogam [sic] alliances and especially incest, was the ideological foundation on which the elaborate laws of succession and inheritance were built.[10]

---

3 Sebastian Brock, "Christians in the Sasanian Empire," 3. Likewise, William Young, in a quantitative analysis of the Church in the Sasanian and the early Muslim Empire from 1974, already pointed out the significant structural expansion of the Eastern Church in the Sasanian Empire; William Young, *Patriarch, Shah and Caliph* (Rawalpindi: Christian Study Centre 1974), 49.

4 Antonio C.D. Panaino, "The 'Persian' Identity in Religious Controversies," 236.

5 Geo Widengren, "The Nestorian Church in Sasanian and Early Post-Sasanian Iran," in *Incontro di Religioni in Asia tra il III e il X Secolo d.C.*, ed. Lionello Lanciotti (Firenze: Leo S. Olschki Editore, 1984), 9.

6 Antonio C.D. Panaino, "The 'Persian' Identity in Religious Controversies," 235–236.

7 Richard E. Payne, *A State of Mixture*, 9.

8 Ibid., 27.

9 Ibid.

10 Maria Macuch, "Zoroastrian Principles and the Structure of Kinship in Sasanian Iran," in *Religious Themes and Texts of pre-Islamic Iran and Central Asia. Studies in Honour*

She convincingly argues that the institutions in Sasanian law, their complex ways of determining kinship, as well as the overall encouragement to endogamic marriages, could only be born out of a society whose dogmatics were Zoroastrian. This would imply that the precepts of Zoroastrianism, its cosmology, were intimately tied to the practical concerns of the Sasanian Empire. As I show in the sixth chapter, the law on matrimony was crucial for establishing this link.

Macuch systematically outlines three main types of marriage in Sasanian jurisprudence: marriage with full matrimonial rights (*pādiḫšāy*), auxiliary marriage (*čagar*), and consensus marriage (*ḫwasrāyēn*). Temporary marriage is not listed as a separate type but a variation, since it may be stipulated for all types.[11] Elsewhere, Macuch contrasts auxiliary and consensual matrimony with the pleasure marriage in Islamic law (*mutʿa*; often rendered as "temporary marriage"). Above all, she concludes that Iranian jurisprudence knew a variety of temporary alliances for different purposes, most of which are, in a way or another, preserved in the pleasure marriage (*mutʿa*).[12] The relevance of matrimony in Iranian society has recently received the attention of other scholars such as Payne. He argues that the jurists aimed at "maximizing elite male access to the reproductive capacities of women."[13] The circulation of women was a substantial concern of elite households, more specifically, to create and maintain their position in the imperial structures of the Sasanian Empire.[14] Payne's findings provide the foundation of my argument that matrimonial institutions in the Sasanian Empire served the specific sociopolitical concerns of the elite, particularly, the maintenance of empire.

Yishai Kiel analyzes the doctrine of next-of-kin matrimony (*ḫwēdōdah*) against the backdrop of Mazdaean cosmological beliefs and Sasanian imperial concerns.[15] Having said that, Kiel does not produce a coherent picture. For instance, he fails to mention that next-of-kin marriages were often fictitious. This was the case, when a daughter was instituted as the intermediary successor (*ayōkēn-stūr*) of her deceased father. Before she could be married

---

of Professor Gherardo Gnoli on the Occasion of his 65th Birthday on 6 December 2002, eds. Carlo G. Cereti, Mauro Maggi and Elio Provasi (Beiträge zur Iranistik, 24, Wiesbaden: Dr. Ludwig Reichert Verlag, 2003), 243.

11 Maria Macuch, "Herrschaftskonsolidierung und sasanidisches Familienrecht: zum Verhältnis von Kirche und Staat unter den Sasaniden," in *Iran und Turfan. Beiträge Berliner Wissenschaftler. Werner Sundermann zum 60. Geburtstag gewidmet*, eds. Chr. Reck and P. Zieme (Iranica, 2, Wiesbaden 1995), 153.

12 Maria Macuch, "Die Zeitehe im sasanidischen Recht – ein Vorläufer der šiʿitischen mutʿa-Ehe in Iran?," in *Archäologische Mitteilungen aus Iran* 18 (1985), 203.

13 Richard Payne, "Sex, Death, and Aristocratic Empire," 522.

14 Ibid.

15 Yishai Kiel, *Sexuality in the Babylonian Talmud. Christian and Sasanian Contexts in Late Antiquity* (Cambridge: Cambridge University Press, 2016), 149–181.

off into an auxiliary marriage to bear children for him, she would legally be held as the *pādiḫšāy*-wife of her deceased father.[16] In other words, in order to connect the children born to her from an auxiliary marriage to the lineage of the juridical father, the Sasanian jurists had to utilize the artifice of a marriage between the deceased and his daughter. This shows that incestuous matrimony did not always constitute an actual marriage between the married parties. Similar to the methodology of Kiel, I situate the Sasanian types of matrimony at the intersection of Mazdaean cosmology and Sasanian imperial concerns in order to shed light on their precise functions in society.

We are not well informed on the status of slaves and their configuration in Sasanian jurisprudence. Macuch specifies four ways of becoming enslaved: the most common being war; second, as a result of children being sold into slavery by the *paterfamilias*; through a transaction in which a person is pledged as security for a limited time; or, by descent.[17] Slavery is not restricted to non-Zoroastrians. To illustrate, the *paterfamilias* of a Mazdaean family is–under extraordinary circumstances such as a shortage of supplies (*adwadād*)–allowed to sell his children into slavery.[18] In addition, a debtor may be enslaved as a result of a transaction in which she pledges a slave.[19] Although Zoroastrians are not safeguarded from being enslaved, it is forbidden to sell a Zoroastrian slave to an infidel.[20] I discuss this particular case in more detail in the seventh chapter to gauge to what extent slave law was negotiated between the cosmological imagery and practical concerns of the rulers.

Macuch observes that the slave is considered an object (*ḫwāstag*). But, Iranian jurisprudence, more generally, acknowledges her human faculties which distinguish her from other forms of property such as immovables. To be more precise, the slave is fully recognized in court as plaintiff, defendant, or witness.[21] Her master can bestow her with limited legal capacity by allowing her to dispose of her own income (*pad windišn pādiḫšāykard*).[22] In

---

16 Maria Macuch, "Incestuous Marriage in the Context of Sasanian Family Law," in *Ancient and Middle Iranian Studies. Proceedings of the 6th European Conference of Iranian Studies, held in Vienna, 18–22 September 2007*, eds. Maria Macuch, Dieter Weber and Desmond Durkin-Meisterernst (Wiesbaden: Harrassowitz Verlag, 2010), 143.

17 Maria Macuch, "Barda and Barda-Dāri. ii. In the Sasanian Period," in *Encyclopædia Iranica*, vol. 3.

18 Maria Macuch, "The adwadād Offence in Zoroastrian Law," in *Shoshannat Yaakov. Jewish and Iranian Studies in Honor of Yaakov Elman*, eds. Shai Secunda and Steven Fine (The Brill Reference Library of Judaism, 35, Leiden and Boston, MA 2012), 259–260.

19 *HazDP*, 149.

20 Maria Macuch, "Barda and Barda-Dāri."

21 Ibid.

22 Ibid.

this thesis, I ascertain whether the (in)capacity of slaves to acquire property is meaningful with regard to creating and assigning a particular societal purpose to the institution as such. To understand the slavery practices of the society of *Ērānšahr* (Sasanian Empire), I scrutinize how Iranian jurisprudence configures slaves legally: their rights and obligations, the ways they differ from free subjects, and how enslavement can be overcome.

The literature on East Syrian jurisprudence is meager, to say the least. In *Orientalisches Kirchenrecht*, Walter Selb comprehensively lists the sources of law and sketches the development of East Christian jurisprudence more broadly. For the Church of the East in Late Antiquity, he distinguishes two types of sources: the synodical records, many of which were compiled in the *Synodicon Orientale*, and the law books written by individual clerics.[23] He rightly observes that, as a formalized institution of lawmaking in the Church of the East, the episcopal synods attained legitimacy with the Synod of Mar Isḥaq (410) or at least shortly after.[24] To support his claim, we can invoke threefold evidence: the reorganization of Church authority decreed at the Synod of Mar Isḥaq, the order to biennially convene all bishops within its jurisdiction in a synod at Seleucia-Ctesiphon, and the interdiction of bishops to appeal to the Western patriarchs at the Synod of Dadishoᶜ (424).[25] Furthermore, Selb claims that by the eighth century the law books–or individual collections of law–had practically replaced the synods as a means of lawmaking.[26] Having said that, Hubert Kaufhold cautiously suggests that the law books might have merely presented an aid to the ecclesiastical jurisdiction of the courts instead of replacing them entirely.[27] It is difficult to see why the mode of lawmaking in the Church of the East progressively moved away from synodical rulings towards individual juridical compilations. The consolidation of its authority and structure after the internecine struggles of the fifth and sixth centuries is perhaps one reason. In the sixth chapter, I show that these individual compilations mobilized scriptural cosmology in order to sanction monogamous marriages

---

23 Walter Selb, *Orientalisches Kirchenrecht*, vol. 1: *Die Geschichte des Kirchenrechts der Nestorianer (von den Anfängen bis zur Mongolenzeit)* (Wien: Verlag der Österreichischen Akademie der Wissenschaften, 1981), 97–115, 165–179.

24 Ibid., 117.

25 *SynO*, [Synod of Mar Isḥaq, canon xxi] 32–35 (*Syr.*)/271–273 (*Fre.*), [canon vi] 24–25 (*Syr.*)/264–265 (*Fre.*), [Synod of Dadishoᶜ] 51 (*Syr.*)/296 (*Fre.*). For a scheme illustrating the structure and organization of the Persian Church as specified in the Synod of Mar Isḥaq see Figure 2, xii.

26 Ibid., 186.

27 Hubert Kaufhold, "Sources of Canon Law in the Eastern Churches," in *The History of Byzantine and Eastern Canon Law to 1500*, eds. Wilfried Hartmann and Kenneth Pennington (Washington: The Catholic University of America Press, 2012), 304–305.

which ties in with my first main argument of cosmology being mobilized by jurists to respond to the specific concerns of the Christian elite.

We are not sufficiently informed about matrimonial customs in the Church of the East. In spite of that, the law on matrimony figures among the most frequently addressed themes in East Syrian writings of jurisprudence. The synodical gatherings, as well as the law books of Mar Aba and Ishoʿbokht, bear witness to this. Noteworthy, our knowledge of matrimonial customs rests almost entirely on the rationale that explicit interdictions imply the existence of the social practices they seek to prohibit. That is, the treatise of Mar Aba (r. 539–52) and his prohibition of close-kin marriage has been taken to imply that this type of matrimony was, in a way or another, practiced among Christians. Antonio Panaino even states:

> In the already mentioned letter [the treatise of Mar Aba], the Katholikos explicitly forbids Christians to maintain unions with relatives just as it was possible according to the Zoroastrian customs, ordering a divorce in the time-span of one year or, in case of refusal, imposing the banishment from the community and the sacraments. These statements patently show the *radical presence* of next-of-kin marriages among the members of the VIth century Christian Persian Church [...].[28]

I agree that the prohibition of close-kin marriage, mainly due to its reiteration in different jurisprudential sources, may indicate that this matrimonial type was occasionally practiced among Christians.[29] However, to claim its "radical presence" among members of the Church of the East is undoubtedly too far-fetched. In particular, due to Mar Aba's defiance of the Sasanian court and his conversion from Zoroastrianism, we cannot rule out a fair amount of polemicism in his writings. Moreover, we should beware of making conclusions with regard to social customs, particularly, when based on this sort of evidence alone. The writings of Mar Aba, his rejection of next-of-kin marriages, will be adduced in support my argument that the Christian elite, through scriptural references, reverted to cosmology to sanction a particular concern–monogamous matrimony.

The process of delimiting matrimonial law in the Church of the East must be seen as an effort by its elite to shape a distinctive notion of community, particularly against the backdrop of an Iranian polity thoroughly invested in promoting next-of-kin unions. Having said that, we might determine dif-

---

28 Antonio C.D. Panaino, "The Zoroastrian Incestuous Unions in Christian Sources and Canonical Laws: Their (Distorted) Aetiology and Some Other Problems," in *Cahiers de Studia Iranica* 36 (2008), 81.

29 On the marital practices of Syriac Christians see Lev E. Weitz, "Syriac Christians in the Medieval Islamic World: Law, Family, and Society" (PhD diss., Princeton University, 2013), 136–143, accessed July 2, 2017, http://arks.princeton.edu/ark:/88435/dsp01ng451h571.

ferent reasons as to why next-of-kin marriage was not an entirely unfamiliar practice among Persian Christians. Manfred Hutter argues that

> [t]he reason for this may be the integration of Christians as 'higher-class' people within Sasanian society, which may have led to that kind of 'Zoroastrianized' Christianity–which seemed to be accepted as 'proper' Persian by Zoroastrian officials [...].[30]

Likewise, Victoria Erhart asserts that certain Christian practices, in particular celibacy and matrimony, had to be made more admissible to the Persian elite and were thus progressively adjusted through canonical reforms.[31] The minutes of the Synod of Mar Babai (497) may attest to this mentioning that the bishops convened at the instigation of the Shahanshah to reform the law on matrimony.[32] In the fifth chapter, I shall focus on precisely how the matrimonial law was laid down and what modifications it underwent with the reforms at the Synods of Mar Aqaq (486) and Mar Babai (497) as well as the prohibitions of Mar Aba in the sixth century.

There are as yet, to the best of my knowledge, no studies focusing on the slavery practices in the Church of the East. Regardless, the Syrian law books are full of references to slaves, in particular, the *Corpus Juris* of Isho^cbokht (d. ca. 800). We thus have a sound basis for conducting more research on them. Even though there are no in-depth studies on slavery laws, we already have a small but indispensable hint at the status of slaves in East Syrian law which perhaps allows us to think of this institution more broadly. In her article on slaves in Iranian jurisprudence, Macuch points out a stipulation in the law book of Isho^cbokht which suggests that slaves are by rule granted a *peculium* (the capacity to property). Furthermore, she rightly states that this stipulation would imply an imbalance with Zoroastrian jurisprudence which does not bestow on slaves the capacity to own property as a rule of

---

30 Manfred Hutter, "Mār Abā and the Impact of Zoroastrianism on Christianity in the 6th Century," in *Religious Themes and Texts of Pre-Islamic Iran and Central Asia. Studies in Honour of Professor Gherardo Gnoli on the Occasion of his 65th Birthday on 6th December 2002*, eds. Carlo G. Gereti, Mauro Maggi and Elio Provasi (Wiesbaden: Dr. Ludwig Reichert Verlag, 2003), 172.

31 Victoria Erhart, "The Development of Syriac Christian Canon Law in the Sasanian Empire," in *Law, Society, and Authority in Late Antiquity*, ed. Ralph W. Mathisen (Oxford: Oxford University Press, 2001), 118.

32 More precisely, the synodical minutes mention that Babai was given instructions by the Sasanian King Zamashp to congregate with all the bishops and reform the laws on legitimate marriage and procreation, *SynO*, 63, ll. 9–13 (*Syr.*)/312 (*Fre.*):
ܘܣܘܦ ܠܗ ܫܢܬܐ ܗܝ ܕܡܢ ܕܢܚ ܟܢܫܐ ܘܩܪܒ ܒܡܠܟܘܬܐ ܕܙܡܣܦ ܡܠܟ ܡܠܟ̈ܐ ܐܬܦܩܕ
ܠܗ ܕܢܬܟܢܫܘܢ ܠܘܬܗ ܐܦܝ̈ܣܩܘܦܐ ܕܬܚܝܬ ܫܘܠܛܢܗ: ܘܢܚܕܬܘܢ ܬܘܪܨܐ ܕܒܢܝܢܐ
ܕܙܘܘܓܐ ܬܟܝܢܐ ܘܡܘܠܕܐ ܕܒܢ̈ܝܐ ܠܒ̈ܢܝ ܥܡܡܐ ܟܠܗܘܢ ܕܒܐܬܪ ܐܬܪ.
Similar to the above, the Synod of Mar Aqaq (486) reports that it convened with the permission of the Shahanshah; cf. *SynO*, 53, ll. 13–15 (*Syr.*)/299–300 (*Fre.*).

thumb.[33] What she is hinting at may be substantial pointing not only to conflicting juridical configurations of slavery but possibly different intentions behind the institution more broadly. In light of the state of the field, I first attempt to systematize the capacities East Syrian law furnishes slaves with, before making assumptions on the relevance of their legal status more broadly. Due to the lack of research on slavery, it is cumbersome to prove that the legal configuration of slavery was tied to the cosmology of Christian religion and the sociopolitical concerns of the Christian elite. By discussing some of the legal stipulations in the primary sources, however, I marshal eidence in support of such an argument.

As mentioned before, recent studies on East Syrian law have gradually challenged the conventional wisdom about the relationship of the Church of the East with the Sasanian Empire. This thesis builds on such new insights. In particular, the third question of this thesis–the relationship of East Syrian to Sasanian law–internalizes the findings of other scholars suggesting that Sasanian and East Syrian law did not operate in isolation from one another, but were in significant dialogue.

When immersing oneself in Islamic law, it is fundamental to be aware of the distinction between *sharīʿa* and *fiqh*. On the *sharīʿa*, al-Khalīl b. Aḥmad (d. 175/791)–the author of the *Kitāb al-ʿAyn* (a phonetically arranged Arabic dictionary)–informs us that:

والشريعة والشرائع: ما شرع الله للعباد من أمر الدين، وأمرهم بالتمسك به من الصلاة والصوم والحج وشبهه [...].

> The *sharīʿa* and the *sharāʾiʿ* [pl.] are what God prescribed to the servants [mankind] on the matter of religion and commanded to them to adhere to with regard to the prayer, the fasting, the pilgrimage and things alike [...].[34]

His definition suggests that the *sharīʿa* primarily encompasses man's relationship to God (*ʿibādāt*), and only subordinately, interpersonal relationships (*muʿāmalāt*). To be clear, while *sharīʿa* is usually regarded invariable divine law as revealed in the *Qurʾān* and through prophetic practice (*Sunna*), the inter-

33 Maria Macuch, "Barda and Barda-Dāri." The stipulation in question in Ishoʿbokht, *CorJ*, 138, l. 27–140, l. 1 (*Syr.*)/139 (*Ger.*) [v, iii, §16]:
ܐܢ ܡܪܐ ܝܗܒ ܠܥܒܕܗ ܐܘ ܠܐܡܬܗ ܒܟܬܒܐ ܐܘ ܫܡܥܐ: ܐܘ ܡܕܡ ܐܚܪܢ. ܥܠܝܗ ܗܘ ܗ̇ܘ ܠܥܒܕܐ ܐܘ ܠܐܡܬܐ ܗܢܘ ܡܕܡ ܠܡܥܒܕ ܐܝܟ ܕܨܒܐ ܒܫܘܠܛܢܗ ܘܐܦ ܒܡܘܗܒܬܗ ܕܝܗܒܗ. ܐܢ ܕܝܢ ܠܐ ܡܘܬܒ ܐܘ ܡܪܐ ܘܡܝܬ. ܗ̇ܢܘܢ ܗ̇ܘ ܡܕܡ ܟܠ ܡܕܡ ܕܠܗ ܕܝܠܗ ܐܬܗܘܢ ܠܒܢܝܗ ܕܡܘܗܒܬܗ ܠܗ.

34 Al-Khalīl b. Aḥmad, *Kitāb al-ʿAyn*, vol 1 (Salsalat al-Maʿājim wa-l-Fahāris [without year]), 253, my translation into English from Arabic.

pretations of divine law, the discipline of jurisprudence, is commonly referred to as *fiqh*.[35]

As to matrimony (and slaves) in the early Islamic context, Kecia Ali has presented a critical study based on a multitude of early Islamic legal texts. On the Islamic legal construction of matrimony, she writes:

> No matter what the understanding of women and their legal capacities in other contexts, when a woman becomes a wife, she inherits a remarkably consistent legal status. The specifics of her rights and duties can differ, sometimes significantly, from school to school, but the basic control over her sexuality and physical mobility that the husband gains by the marriage contract–with due modifications in the case of enslaved wives whose owners' claims must be considered–is the same. Along with his sole prerogative to end the marriage unilaterally, this control is the most basic element of marriage as regulated by the jurists.[36]

Most importantly, her findings on the nature of marriage are based on, among many others, the same primary sources as the chapter on Islamic law in this thesis. I use her analytical findings to support the central argument of this thesis which is that the legal notion of matrimony is located at the nexus of cosmological beliefs and the sociopolitical concerns of the Muslim community.

Several studies on slavery in Islamic law are available. Until recently, however, we lacked a copious roadmap of the legal configuration of slaves. Filling this gap, Rainer Oßwald, based on a large variety of Mālikī legal texts, has provided a yet unrivaled introduction titled *Das islamische Sklavenrecht*.[37] Other studies such as Patricia Crone's *Slaves on Horses* and Bernhard Lewis' *Race and Slavery in the Middle East* deal with the institution of slavery throughout the centuries.[38] A very important article was written by Daniel Pipes (before his political career) on the so-called clients (*mawālī*).[39] This legal status, somewhat in between freedom and slavery, attained increasing prominence after the first century of Islam, when many non-Muslims converted to Islam in order to overcome slavery. In light of these studies, I try to ascertain the role and function of slavery in the early Islamic Empire. In addition, I attempt to gauge whether the legal configuration of slavery is in

---

35 Al-Khalīl's less useful entry on *fiqh*, ibid., vol. 3, 370:
الفقه : العلم في الدين. يقال : فقه الرجل يفقه فقها فهو فقيه. وفقه يفقه فقها إذا فهم.

36 Kecia Ali, *Marriage and Slavery in Early Islam* (Cambridge, MA and London: Harvard University Press, 2010), 185–186

37 See Rainer Oßwald, *Das islamische Sklavenrecht* (40, Mitteilungen zur Sozial- und Kulturgeschichte der islamischen Welt, Würzburg: Ergon Verlag, 2017).

38 See Patricia Crone, *Slaves on Horses*; see also Bernard Lewis, *Race and Slavery in the Middle East.*

39 See Daniel Pipes, "Mawlas," 132–177.

any way integrated into Islamic cosmological imagery and to what extent it is overlapping with the sociopolitical aspirations of the Muslim elite.

First and foremost, research on Islamic law has been concerned with exploring its relationship to other systems of jurisprudence. The discussion mainly centered on foreign elements. Goldziher (d. 1921), Bergsträsser (d. 1933), and Schacht (d. 1969) were the intellectual pioneers of examining the possibility of Roman-Byzantine elements in Islamic law. For different reasons, it has proved to be a difficult undertaking to determine through what channels such transmission could have occurred. Initially, Joseph Schacht suggested that Roman legal elements would have most likely entered through the discipline of rhetorical studies in Iraq, which he claims was profoundly imbued with the spirit of Hellenism.[40] Patricia Crone persuasively dismantled this theory. She concedes that rhetorical studies loomed large concerning transmitting Late Antique culture into Islam. However, the purpose of rhetorical studies was not to acquaint students with the precepts of Roman law, but rather to convey techniques of debate and how to argue effectively.[41]

Arguing for the pervasion of foreign elements into Islamic jurisprudence, some studies have been informed by highly questionable methodologies. For instance, commonalities in Islamic law with other, earlier legal systems are sometimes alone taken as indicators that these influenced Islamic law. The unspoken assumption is usually that the later coming into existence of a legal system, its temporal succession to another, justifies the tracing of such commonalities. In other words, the legal texts themselves then merely confirm what is already known, namely that Islamic law is chronologically speaking the latest revealed Late Antique legal system. Thus, when commonalities with other earlier legal systems are found, they merely come to validate scholars' initial assumption that the previous legal system provided tools for the later, in this case, the Islamic.[42] This Orientalist method tends to repeatedly deny Islamic law any kind of originality. The origins of originality, according to this method, are situated in a genealogy of power, in which Roman and Jewish law, blossoming with creativity, throne over the achievements of later legal systems, particularly Islamic law, which come to

40 For the full argument see Joseph Schacht, "Foreign Elements in Ancient Islamic Law," in *Journal of Comparative Legislation and International Law* 32/3-4 (1950), 13–14.

41 Patricia Crone, *Roman, Provincial and Islamic Law, The Origins of the Islamic Patronate* (Cambridge: Cambridge University Press, 1987), 8–12.

42 An article by Judith Wegner is indicative of this scholarship. Taking as a point of departure the classical *uṣūl al-fiqh*, Wegner embarks on a dubious journey identifying for each 'root' of Islamic law its Talmudic equivalent. In her conclusion, she denies any originality to Islamic law by stating that the entire concept of analogy (*qiyās*) was merely copied from Judaic law; Judith Wegner, "Talmudic Jurisprudence," in *AJLH* 26/1 (1982), 45–47.

be perceived as devoid of any significant innovations.[43] The flaw of such comparative studies is not so much their claim that foreign elements were adopted, but their lack of specifying the channels through which this alleged influence took place. On this, Ṣūfī Ḥasan Abū Ṭālib rightly states:

لكي يمكن قبول هذه الحجة على أنها دليل على تأثر الفقه الإسلامي بالقانون الروماني يجب إثبات أمرين: أن العرب لم يكن لهم نظام قانوني قبل الإسلام وأن الفقهاء المسلمين أمكنهم معرفة القانون الروماني والتأثر به [...].

> In order to be able to accept this argument [traces of Roman in Islamic law], although it points towards the influence of Islamic law by Roman law, two things must be proven: (1) that the Arabs did not have a legal system before Islam, and (2) that the Muslim jurists could have known Roman law and be influenced by it […][44]

To make a case for foreign influences in Islamic law, scholars should identify the specific channels through which this influence could have taken place. Just because legal institutions, concepts, and principles in legal writings from different traditions resemble each other, these alone do not suffice to make an argument that one legal system necessarily influenced the other. Building on these studies and taking their flaws into consideration, I attempt to sketch a different methodological approach to comparative Near Eastern law in the fourth, methodological chapter.

This literature review fulfilled two purposes. It intended to show the current state of research identifying some of the significant findings scholars have made as to matrimony and slavery in Sasanian, East Syrian, and Islamic law. This thesis seeks to consider these findings to develop its main research questions: What legal forms do the laws of matrimony and slavery cultivate? How are these legal forms related to the practical concerns of the community/empire which engenders and enables them? What patterns of interaction mark the relationship between Sasanian, East Syrian, and Islamic law? Secondly, I outlined some of the methods other scholars have used to approach comparative legal issues. Taking these into consideration, I now explain how the theoretical insights gained from legal culture and legal pluralism can enable us to carve out a fresh methodological approach to the comparative study of Near Eastern law.

43 The domination of the narrative of borrowings in the academic field concerned with the formative period of Islam has also been pointed out by Wael Hallaq, *Restating Orientalism. A Critique of Modern Knowledge* (New York: Columbia University Press, 2018), 259.

44 Ṣūfī Ḥasan Abū Ṭālib, *Bayna al-Sharīʿa al-Islāmīya wa-ʾl-Qānūn al-Rūmānī* (al-Qāhira: Maktabat Nahḍat Miṣr), my translation into English from Arabic, 13.

Chapter IV Methodology

Much has been written in the quest for the origins of Islamic jurisprudence. However, the manner some scholars have approached the issue frequently led to flawed conclusions. The implications of assigning the achievements of civilization to another world of thought or jurisprudence–more specifically, the hierarchization and claims of superiority that come with condensing religious systems into genealogical tables–are too sweeping and dangerous to accept unsubstantiated claims. As George Hourani aptly points out:

> To reach an adequate proof of affiliation of ideas, an intellectual historian needs one or both of two kinds of evidence: *(i) external evidence of affiliation; for example, a report of a biographer that one scholar was taught by another or was favorably impressed by his works;* (ii) detailed resemblances so close that they could not be accidental; for example, exact correspondence of sentences, or numerous correspondences in technical terms. No precise rules can be set. Combinations of external evidence with several general resemblances may give conclusions of various degrees of probability.[1]

Especially the first point has often been overlooked. In other words, commonalities alone cannot suffice as evidence for influence; rather, to pinpoint foreign influences or "borrowings"–and this applies not exclusively to Islamic law–the channels or means of transmission would have to be identified. I do not think that tracing influences alone is conducive to our understanding of the meaningfulness of legal concepts and institutions. I, therefore, suggest that we deliberate more broadly on why societies may at times adopt similar resolutions to juridical problems, whereas they do not in other instances. In this thesis, I take a combined approach considering legal culture and legal pluralism as alternatives to the overused 'influence paradigm' which has significantly dominated the field of Near Eastern comparative law.

The methodological approach that David Nelken and others coin as "legal culture" examines the interaction of the law, its institutions, and upholders with society, legal mechanisms of enforcing the law in society, and cultural values conditioning legal boundaries.[2] Regarding the objectives of legal culture, Lawrence Friedman ingeniously states:

---

1 George Hourani, "Muʿtazilite Ethical Rationalism," in *IJMES* 7/1 (1976), 63. Ṣūfi Ḥasan Abū Ṭālib exemplifies the argument regarding the debate on Roman influences in Islamic law; see *supra* note 95.

2 David Nelken, "Using the Concept of Legal Culture," 1–3, 8. For more literature on the concept of legal culture: see David Nelken (ed.), *Using Legal Culture* (London: Wildy, Simmonds & Hill, 2012); David Nelken (ed.), *Comparing Legal Cultures* (Aldershot: Dartmouth, 1997); also, Henry W. Ehrmann, *Comparative Legal Cultures*

> The vocation of legal scholarship should be (in my opinion) heavily canted toward understanding how the legal system, as an operating system, actually works; what made it this way; and how it affects the social order in which it is embedded.[3]

The primary assumption I must make to apply legal culture is that the jurisprudential writings I deal with, in a way or another, furnish insights into the realities of the society and community that engenders them and which they have a stake in shaping. Because a multitude of my sources claims to be idealized sets of law, written with the intent to harmonize the legal practices of a community, I cannot necessarily assume that they are congruent with the law applied. In the fifth chapter, in which I discuss my sources, I carefully revisit this assumption for each source. First and foremost, they are jurisprudential texts, recommendatory in nature. In other words, it is doubtful that the laws would be enacted precisely the way a jurist describes it and more apt to reason that their presence in a jurisprudential text, to some extent, resonates with the investment of lawmakers in such legal matters.

I deploy legal culture as an interpretative method by which I situate my primary sources in a reciprocal relationship with the societies engendering them and on which they left their imprint. My research indicates that the laws on matrimony and slavery were affected by cosmology and the sociopolitical efforts of the elite. Building on that, legal culture, analytically, serves as a lens through which I can gauge how the legal stipulations on marriage and slaves were mediated in a triangular relationship with cosmology and the practical concerns of community/empire. Using legal culture, I tackle how the taxonomy of marital relations and the legal configuration of slavery relate to the sociopolitical concerns of the community/empire that engenders and enables them.

The second intervention this thesis seeks to make is theoretically underpinned with legal pluralism. Legal pluralism is opposed to legal centralism which is premised on the notion of a single overarching authority and jurisdiction to which individuals in a society relate. On the contrary, legal pluralism assumes that individuals connect to multiple, coexisting points of power, each of which maintains its own jurisdiction.[4] Accordingly, in such societies, individuals are, at least in theory, exposed to different legal regimes which, more broadly, indicates

---

(Englewood Cliffs: Prentice Hall, 1976). For a critical appraisal of the concept: cf. David Nelken, "Thinking about Legal Culture," in *Asian Journal of Law and Society* 1 (2014), 255–274.

3 Lawrence M. Friedman, "Is there a Modern Legal Culture?," in *Ratio Juris* 7/2 (July 1994), 118.

4 John Griffiths, "What is Legal Pluralism?," in *JLPUL* 24 (1986), 3–4, 14–15.

> that the 'law' which is actually effective on the 'ground floor' of society is the result of enormously complex and usually in practice unpredictable patterns of competition, interaction, negotiation, isolationism, and the like.[5]

The *de facto* capacity of individuals to bypass an administration of justice may vary significantly. That is, even though a person may skirt the legal regime allocated to her by birth, its jurisdiction would usually develop mechanisms for preventing or making skirting more difficult. Conversion to another religion is the example *par excellence*. While, upon conversion, the convert becomes affiliated with another administration of justice, this very act may be punished by death in the legal system from which she converted. Therefore, capital punishment as a measure of preventing believers from skirting may, in some instances, be the result of competition and interaction between different legal regimes.

In *A Common Justice*, Uriel Simonsohn recently deployed the theory of legal pluralism to the jurisdiction of Jews and Christians in the early Islamic Empire.[6] His work and method have significantly inspired this thesis. To set out his approach, Simonsohn questions the notion of autonomous communities which is usually acknowledged as a given in the early Islamic Empire. In other words, he tries to do away with the idea that Jews and Christians lived in isolated communities which were exclusively ruled by the laws of their religious elite and the regulations for *dhimmīs*.[7] Simonsohn states that many primary sources, in fact, suggest otherwise. Thus, he builds his argument stating that the principle of legal autonomy is one that grew as an ideal at the hand of Muslim writers, rather than reflecting social reality, in which autonomous authority was wishful thinking of the respective elites, but never completely effectuated.[8]

For the application of legal pluralism as a theoretical framework in this thesis, we must assume that individuals living in the Sasanian and the Muslim Empires were capable of navigating between jurisdictions. This assumption I make based on Simonsohn's and the findings of other scholars such as Payne. For instance, a Christian living in the Sasanian Empire, although by birth affiliated with the legal authorities of the Church of the East, was exposed to the law of the Zoroastrian authorities.[9] Besides, the finding that

---

5 Ibid., 39.

6 See Uriel I. Simonsohn, *A Common Justice*, 2011.

7 Ibid., 7–8.

8 Ibid., 9.

9 Payne provides significant evidence in support of this assumption. Based on the minutes of the Synod of George (676), he argues that the bishops condemned Christians who were using the courts of other confessions first in 676, Richard E. Payne, "East Syrian Bishops, Elite Households, and Iranian Law after the Muslim Conquest," in *Iranian Studies* 48/1 (2015), 7, 12–3. For the synodical minutes, see *SynO*, 214–226 (*Syr.*)/480–490 (*Fre.*). Also cf. Mario Kozah who states that the Synod of

next-of-kin marriages were not at all uncommon among the Christian minority in the mid-sixth century strongly points towards this social reality.[10] Thus, a Christian would effectively navigate between two centers of authority in which different ideas of matrimony prevailed. Whereas the Zoroastrian authorities highly promoted next-of-kin marriage, it was despicable to the Christian bishops. On the other hand, the strict notion of monogamy advocated by Church authorities was in stark contrast to the practice of the Zoroastrians. In my analysis, I will show that the prolonged coexistence of these legal systems led to different patterns of interaction between them which were not merely a matter of adopting foreign elements. In other words, instead of arguing that next-of-kin marriage influenced Christian law simply and only in the sense that the Christian elite began to imitate this distinctly Sasanian practice, I show that, in fact, the law of the Church of the East merely had to be made more permissible to Sasanian authorities. Most peculiarly, this led Christian elites to make essential changes to the matrimony laws of its Church hierarchy.

To sum up, in this thesis, I proceed in three steps. I first carve out the types of marriage and the legal configuration of slaves in Sasanian/East Syrian/Islamic law by discussing relevant passages in the primary sources. Secondly, I use legal culture to examine how matrimony and slavery were negotiated through the triad of cosmology, lawmaking, and the practical concerns of maintaining community/empire. Thirdly, I use the insights of the theory of legal pluralism to ascertain patterns of competition, interaction, and negotiation between the jurisdictions of the Sasanians, the Church of the East, and the Arab Muslims.

George resolved the internal struggles of the Church of the East with respect to the authority of the catholicos, Mario Kozah, "Introduction," in *The Syriac Writers of Qatar in the Seventh Century*, eds. Mario Kozah et al. (Piscataway: Gorgias Press, 2014), 15.

10 Manfred Hutter, "Impact of Zoroastrianism on Christianity in the 6th Century," 172.

Chapter V
Jurisprudence in Late Antiquity

A. *Jurisprudence, legal practice, and the modality of lawmaking*

Before looking at matrimony and slaves more closely, we need to reflect on the sources of and the principles fundamental to jurisprudence. The latter are not legislation in the proper sense, but rather distinctions or methods the jurist uses conceptually to analyze, discuss, or judge in particular legal cases.

Jany Janós has made an ambitious attempt at collating the sources and methods of legal reasoning in Iranian jurisprudence by drawing parallels to the principles of Islamic jurisprudence (*uṣūl al-fiqh*).[1] His study is perhaps the closest the field has yet come towards a legal theory of Iranian jurisprudence. He first establishes that the *Avesta*, in theory, stands above all other sources of law.[2] Practically more important than the *Avesta*, according to Janós, is the role of consensus of the learned (*hamdādestānīh*). Effectively, it signified a source independent of the *Avesta* for making legal judgements. Janós identifies these learned men as sages who were, in one way or another, involved in circles of learning.[3] We do not know exactly what consensus meant in this context or how it was negotiated; however, we are informed that individual sages proclaimed their own doctrines (*čāštag*). As a legal source, doctrines epitomized the interpretations of a sage and, most importantly, constituted the main body of oral law pertaining to a circle of learning. Janós then proceeds to the tools of legal reasoning in Iranian jurisprudence: analogy, legal fiction, and presumption.[4] At last, he brings into focus the established practice of the courts (*kardag*) which, not always in compliance with the theoretical doctrines of the sages (*čāštag*), developed into an additional reference point for lawmakers.[5] In brief, this indicates that Sasanian law had internalized the tension between law in theory and law in practice. Refering to the legal practice of the courts as a source of law, the jurists, notably in post-Sasanian times, transformed *kardag* into an inlet through which the changing realities of jurisdiction could penetrate into the realm of theoretical law. With regard to Islamic law, this phenome-

1 See Jany János, "The Four Sources of Law in Zoroastrian and Islamic Jurisprudence," in *Islamic Law and Society* 12/3 (2005), 291–332.

2 Ibid., 296.

3 Ibid., 299.

4 Ibid., 307.

5 Ibid., 310–313.

non is later rivaled by the Mālikīs who perhaps as the only Muslim legal school (*madhhab*) acknowledge customary law (*ʿamal*) as a source of lawmaking.[6]

Legislating in the Church of the East presupposed the convention of all metropolitans and bishops residing within its jurisdiction in a council or synod. These gatherings were usually headed by the Catholicos (later: Catholicos-Patriarch) or his vicar. The bishops could stipulate laws or canons only through consensus.[7] This modality of lawmaking was accompanied by a formal procedure of writing, signing, and confirming–qualified in the Synod of Mar Isḥaq (410):

ܘܒܬܪܟܢ ܡܪܝ ܡܪܘܬܐ ܐܡܪ ܠܟܠܢ: ܕܟܠܗܘܢ ܙܘܗܪܐ ܘܢܡܘܣܐ ܘܩܢܘܢܐ ܗܠܝܢ
ܡܬܟܬܒܘ ܢܬܟܬܒܘܢ. ܘܟܠܢ ܐܢܚܢ ܢܪܫܘܡ [ܐܪܫܘܡ] ܚܬܡ ܒܣܘܦܗ ܠܦܘܪܫܢܐ ܒܟܬܒܬܐ
ܢܩܝܡ ܘܢܫܪܪ ܒܩܝܡܐ ܕܠܐ ܡܫܬܚܠܦ.

Then, Mar Marutha said to all of us [the bishops] that all of these admonitions, laws, and canons must be written down and that we all should sign at the end of the judgement and conclude an invariable covenant.[8]

This procedure is likely to have been applied throughout most of the synods in the Church of the East because the synodical minutes in the *Synodicon Orientale* display significant structural and formal resemblances. It is worth noting that the stipulations made in a council or synod were, first and foremost, morally as opposed to juridically binding.[9] Most importantly, the act of lawmaking was considered authoritative due to the supposed presence of the divine spirit which led the congregation on the right path.[10] We can assume that the episcopal assembly collectively perceived of itself as the representation of Christ's flesh from which it allegedly obtained its authority, guidance, and truth.

The synodical councils occasionally position themselves in a particular juridical legacy by mentioning the episcopal synods or canons they recognize as legitimate precedents.[11] On that note, Hamilton Hess indicates the signifi-

6 Joseph Schacht, *The Origins of Muhammadan Jurisprudence* (Oxford: Clarendon Press, 1950), 62–63.

7 Hamilton Hess, *The Early Development of Canon Law and the Council of Serdica* (Oxford Early Christian Studies, Oxford: Oxford University Press, 2002), 30.

8 *SynO*, 21, ll. 12–15 (*Syr.*)/260 (*Fre.*), my translation into English from Syriac. The passage is referring to Marutha of Maypherqaṭ, cf. Sebastian P. Brock, "Marutha of Maypherqaṭ," in *Gorgias Encyclopedic Dictionary of the Syriac Heritage*, eds. Sebastian Brock et al. (Piscataway: Gorgias Press, 2011), p. 273.

9 Hamilton Hess, *The Early Development of Canon Law*, 73.

10 Ibid., 76–77.

11 Cf. for instance the Synods of Yahbalaha I (420) and Mar Babai (497), *SynO*, 38 (*Syr.*)/278 (*Fre.*) and 63 (*Syr.*)/312 (*Fre.*).

cance of the Council of Nicaea in the process of developing the theoretical notion of 'the council':

> First, it [the Council of Nicaea] introduced by precedent the concept and the practice of a deliberative and legislative gathering of the oecumene. Second, some fifty years after it met, Nicaea came to be regarded as the divinely inspired touchstone of orthodoxy consequent to the acceptance of Nicaea's terminological solution to the Arian problem by the council of Constantinople in 381.[12]

The role of Nicaea as a lawful template for later councils is evident because of its frequent mention in the synodical minutes of the Church of the East.[13] Lastly, it is important to note that a synod may choose to codify its resolutions and episcopal norms in the form of canons, however, not as a general rule. Besides the synodical gatherings, the Church of the East, beginning in the mid-sixth century, was witness to the burgeoning of legal handbooks written at the hands of individual bishops such as Mar Aba, Mar Shemᶜon, and Ishoᶜbokht.[14] It is challenging to theorize or extract a common legal ideology about these law books due to their differing characters. We can only tentatively claim that they more or less attempted to codify the diverging and rapidly transforming legal practices in the jurisdiction of the Church of the East.[15]

The Islamic legal tradition, like the Sasanian, internalizes the tension between jurisprudence and legal practice. To clarify, it is worth taking into account the position of Joseph Schacht:

> They [the *qāḍīs*] considered possible objections that could be made to recognized practices from the religious and, in particular, from the ritualistic or the ethical point of view, and as a result endorsed, modified, or rejected them. They impregnated the sphere of law with religious and ethical ideas, subjected it to Islamic norms, and incorporated it into the body of duties incumbent on every Muslim. [...] As a result the popular and administrative practice of the late Umayyad period was transformed into the religious law of Islam. [...] The circumstances in which the religious law of Islam came into being caused it to develop, not in close connexion with the practice, but as the expression of a religious ideal in opposition to it.[16]

---

12 Hamilton Hess, *The Early Development of Canon Law*, 46.

13 Walter Selb, *Orientalisches Kirchenrecht*, vol. 1: *Nestorianer*, 105.

14 Cf. Nima Jamali, "Book VI of Īšōᶜ-Bokht's Corpus Juris and the Emergence of Procedural Laws in the Church of the East," in *Journal of the Canadian Society for Syriac Studies* 17 (2017), 37–47.

15 Ishoᶜbokht makes this explicit, *CorJ*, 10, ll. 6–9 (*Syr.*)/9 [i, i] (*Ger.*):
ܐܝܠܝܢ ܕܐܝܬܘܗܝ [ܕܐܝܬܝܗܘܢ] ܐܦ ܗ̇ܢܘܢ ܡܫܠܡܝܢ ܗ̄ܘܘ ܠܟܠ ܚܘܫܠܦܐ ܕܕܝܢ̈ܐ ܕܐܝܬ ܠܗ ܒܗ
ܠܟܠܗ ܕܦܘܩܕܢ̈ܐ. ܘܐܬܬܪܝܪܘ ܕܝܢ ܕܗܘܝܘ [ܘܗܘ] ܗܘ ܕܝܢ ܢܡܘܣܐ ܗܘܐ ܚܠܦ ܡܫܘܕܥܢܘܬܐ
ܕܡܠܟܐ. ܐܦ ܠܐ ܡܝܬܪܐ ܕܡܘܬܐ ܕܗܘܝܘ ܗܘ ܕܝܢ ܢܡܘܣܐ. ܡܛܠ ܕܐܝܬ ܠܗ ܕܫܘܚܠܦ ܚܝܠܐ.
Also, cf. Walter Selb, *Orientalisches Kirchenrecht*, vol. 1: *Nestorianer*, 214.

16 Joseph Schacht, *An Introduction to Islamic Law* (Oxford 1964), 26–27.

In other words, Schacht claims that the religious law of Islam, by which he means jurisprudence (*fiqh*), took shape against the backdrop of the customs and administrative practices of the Umayyads. However, lawmakers did not simply incorporate but collated the ideas that came about in this setting with the rituals and ethics of Islam; the normative plain of jurisprudence developed as a result of this process and not infrequently in semantics that opposed contemporary juridical practices. Islamic jurisprudence, therefore, presents an idealized state of the law which does not necessarily reflect legal practice on the ground but should instead be read in conversation and perhaps opposition to it.

By the end of the second/eighth century, the Muslim legal specialists (*fuqahāʾ*) had begun to theoretically develop the tools of legal reasoning which would later become the linchpins of the Islamic legal schools (*madhāhib*). These tools were formed, particularly, against the backdrop of the controversy between the *ahl al-ḥadīth/ahl al-sunna* (traditionalists) and the *ahl al-raʾy* (rationalists).[17] This controversy was, more largely, rooted in the debate on the relationship between transmitted (*manqūl*) and demonstrative (*maʿqūl*) knowledge. Accordingly, the traditionalists (*ahl al-ḥadīth*) advocated precedence of the *Sunna* of the Prophet, whereas the rationalists (*ahl al-raʾy*) prioritized the living tradition and were thus more inclined towards demonstrative (*maʿqūl*) reasoning.[18] More importantly, this debate was a prelude to the conceptualization of the more specific tools of legal reasoning, in particular, analogy (*qiyās*), approval/preference (*istiḥsān/istiḥbāb*), consensus (*ijmāʿ*), and individual reasoning (*ijtihād*).[19] These are, according to the particular school of law (*madhhab*), ranked and prioritized differently.

The legal theory of al-Shāfiʿī, as developed in his *Risāla*, expounds that every act of the believer, which is within the scope of jurisdiction, corresponds to a legal statute (*ḥukm*) contained in the divine law (*sharīʿa*).[20] The statute (*ḥukm*) must either be identified directly in the divine scripture (*Qurʾān* and *Sunna*) or may, subordinately, be inferred from these through analogy (*qiyās*).[21] As a result, he allocates priority of transmitted (*manqūl*) over demonstrative (*maʿqūl*) knowledge. By contrast, the Mālikīya make al-

17 Wael B. Hallaq, *The Origins and Evolution of Islamic Law* (Cambridge: Cambridge University Press, 2004), 74.

18 Joseph Schacht, *Introduction to Islamic Law*, 34.

19 Ibid., 37; also, cf. Wael B. Hallaq, *The Origins and Evolution of Islamic Law*, 140–147.

20 On the development of Shāfiʿī legal doctrine, cf. Ahmed El Shamsy, "From tradition to law: The origins and early development of the Shāfi'ī school of law in ninth-century Egypt" (PhD diss., Harvard University, 2009), accessed August 19, 2017, https://search-proquest-com.ezproxy.cul.columbia.edu/docview/304889761?accountid=10226.

21 Éric Chaumont, "al-Shāfiʿī," in *EI²*.

lowance for local customs (*ʿamal*) which tends to result in the heigher weighting of demonstrative (*maʿqūl*) knowledge.[22] The means of reasoning undoubtedly do not constitute invariant templates but should rather be seen as more or less pliable guideline principles.

B. Legal sources: a survey

For Iranian jurisprudence, the number of legal writings that have come down to us is meager. The principal source, which is also employed here, is a not entirely preserved legal manual with the title *A Thousand Judgments* (*Hazār Dadestān*). The *Hazār Dadestān* was written by a certain Farroḫmard i Wahrāmān at the beginning of the seventh century right before the Arab conquests.[23] Anahit Perikhanian and Maria Macuch have both edited and translated the *Hazār Dadestān*. In addition to her translation, Macuch provides an indispensable commentary to the *Hazār Dadestān* in which she discusses each stipulation in terms of its significance within Iranian jurisprudence more generally. In this thesis, I utilize Perikhanian's English translation for the convenience of the reader but will adduce the German translation by Macuch at points where the English version significantly differs from the German. The text of the *Hazār Dadestān* is highly sophisticated and presumes familiarity of the reader with the complex institutions and principles of Iranian law.[24]

For the jurisprudence of the Church of the East, I use the *Synodicon Orientale* which is a collection of the synodical minutes of the Eastern Church. The corpus was supposedly compiled between 775 and 790 and has been edited and translated into French by J.B. Chabot in 1902.[25] It begins with the

22 Similarly, cf. Joseph Schacht, *Introduction to Islamic Law*, 61–62.

23 Name and author of the book are mentioned in the MS itself, *HazDP*, 193 (79,3–13) and ibid., 195 (79,16-80,17). Importantly, Macuch points out that the title of the MS is often erroneously rendered *The Book of a Thousand Judgements (Mādigān-i-Hazār Dādistān)*. For the debate cf. Maria Macuch, *HazDM*, 10–11. As concerns the dating, the latest king mentioned in the *HazD* is Husraw i Ohrmazdān (r. 591–628). In the 26th year of his reign, the author states, a certain document was written and sealed. Thus, the *HazD* cannot have been written before that; Farroḫmard i Wahrāmān, *HazDP*, 227 [99,17–100,5]; also, cf. Maria Macuch, *HazDM*, 9–10.

24 Bartholomae claims that the author of the *HazD* does not master the content of his writings because several judgements are mentioned more than once. However, his argument fails to take into account the particular purpose of the *HazD* as a manual that is designed for legal practitioners, rather than attempting to be a succinct theory of Sasanian law. Cf. Christian Bartholomae, *Über ein sasanidisches Rechtsbuch* (Heidelberg: Carl Winter's Universitätsbuchhandlung, 1910), 4.

25 While the date is not entirely clear, Chabot argues convincingly that the compilation must have taken place sometime between 775 and 790 due to a note of the author on the Synod of Barṣawma (484), in which he mentions that his corpus includes all ori-

Synod of Mar Isḥaq (410) and ends with the Synod of Ḥenanishoᶜ (775). Therefore, it is a useful historical overview of the developments in the Church of the East more generally. Other than the *Synodicon Orientale*, I use the law books of Mar Aba (*Eherecht des Patriarchen Mâr Abhâ*) and Ishoᶜbokht (*Corpus Juris des persischen Erzbischofs Jesubocht*), both of which have been edited and translated into German by Eduard Sachau in 1914. The treatise written by the Patriarch Mar Aba (r. 539–52) is a collection of 20 legal statutes on issues pertaining to congress and matrimony.[26] Ishoᶜbokht was ordained Metropolitan of Rev Ardashir about 780 and probably composed his *Corpus Juris* during his tenure as metropolitan.[27]

Concerning Islamic jurisprudence, I use the *Risāla fī Uṣūl al-Fiqh* by Muḥammad b. Idrīs al-Shāfiᶜī (d. 204/820). Apart from being known as the eponym of the Shāfiᶜīya, he made significant theoretical contributions to Islamic law.[28] This landmark in the history of Islamic jurisprudence has re-

ental synods except this particular one due to it being illicit. Therefore, he would have certainly added the Synod of Timothy I (790) after the Synod of Ḥenanishoᶜ (775) which is the last he includes; see *SynO*, 61, ll. 28–29 (*Syr.*)/309 (*Fre.*):

ܐܫܬܒܩ ܠܗ ܠܟܠܗܘܢ ܕܥܕܬܐ ܣܘܢܗܕܘܣ ܕܡܕܢܚܝܬܐ ܠܒܪ ܡܢ ܡܢܗ ܡܛܠ ܕܠܐ ܢܡܘܣܝܐܝܬ

ܕܚܢܢܐ ܒܠܚܘܕ ܣܘܢܗܕܘܣ ܠܒܬܪܝܬܐ.

Also, cf. J. B. Chabot, *SynO*, 13.

26 From the last line of the treatise, we know that Mar Aba must have written it himself, Mar Aba, *EheM*, 284, ll. 6–8 (*Syr.*)/285 [§ 20] (*Ger.*):

ܟܬܒܬܗ ܐܓܪܬܐ ܕܡܪܝ ܐܒܐ ܩܬܘܠܝܩܐ ܦܛܪܝܪܟܝܣ ܕܡܕܢܚܐ. ܕܡܢܗ ܠܗ ܠܟܠ ܬܩܢܬܐ

ܕܥܬܩܬܐ ܕܙܘܘܓܐ ܘܥܠ ܡܫܒܩܢܐ ܕܢܫ̈ܐ.

Most of the information that has come down to us about Mar Aba is from his biography which was composed shortly after his death, *Histoire de Mar-Jabalaha: de Trois Autres Patriarches, d'un Prêtre et de Deux Laïques, Nestoriens*, ed. Paul Bedjan (Paris: Otto Harrassowitz, 1893), 206–274. We are also informed that Mar Aba was a Christian convert from Zoroastrianism.

27 Ishoᶜbokht composed the *Corpus Juris* in Middle Persian (Pahlavi). From the anonymous translator's preface, we know that a certain Timothy instigated its translation into Syriac. Based on other information by the translator, scholars concluded that the Timothy in question, is probably the Catholicos-Patriarch Timothy I (r. 780–823). Thus, the translation would have taken place sometime between 780 and 823. In addition, the translator informs us that Ishoᶜbokht was ordained Metropolitan of Rev Ardashir at the hands of Ḥenanishoᶜ. Looked at in conjunction with the reference to Timothy I, scholars have mutually agreed that this is by all means a reference to the latter's immediate predecessor Ḥenanishoᶜ II (r. 775–80); see Ishoᶜbokht, *CorJ*, 4, ll. 9–11 (*Syr.*)/5 (*Ger.*).

28 The life of al-Shāfiᶜī is quite well-known and has been thoroughly researched. Wüstenfeld points out the disagreement about al-Shāfiᶜī's birthplace. It is most likely Ghazza. From an early age, he had memorized the *Qur'ān* and Mālik's *Muwaṭṭaʾ*. Mālik proposed to him to join his circle of students which he remained in until the latter's death in 179/795. After his stay in Medina, we are informed about a journey to Baghdād where the teachings of the *Ḥanafiya* had gained currency. Here he was initially on friendly terms with Muḥammad b. al-Ḥasan al-Shaybānī who later opposed him resolutely. In 195/811, he began teaching in the disciplines of *ḥadīth*,

cently been edited and translated into English by Joseph E. Lowry.[29] It is important to realize that the *Risāla* is primarily a theoretical compendium interested in the epistemological and methodological dimensions of lawmaking. Consequently, the *Risāla*–unlike the *Mudawwana* of Saḥnūn–does not address the manifold particulars and variations pertaining to different legal cases. However, it incidentally discloses some important theoretical notions governing matrimony and the juridical configuration of slaves. The multivolume *Mudawwana al-Kubrā* of Saḥnūn b. Saʿīd al-Tanūkhī (d. 240/854) constitutes the main source against which I analyze matrimony and slaves in the Islamic tradition.[30] The *Mudawwana* allocates to matrimony three comprehensive chapters (*kutub al-nikāḥ*) on various aspects. With regard to slaves, identifying the relevant passages is more tedious because slave law runs through the entire compendium rarely restricted to a particular chapter or section.[31]

In this chapter, I discussed and theorized the modes of lawmaking in the Sasanian, East Syrian, and Islamic legal tradition. This provided essential insights into the modality of lawmaking which is crucial for analyzing stipulations in the jurisprudential material. Besides, I laid out the primary sources deployed in this thesis.

---

kalām, and *fiqh* acquiring a circle of enthusiasts who openly advocated his views. While in Baghdād, al-Shāfiʿī supposedly compiled the first version of his *Risāla*. We are not well informed about the reasons of his later emigration to Egypt; however, Chaumont suggests that it may be related to the popularity of the teachings of Mālik in the Ḥijāz. Therefore, Egypt would have provided a more fertile soil for al-Shāfiʿī's doctrine to flourish. He died on a Friday in Rajab 204/820 in Fusṭāṭ; Ferdinand Wüstenfeld, *Der Imâm el-Schâfiʿî seine Schüler und Anhänger bis zum J. 300 d. H.* (Göttingen: Dieterich'sche Verlags-Buchhandlung, 1890), 32–35, 41 and Éric Chaumont, "al-Shāfiʿī," in *EI*²; also, Fuat Sezgin, *GAS*. Vol 1: *Qurʾānwissenschaften, Ḥadīṯ, Geschichte, Fiqh, Dogmatik, Mystik bis ca. 430 H.* (Leiden: E. J. Brill, 1967), 484–485.

29 See Muḥammad b. Idrīs al-Shāfiʿī, *The Epistle on Legal Theory. Muḥammad ibn Idrīs al-Shāfiʿī*, ed. and tr. Joseph E. Lowry (New York and London: New York University Press, 2013).

30 Saḥnūn was born in Qairawān in 160/776. Although, we know that Saḥnūn travelled to Medina and Mecca, it is uncertain whether he was ever taught by Mālik himself. Based on his intellectual exchanges with Ibn al-Qāsim al-ʿAtakī (d. 191/807) and Asad b. al-Furāt (d. 212/827), he penned what was initially called the *Asadīya*. Due to the widespread impact of the *Asadīya* within North Africa, the text was again revised by Ibn al-Qāsim and given the name *Mudawwana*. Saḥnūn is, even today, affiliated with the spread and triumph of the Mālikīya in Ifrīqiyā and the development of Qairawān into an important center of learning for Mālikī jurisprudence; Fuat Sezgin, *GAS*. Vol 1: *Fiqh*, 468 and Mohamed Talbi, "Saḥnūn," in *EI*². For matrimony in other legal schools such as the Ḥanbalīya, see Susan A. Spectorsky, *Chapters on marriage and divorce: responses of Ibn Ḥanbal and Ibn Rāhwayh* (Austin: University of Texas Press, 1993).

31 This can be attributed to the fact that slaves are considered property while possessing undeniable human qualities which make them surface not merely in sections on property law but also in such concerned with other regulations.

Chapter VI
Matrimony

A. Sasanian law: utilizing female reproductive capacities

1. Cosmogony and eschatology: the origins and benefits of marriage

In this chapter, I discuss the various types of matrimony in Sasanian law arguing that these are closely tied to the notion of maintaining empire while being integrated into the cosmic idiom of Zoroastrianism. The *Avesta* and the Pahlavi books indicate that the reproduction of the creatures supporting Ohrmazd is beneficial for the cosmos and, more importantly, protects the earth from the expansion of the evil forces of Ahriman.[1] To be more precise, it is considered the private duty (*ẖwēškārīh*) of every Zoroastrian to contribute to the proliferation of human creatures.[2] According to the myth of creation, all human creatures that were and will be, originated from the first semen of next-of-kin marriage (*ẖwēdōdah*).[3] Most significantly, the religious books sanctify this particular form of marriage which is well summarized by Prods O. Skjærvø:

> Marrying one's closest relatives (parents, siblings, children) was said to be one of the foremost good deeds [...], the model for which was provided by three divine and mythical unions: Ohrmazd and his daughter Spandārmad (the earth), Gayōmard and his mother Spandārmad, and the two first humans Mashī and Mashiyānī [...].[4]

Cosmogony, in fact, provides for each kind of incest with first-degree relatives an archetype: Ohrmazd and Spandārmad (father and daughter),

---

1 *[Vidēvdad] Wrestling with the Demons of the Pahlavi Widēwdād*, ed., tr., and ct. Mahnaz Moazami (Leiden and Boston: Brill, 2014), 353 (14.15). Also, *Dēnkard. Book 4. Zoroastrian Religious Writings from the Arsacid and Sasanian Periods*, tr. Dastur Peshotanji Behramji Sanjana, 24 (113), accessed online: http://www.avesta.org/denkard/dk4.html, July 10, 2017: "Every man that has a material body should regard his own marriage as a good work incumbent on him to perform [...]. And he should promote the marriages of others."

2 *Dēnkard, Book 7*, 1, 9, accessed online: http://www.avesta.org/denkard/dk7.html, July 10, 2017: "[Mashī and Mashiyānī] also performed the will of the creator, enjoyed the advantage of the many duties of the world, and practiced next-of-kin marriage for procreation, union, and the complete progress of the creations in the world, which are the best good works of mankind." Likewise, cf. Maria Macuch, "Herrschaftskonsolidierung und sasanidisches Familienrecht," 157.

3 *Le Troisième Livre du Dēnkart*, ed. Jean de Menasce (Paris: Librairie C. Klincksieck, 1973), 86, 17–20.

4 Prods O. Skjærvø, *The Spirit of Zoroastrianism*, 33–34.

Gayōmard and Spandārmad (son and mother), Mashī and Mashiyānī (brother and sister). According to Zoroastrian dogma, these are all desirable forms of matrimony. Maria Macuch indicates that the term for incestuous marriages figures five times in the *Avesta*. However, she states that it is unclear whether it is used in the precise meaning of next-of-kin marriage.[5] The Pahlavi books support the notion of benefit that comes through instituting next-of-kin marriage, and, moreover, make evident that it is among the most meritorious deeds a believer can commit. In a law book on the proper and improper behavior of Zoroastrians, probably written in late Sasanian times, a story is quoted in which Ahriman, the representative of darkness himself, concedes the virtue and merit of next-of-kin marriage:

> Aharman [Ahriman] exclaimed thus: 'Enter into the season-festival! [...] enter into the sacred feast! [...] but avoid next-of-kin marriage! because I do not know a remedy for it; for whoever has gone four times near to it will not become parted from the possession of Aûharmazd [Ohrmazd] and the archangels.'[6]

Elsewhere, it is stated that next-of-kin marriage is in an inverse relationship with anal intercourse (*kunmarz*). Accordingly, the creatures of Ohrmazd, practicing next-of-kin marriage to recreate the cosmos, counteract the followers of Ahriman who engage in sinful anal intercourse to spread evil.[7] Furthermore, next-of-kin marriage is embedded in the eschatological vision of Mazdaism. This becomes evident from *The Pahlavi Rivāyat*:

> Just as today the most evil (comes) from sodomy, so when the Sōšāns [the Messiah] comes, all men will practise *xwēdōdah* [next-of-kin marriage], and every demon will be destroyed through the miracle and power of *xwēdōdah*.[8]

This chapter, more broadly, sheds light on the stipulations on matrimony in the *Hazār Dādestān*. Moreover, I investigate to what extent the cosmological sanctioning of particular types and institutions of matrimony ties in with the practical concerns of the Sasanian elite. This inquiry illustrates that the legal authorities utilized, and were forced to utilize, the idiom of cosmology for the sake of justifying the marital practices and institutions they propagated.

---

5 Maria Macuch, "Inzest im vorislamischen Iran," 150. The passages she points at: *Yasna*, 12, 9; *Vidēvdad* 8, 13; *Visperad* 3, 3; *Gāh* 4, 8; *Yašt* 24, 17.

6 [*Šāyest nē šāyest*] *The Sacred Books of the East*, vol. 5, tr. E.W. West (Oxford: Clarendon Press, 1880), 389. For a brief discussion of this passage, cf. Maria Macuch, "Inzest im vorislamischen Iran," 150.

7 Maria Macuch, "Inzest im vorislamischen Iran," 150, also, Yishai Kiel, *Sexuality in the Babylonian Talmud*, 161. Noteworthy, it is doubtful whether or not anal intercourse can be compensated for by entering a next-of-kin marriage.

8 *The Pahlavi Rivāyat. Accompanying the Dādestān ī Dēnīg. Part II: Translation, Commentary and Pahlavi Text*, ed., tr. and ct. Alan V. Williams (Copenhagen: Munksgaard, 1990), 12 (8c6).

2. *Marriage types*

a. *Full marriage (pādiḫšāy)*

To enter a marriage with full matrimonial rights (*pādiḫšāy*), a woman is required to obtain approval by her legal guardian (*sālār*).[9] The formulation of the stipulation in the *Hazār Dādestān*–the "sister" or "daughter"–indicates that the guardianship (*sālārīh*) over her is usually held by her brother or father. In case she enters a marriage without the approval of her legal guardian, it is considered invalid.[10] The approval is required because, when entering a *pādiḫšāy*-marriage, the guardianship over the woman is transferred from her former guardian to the *pādiḫšāy*-husband.[11]

The appropriation of the legal guardianship by the husband is a necessary condition of a *pādiḫšāy*-marriage. A stipulation in the *Hazār Dādestān* with regard to a certain Farroḫ makes this evident:

> If he declares: 'I have dissolved my marriage with (this) woman and have given her in marriage and guardianship to Farraxv [Farroḫ]', and (if) Farraxv takes the woman as a wife but declares regarding the guardianship: 'there is no need ('not needed')'; some (authorities) have stated that (in such a case) the divorce is not valid. Vahrām has stated that the reason for this is that to declare: 'not needed' with regard to the guardianship is to declare (the same) with regard to the marriage. *For a marriage cannot ('may not') exist without guardianship* [my emphasis] [...].[12]

In the case at hand, a man dissolves the marriage with his *pādiḫšāy*-wife giving her in marriage and guardianship to Farroḫ who accepts her as his wife but not the guardianship over her. Farroḫmard informs us that, according to some authorities, this marriage does not come into effect, since a *pādiḫšāy*-marriage is concomitant with the guardianship over the wife. The marriage of the husband who wanted to divorce his *pādiḫšāy*-wife is, in turn, not dissolved.

We can adduce at least two other stipulations showing that the validity of the *pādiḫšāy* is intertwined with the transfer of the legal guardianship to the *pādiḫšāy*-husband. The first states that a marriage can only be terminated with the assignment of a new legal guardian over the wife and the verbatim statement "let (her) be given (in guardianship to such a one?)."[13] The other features an interesting, more complex case. If a woman remarries after

---

9 Farroḫmard, *HazDP*, 101 (36, 2–5).

10 Ibid.

11 Ibid., 35 (4, 15–5, 3).

12 Farroḫmard, *HazDP*, 35 (4, 15–5, 3); see the commentary of Maria Macuch, *HazDM*, 85-86.

13 Farroḫmard, *HazDP*, 35 (4, 9–10).

being divorced by her *pādiḫšāy*-husband and the former husband for whatever reason failed to transfer the guardianship over her, then any children born to her are legally considered his, irrespective of whether or not he is the natural father.[14] This illustrates that a marriage with full matrimonial rights is valid for as long as the legal guardianship over the wife is with the *pādiḫšāy*-husband.[15]

Once the *pādiḫšāy* is valid, both spouses have certain rights and obligations. First, it is important to note that all children born from this type of marriage are affiliated with the lineage of the husband. Macuch points out that due to the absence of primogeniture in Iranian law, all sons equally are considered his legal successors and heirs.[16] Concerning the husband, the law book explicitly states that he is obliged to provide maintenance to his *pādiḫšāy*-wife:

> A well-behaved and pious wife from a *pātixšāyih*-marriage [marriage with full matrimonial rights] (must be supported) year after year at her husband's expense, and the husband may not say: 'do not give (funds for her) support!'[17]

The *pādiḫšāy*-wife, on the other hand, commits to sustaining her husband's lineage, should he, for whatever reason, remain childless.[18] This obligation is valid even beyond his death and, as we will see, led to the development of the complex institution of the intermediary successor (*ayōkēn*). For instance, in case of the death of her childless husband, the *pādiḫšāy*-wife would be appointed his *ayōkēn* whose responsibility it was to enter an auxiliary marriage (*čagar*) the children of which are considered offspring of her deceased *pādiḫšāy*-husband.[19] Essentially, the *pādiḫšāy* implements an exchange of financial securities on the part of the husband for the lifelong commitment to producing offspring on the part of the wife.

The laws on property indicate that the termination of the *pādiḫšāy* results in the suspension of this exchange. While married, the husband can convey to his *pādiḫšāy*-wife anything he likes except land, water, plants, the house

14 Ibid., 33 (3, 15–4, 1).

15 The conjunction of the *pādiḫšāy*-marriage with the legal guardianship over a woman is attested elsewhere. For instance, another provision stipulates that a divorce is only valid once the question concerning the legal guardianship is settled; ibid., 295 (87, 7–10). For a further discussion of the features of the *pādiḫšāy*-marriage; see Maria Macuch, "Herrschaftskonsolidierung und sasanidisches Familienrecht," 152–153.

16 Maria Macuch, "Zoroastrian Principles and the Structure of Kinship in Sasanian Iran," 236.

17 Farroḫmard, *HazDP*, 95 (33, 9–11). Elsewhere, it is stated that the husband has the duty to maintain his *pādiḫšāy*-wife as well as minor *pādiḫšāy*-children; ibid., 89 (30, 10–11); also, ibid, 91 (31, 4–6).

18 Maria Macuch, "Herrschaftskonsolidierung und sasanidisches Familienrecht," 152–153.

19 Ibid., 154.

and a maximum of two slaves.[20] However, there is disagreement on what property the wife is entitled to take away with herself in the case of a divorce. What is certain, is that if the divorce is consensual, she cannot raise any claim to property acquired during the marriage.[21] For different circumstances, varying opinions prevail. Farroḫmard notes that some authorities rule that the wife cannot take away with her any property obtained during the marriage, but that she is permitted to return with the dowry, meaning the share in her father's inheritance that she brought into the marriage.[22] He also states that the proper procedure is to make sure that she leaves the marriage provided for.[23] While married, therefore, the wife can expect to be compensated and provided for financially–probably due to her commitment to produce offspring even beyond the death of her husband. However, once that commitment is not sustained, meaning the marriage terminated, she is only entitled to the property that she herself brought into the marriage (the dowry) and can hardly make any claims to the financial assets of her husband.

b. Auxiliary marriage (čagar)

This brings us to the second type of marriage: the auxiliary marriage (*čagar*). The primary purpose of this marriage is most likely to assure the continuation of a man's lineage. Accordingly, this form of matrimony is instituted especially in the case that a *pādiḫšāy*-husband dies without a male successor. It is not limited to the wife of the deceased but could also be entered by his daughter or sister who would, similarly to his wife, be instituted as his intermediary successor (*ayōkēn*).[24] Furthermore, any other member inside or outside the family could be instituted as his substitute-successor (*stūr*)[25] and likewise procreate or bear children in an auxiliary marriage who would legally be considered children of the deceased.

In general, children born from an auxiliary marriage are not affiliated to the lineage of their natural father (*čagar*-father). The law book is unmistakably clear on this. They are thus authorized neither to legal claims towards him, nor to the appointment as family guardians or substitute-successors

20 Farroḫmard, *HazDP*, 95 (33, 9–11).

21 Ibid., 35 (4, 13–14).

22 Ibid., 35 (4, 11–13).

23 Ibid.

24 Ibid., 69 (21, 5–8 and 21, 8–10).

25 Ibid., 119 (44, 2–3): "If [...] they [the kinsmen] do not wish (to accept) the *stūr*ship [...], (then), [...] a fellow-citizen [...] must be appointed (as *stūr*) in accordance with the procedural norms [...]."

(*stūr*) in the lineage of the *čagar*-father.[26] This indicates that in a legal sense these children are not in any way related to their natural father. However, it seems that, occasionally, their status, and even that of the wife, would have been modified. More specifically, Farroḫmard informs us about the authorities' opinions with regard to elevating the status of the *čagar*-wife and *čagar*-children to the *pādiḫšāy*-type:

> [...] [I]n the chancellery of the magupat [chief-priest] of Artaxšahr-Xvarreh, it has been decreed to take into account [...], that if (anyone) declares as regards a wife and child from a *čakar*-marriage: 'I have received (her/him) as a *pātixšāy*-wife and as *pātixšāy*-children', then such a decision should not be considered to have legal force [...].[27]
>
> Besides that, Pusānveh ī Burzatūr Farnbaγān has said, that when (a question of the taking) a wife or child from a *čakar*-marriage as a *pātixšāy*-wife and *pātixšāy*-children (is examined), then this question is resolved in accordance (with the existing general rules) for the adoption of a son or daughter. And the wife, if she becomes a *pātixšāy* one, shall inherit (her husband's) estate and it must go to her.[28]

The articles seem to disagree with each other. In the opinion of the chancellery, statements in which the husband indicates his willingness to accept both, the *čagar*-wife and *čagar*-children, as part of a *pādiḫšāy*-agreement are not legally valid. By contrast, Pusānweh i Burzādur-Farrbayān clarifies that the official procedure in this case is for the *čagar*-father to adopt the children; whereas the wife–presumably if not yet in another *pādiḫšāy*-relation–is recognized as his *pādiḫšāy*-wife. Regarding the acceptance of the wife into a *pādiḫšāy*-wedlock, another authority, Māhdād-Gušnasp mentions that a decision on this matter must be taken in the city of Darabgird.[29] It is noteworthy that Macuch comments on this passage arguing that, according to Iranian legal theory, the transformation of a *čagar*-marriage into a *pādiḫšāy* is generally not permissible, however, as the above stipulations attest, it was probably common in practice.[30]

Lastly, an auxiliary marriage is not contracted solely to produce offspring for a deceased *pādiḫšāy*-husband who remained childless. Put differently, it could also come into effect during his lifetime, as the following passage indicates:

---

26 Ibid., 271 (A14, 9–10), 83 (27, 14–15).
27 Ibid., 321 (A40, 9–11).
28 Ibid., 321 (A40, 11–14).
29 Ibid., 175 (70, 3–12).
30 Maria Macuch, *HazDM*, 473–4.

> If he declares to his wife: 'I have granted you the right of 'self-guardianship,' the marriage is not dissolved (thereby), but she is given the right to enter into a *čakar* marriage.[31]

The stipulation is hard to analyze because we do not know due to what purpose a husband would allow his *pādiḫšāy*-wife to enter a *čagar*-marriage. We can think of at least two reasons. First, if the husband is sterile and yet without children, it would make sense for him to allow her to enter another marriage to bear him children. However, due to the transfer of the legal guardianship to her, we can assume that the children conceived in such a marriage would not be his–as we saw in one of the above stipulations which made clear that children born from other marriages are affiliated to the *pādiḫšāy*-husband only while he holds the legal guardianship over his *pādiḫšāy*-wife.[32] The second more likely reason is quite different. In this case, he would allow his wife to enter a *čagar*-marriage with the purpose of bearing children by and for another man who is yet childless. This is plausible against the backdrop of the legal guardianship being bestowed on her which would allow her to pass it on to the *čagar*-husband so that the children she gives birth to are affiliated to the latter's lineage.[33]

The cases and different regulations I have discussed here are not exhaustive. It is undoubtedly beyond the scope of this thesis to deal with the vast variety of these cases in more detail. What becomes apparent though is that the auxiliary marriage was a highly developed and complex institution in Sasanian law. Furthermore, we will see that it is central to the Sasanian law on matrimony and inheritance and an indispensable institution for the intricate laws on intermediary and substitute-successors.

c. Consensus marriage (ḫwasrāyēn)

The last distinct type of matrimony mentioned by Macuch is the consensus marriage (*ḫwasrāyēn*). This marriage is particularly noteworthy because a daughter does not need permission by her legal guardian (*sālār*) to become a *ḫwasrāyēn*-wife.[34] The most pertinent stipulation on this type of marriage in the *Hazār Dādestān* is as follows:

> If the daughter, without the authorization of the father, marries a *gādār*(-husband): provided that she enters the marriage temporarily [...], then the guardianship and

31 Farroḫmard, *HazDP*, 33 (3, 10–11).

32 Ibid., 33 (3, 15–4, 1).

33 This could, perhaps, be the case when the *pādiḫšāy*-wife was called to serve as the substitute-successor (*stūr*) of her father or brother. Macuch investigates this possibility; Maria Macuch *HazDM*, 75–76 (3.10–11).

34 Maria Macuch, "Die Zeitehe im sasanidischen Recht," 198.

her inheritance share in the estate of the father are not altered. However, if she enters the marriage without a stipulated time limit [...], then the estate of the father does not pass to her and the father loses the work income of the daughter. [35]

First, the passage indicates that a habitual sexual relationship of the daughter with another man who has not been approved by her father is allowed.[36] Moreover, such an association does not release the daughter from the lineage of the father with all the implications this entails. In other words, in spite of being in wedlock, the daughter may still assume the intermediary successorship (*ayōkēnīh*) of her father and continues to have an inheritance share in his estate. This applies as long as the consensus marriage is temporary. Should it be contracted without a time limit, the daughter forfeits her share in the estate of the father. In the same way, any property she acquires cannot be claimed by him. The explicit mentioning that, in the case the consensus marriage is stipulated temporarily, the daughter stays within the lineage of the father, may imply that this is not the case when it is stipulated with no time limit. Judging from the loss of her inheritance share of the estate of the father and the fact that the latter cannot claim property acquired by her, we can probably assume that, in that case, she leaves her father's lineage.

More specifically, it would be useful to know whether–in the case that the consensus marriage is contracted without a time limit–the daughter is affiliated to the lineage of her *ẖwasrāyēn*-husband. Having said this, I have not come across any judgments in the *Hazār Dādestān* which would help to resolve this question.[37] Relying on evidence from the *Rivāyat-ī Hēmīt-ī Ašavahištān*, Maria Macuch answers it in the negative. Therefore, a son

35 Farroẖmard, *HazDM*, 179 (24, 7–10), my translation into English from German. Note that Macuch translates with "Beischlaf" (sexual intercourse) instead of the more tendentious "adultery." Farroẖmard, *HazDP*, 75 (24, 7–10): "If a daughter enters into a sexual relationship without her father's sanction, then–if it is not a case of adultery as a habitual offence–this will not result in an alteration of her status as ward and as successor to (her) father. But if (it is a case) of adultery continually committed by her, then she will not receive the inheritance and the succession of her father, and her father shall likewise lose his right over the daughter's income (= revenue)." Also note that the text states "enters into a sexual relationship without her *father's* sanction," instead of referring to the legal guardian. Macuch equally employs "Vater" in the German translation.

36 The law book, more generally, underscores that "(the decision regarding) sexual intercourse belongs to the daughter;" ibid., 103 (36, 12–16). In other words, the father cannot interfere with the right of his daughter to make decisions about her sexual relationships.

37 A stipulation dealing with the selection of the substitute-successor (*stūr*), in case there are multiple candidates, incidentally mentions the *ẖwasrāyēn*-marriage. However, it does not seem to convey information that would be relevant here; Farroẖmard, *HazDP*, 113 (41, 9–13A); also, see the commentary of Maria Macuch, *HazDM*, 333–334.

born from a consensus marriage, she argues, is juridically considered a "nobody's son" due to his lack of affiliation with the lineage of the father or mother. In addition, her evidence illustrates that the wife is neither entitled to maintenance by her *ḫwasrāyēn*-husband, nor to a share in his estate upon his death.[38]

We do not know precisely about the function of the consensus marriage in Sasanian law. However, the fact that neither husband nor wife seems to obtain material or juridical benefits from this type of matrimony is most striking. As for the husband, the children he begets are presumably not affiliated with his lineage and can therefore not serve as his legal successors or heirs. As for the wife, she is not eligible for maintenance or an inheritance share in the estate of her *ḫwasrāyēn*-husband. Hence, it is reasonable to assume that the primary intent of the *ḫwasrāyēn* was perhaps to sanction sexual relationships which were not authorized by the legal guardian of the daughter. This is plausible, in particular, when looking at other legal systems which similarly developed matrimonial forms making allowance for sexual relationships which could otherwise not be sanctioned.[39] Even though a daughter may enter a *ḫwasrāyēn*-wedlock without the consent of her father, it should again be noted that, under no circumstances, can she contract a marriage with full matrimonial rights without the approval of her guardian.[40]

d. Temporary marriage (*nē az ān ī hamēig*)

Macuch rightly states that the temporary marriage (*nē az ān ī hamēig*) is not a distinct type of matrimony but a variation, since all of the above can be contracted temporarily.[41] The temporary marriage is highly interesting with regard to its implications on the lineage of the daughter. Farroḫmard tells us:

---

38 Maria Macuch, "Die Zeitehe im sasanidischen Recht," 199.

39 The pleasure marriage (*mutʿa*) in Islamic jurisprudence is a case in point. Von Denffer argues that the *mutʿa* does, in fact, have a number of functions but most prominently the legalization of sexual relationships otherwise prohibited (e.g. prostitution); Dietrich von Denffer, "Mutʿa – Ehe oder Prostitution? Beitrag zur Untersuchung des šiʿitischen Islam," in *Zeitschrift der Deutschen Morgenländischen Gesellschaft* 128/2 (1978), 299–325.

40 Farroḫmard, *HazDP*, 101 (36, 2–5): "It is written thus in the Dātastān-nāmak: if a sister or ('and') a daughter enters into a marriage [...] without the permission of her guardian, then (this) marriage is invalid ('not good') [...]." This stipulation must not be confused with the provisions pertaining to the *ḫwasrāyēn*. In other words, it does not encompass the *ḫwasrāyēn*-marriage because it is listed right under the chapter title "[...] concerning a wife with full-rights [...]."

41 Maria Macuch, "Judicial and Legal Systems. iii. Sasanian Legal System," in *Encyclopædia Iranica*, vol. 15, 181–196.

Vāyayār has written that if a daughter–empowered by her father–concludes (the following agreement) with someone: 'I shall be your wife for ten years', and (if) the father dies before the ten years are up, (then) a *stūr* [substitute-successor] must be appointed for the father until the (end of the) ten years limit. At the end of the ten years, however, she ceases to be that man's wife and becomes her father's *epikleros* [heiress].[42]

The case indicates that upon entering a temporary marriage, a daughter probably leaves the lineage of her father and is affiliated to the lineage of her temporary husband.[43] Therefore, if her father dies before the expiration of the temporary marriage, she cannot instantaneously be appointed his intermediary successor. However, once the temporary marriage expires, the daughter again switches to the lineage of the father and reassumes her obligation to serve as intermediary successor. In other words, the duty to intermediary successorship is merely suspended for the duration of the temporary marriage.[44]

The traits of the temporary marriage are ultimately determined by how it is contracted–as a marriage with full matrimonial rights, an auxiliary, or a consensus marriage. In spite of the meager evidence in the law book about the temporary marriage, there is reason to assume that it significantly increased the flexibility of the marital system.[45] For instance, temporary marriages were indispensable with regard to ensuring that the substitute-successors of a deceased could–for a limited duration–attend to their duty of producing offspring for him; however, once birth was given to a male successor (or probably multiple ones considering the high infant mortality rate), their reproductive capacities were more useful elsewhere. Therefore, to prevent these women from ending up in a marital deadlock, the temporary marriage, right from the very start, assured their recirculation with its expiration. Again, it is rather important to note that marriages stipulated with a time limit could have different functions and probably increased the flexibility of the legal system.

---

42 Farroḫmard, *HazDP*, 73 (23, 1–4).

43 The law book, in fact, makes evident the disagreement among authorities on whether or not a daughter is affiliated to the lineage of her husband during a temporary marriage; ibid., 249 (A2, 7–11). The question here is whether the possessions of the daughter, in particular her dowry, stay with her temporary husband in case she dies during the marriage. Accordingly, her property would stay with the temporary husband which strongly indicates her affiliation with his lineage. Some authorities, however, as the case goes, have ruled that this is not the case.

44 In accordance with this, it is stated elsewhere that she remains in the status of intermediary successor (*ayōkēn*) during the temporary marriage; ibid., 203 (87, 2–3).

45 Similarly, cf. Maria Macuch, "The Function of Temporary Marriage in the Context of Sasanian Family Law," in *Proceedings of the Fifth Conference of the Societas Iranologica Europaea held in Ravenna, October 6–11, 2003, vol.* I: *Ancient and Middle Iranian Studies*, eds. A. Panaino and A. Piras (Milano 2006), 594.

3. *Intermediary (ayōkēn) and substitute-successors (stūr)*

The intermediary (*ayōkēn*) and substitute-successor (*stūr*) are perhaps among the most peculiar and intricate institutions in Iranian family law. The purpose of these institutions, more largely, is to assure the continuation of the lineage of a deceased *paterfamilias* (head of household) who does not have a male successor to whom his position and estate can be passed on. The intention inscribed in this institution is, therefore, to make sure that someone produces for him a male successor to take on the responsibility as *paterfamilias*. It is important to realize that the intermediary and the substitute-successor only create the link between the deceased *paterfamilias* and the actual successor.[46] In other words, their positions do not come with the right to successorship or a share in the estate of the deceased. They are, however, endowed with material benefits for which a portion in the estate of the deceased is retained.[47]

The distinction between intermediary and substitute-successor is not always clear throughout the law book. While it mostly distinguishes between them, it occasionally conflates both institutions.[48] Most likely, this is related to the fact that their functions are, for the most part, identical. To be more precise, the intermediary successor constitutes a particular variant of the substitute-successor to be performed exclusively by the wife, the daughter, or the sister of a *pādiḫšāy*-husband. On the contrary, the position of the substitute-successor can, more broadly, be assumed by any person, male or female, inside or outside the family.[49] The law book is clear on the necessity of installing a substitute-successor (*stūr*) in the case that the deceased, at the time of his passing, does not have a wife or children.[50] Having said that, the

46 Maria Macuch, "Herrschaftskonsolidierung und sasanidisches Familienrecht," 154.

47 For the material benefits of *stūr*ship; Farroḫmard, *HazDP*, 113 (41, 8–9): "[...] the *stūr*ship also (presents/gives) an advantage, and that which (presents/gives) an advantage is to be received as though it were needed for the minor [...]." Also, ibid., 113 (41, 16–42,1): "If he declares the following: 'I have declared this thing conveyed for *stūr*ship', and he has two daughters, (then) that (part of the estate) regarding which he made no disposition passes as personal inheritance-shares (= 'daughter's' shares) to both daughters, but that (estate) regarding (whose transfer for *stūr*ship) he made the declaration, shall go to the elder daughter on the basis of a *stūr*'s possession [...]." The stipulation indicates that the share allocated for the substitute-successor (*stūr*) is independent of inheritance shares. Also, cf. Maria Macuch, "Herrschaftskonsolidierung und sasanidisches Familienrecht," 155.

48 Cf. Macuch who states that while the law book distinguishes between intermediary (*ayōkēn*) and substitute-successor (*stūr*), these are, particularly in later texts, usually used interchangeably; Maria Macuch, "Zoroastrian Principles and the Structure of Kinship in Sasanian Iran," 238.

49 Farroḫmard, *HazDP*, 119 (44, 2–3).

50 Ibid., 33 (3, 14–15): "If at the time of his death he had neither a wife nor children, a *stūr* must be appointed."

position only comes into effect when the minimum amount of property owned by the deceased is either 60 or 80 *satērs*.[51] This points to the fact that the meticulous and complex rules pertaining to the continuation of the successor line, which are epitomized in the institutions of the intermediary and substitute successor, did, in fact, only apply to a group that had amassed a minimum amount of material wealth. This is evidence to support my main argument that the particular forms of marriage propagated in Sasanian law are indicative of the imperial aspirations of the ruling elite.

In view of selecting the most suitable candidate for intermediary/substitute-successorship, the *Hazār Dādestān* sets out a multitude of regulations and instructions.[52] In this inquiry, we only focus on the laws pertaining to an *ayōkēn*-daughter. To serve as an intermediary successor to her father, she must be assigned to his lineage. For instance, if she is bound in *pādiḫšāy*-wedlock, her obligation to intermediary successorship ceases because she is not part of her father's lineage. However, in the case the *pādiḫšāy* is dissolved and the legal guardianship over her returned to her father's lineage, she can reassume her obligation as *ayōkēn*.[53] The same rules–as stated above–apply to the temporary marriage. For as long as the daughter is bound in a temporary union, she cannot become the *ayōkēn* of her father. Meanwhile, a placeholder is appointed whom she, once the temporary marriage expires, replaces as the *ayōkēn* of her father.[54] With regard to the consensus marriage, the case is clear because the daughter–provided the *ḫwasrāyēn* is not contracted without a temporal limit–does not leave her father's lineage. These stipulations regarding the *ayōkēn*-daughter come into effect, particularly, in the case that the deceased does not have anyone else in his family who could assume the intermediary successorship (*ayōkēnīh*) for him, meaning a wife or other daughters. Following the appointment as intermediary successor, the *ayōkēn*-daughter is given into an auxiliary marriage, preferably with an agnate, to produce male offspring for the deceased she is appointed for. To make sure the children born from this marriage are correctly affiliated with the lineage of the deceased, the *ayōkēn* first needs to be placed in a *pādiḫšāy*-wedlock with the deceased. This does not apply if the intermediary successorship passes to the wife of the deceased, since she already finds herself in a *pādiḫšāy*-marriage with him. However, in the case it passes to the daughter or sister, she has to enter a *pādiḫšāy* with him. In other words, she fictionally weds her deceased father or brother, respective-

51 There is disagreement among the editors/translators. Perikhanian edits 60, Macuch 80 *satērs*; ibid., 117 (43, 11–13) and Maria Macuch, *HazDM*, 318, 343–344.

52 For instance, Farroḫmard, *HazDP*, 33 (4, 1–4); 71 (22, 6–8); 75 (24, 4–7); 111 (41, 2–5); 113 (41, 5–8); 113 (41, 9–13); 113 (41, 15); 115 (42, 1–5); 115 (42, 5–9).

53 Ibid., 69 (21, 5–8).

54 Ibid., 203 (87, 2–3).

ly. More importantly, this is an instance *par excellence* in which a next-of-kin marriage is employed as a legal strategy to ensure that children end up in the lineage desired by the legal authorities.

In his *Corpus Juris*, Ishoʿbokht hints at Zoroastrian marital practices. To be more precise, he unmistakably refers to intermediary/substitute-successors in Sasanian law. With his recurring polemical tone against the followers of Zarathustra, he states:

> ܐܦܠܐ ܕܐܦ ܠܡܢ ܠܗ ܐܢܬܬܐ ܠܗܘ ܕܡܝܬ: ܐܘ ܠܐ ܡܫܟܚܐ ܐܢܬܬܗ ܕܬܐܠܕ ܡܛܠ ܣܝܒܘܬܐ ܘܥܩܪܘܬܐ: ܢܐܒܕ ܐܦܠܐ ܫܡܗ ܕܗܘ ܕܐܙܠ ܡܢ ܒܝܬ ܚܝ̈ܐ. ܐܠܐ ܡܢ ܒܪܬܗ ܐܘ ܡܢ ܚܬܗ. ܐܘ ܡܢ ܐܚܐ ܟܕ ܢܣܒ ܐܢܬܬܐ ܒܫܡܐ ܕܐܚܘܗܝ: ܐܘ ܒܟܠ ܦܘܪܣ ܡܢ ܐ̄ܢܫ ܡܢ ܒܢ̈ܝ ܓܢܣܗ ܕܡܝܬ [ܕܡܝܬܐ] ܠܗ ܐܦܩ ܙܪܥܐ ܕܡܝܬܐ ܘܫܡܐ ܠܗܘ ܕܐܙܠ.
>
> Not even the name of him who does not leave behind a widow when he dies or whose widow cannot give birth due to age or sterility may perish from among the living. Instead, he [Zarathustra] commanded that [the deceased's] daughter, sister, brother–by entering a marriage with a woman in the name of his [deceased] brother–or, in any case, someone from his lineage should restore the seed of the deceased.[55]

What he asserts to be a command of Zarathustra–to give the daughter, sister, or brother of the deceased in marriage with someone to prevent the deceased's name from disappearing from among the living–can be taken as an explicit reference to the practice of intermediary and substitute-successors. This is telling. First, it indicates that Ishoʿbokht was familiar with these practices. Secondly, it *may* point towards both institutions not being merely a theoretical construct of Sasanian law but, in fact, applied legal practice.

Lastly, we must deliberate on the question of what the laws on intermediary/substitute-successorship indicate about Sasanian law and society more broadly? It is evident that both institutions are, more largely, indicative of the proclivity to maintain agnatic lineages and the reproductive pressure inscribed in Sasanian law. This is initially achieved by obliging women to maintain their husband's lineage when entering a marriage with full matrimonial rights. In fulfillment of this obligation, they are, upon his death, instituted as intermediary successors to produce for him children in an auxiliary marriage. Noteworthy, the position of the intermediary (and substitute) successor is endowed with significant material incentives. The highly complex laws pertaining to this institution, in conjunction with the sophisticated legal idiom it is expressed through, indicate its centrality and importance in Sasanian law.

---

55 Ishoʿbokht, *CorJ*, 96, ll. 26–31 (*Syr.*)/97 [iv, i, §5] (*Ger.*), my translation into English from Syriac.

4. *The practice of next-of-kin marriage (ḫwēdōdah)*

The practice of next-of-kin marriage (*ḫwēdōdah*) in Iranian law and society has received the attention of many scholars. Peculiarly, the regulations pertaining to it and their reinforcement by Zoroastrian authorities, at first glance, quite significantly oppose the general prohibition of incest present in most societies which is succinctly described by Helmut Schelsky:

> The prohibition of incest applies in the first place to the three primary relationships, father-daughter, mother-son, and brother-sister, but affects other, more distant relationships in many cultures […].[56]

It appears that, in fact, the incest "taboo" subscribed to by other societies and their legal systems was absent in the Sasanian context reflected in the sanctioning and promoting of marriages between father and daughter, mother and son, and brother and sister.

This begs the question to what extent the legal doctrine of next-of-kin marriage was able to penetrate into Sasanian society. The answer is unsatisfactory. Some references, particularly in non-Zoroastrian sources, strongly indicate that next-of-kin relationships were, in all likelihood, practiced in Sasanian Iran. Ishoᶜbokht, for instance, asserts that:

> ܕܠܝܛ ܗܘ ܡܢ ܕܕܡܟ ܥܡ ܐܡܗ [ܐܡܗ] ܐܘ ܚܬܗ ܐܘ ܒܪܬܗ ܐܘ ܐ̄ܚܪܢܝܬܐ ܕܐܟܘܬܗܝܢ
> ܗܠܝܢ. ܕܐܦ ܡܡܪܚܝܢ ܒܢܝ̈ܢܫܐ ܒܡܬܪܥܝܬܐ [ܕܒܠܠܗܘܢ ܒܡܬܪܥܝܬܐ] ܕܒܚܕ ܡܢ ܫܘܪ̈ܐ
> ܕܢܡܘܣܐ. ܢܛܝܪܝܢ ܡܢ ܗܠܝܢ ܕܫܪܟܐ. ܡܛܠܗܢܐ ܠܝܛ ܙܪܕܘܫܬ ܕܐܙܝܢ ܒܪܓܬܐ
> ܒܪܢܫܝܬܐ: ܗܘ ܕܒܗ ܐܫܬܒܚ ܣܓܝ ܡܢ ܣܓܝ̈ܐܐ : ܒܗ ܡܢ ܡܥܒܕܢܘܬܐ ܘܡܣܝܥܢܘܬܐ
> ܕܫܐܕ̈ܐ. ܗܢܘܢ ܕܚܕܝܢ ܡܢ ܒܗ ܡܛܠ ܚܕܝܢ ܗܘܘ ܒܪܓܬܐ ܐܬܠܒܒ. ܗܘ ܥܡ ܒܢܝ̈
> ܠܒܗ ܐܡܪܚܘ ܠܡܥܒܪ ܠܒܪ ܡܢ ܗܠܝܢ ܬܠܬ ܫܘܪ̈ܐ ܕܢܡܘܣܐ.

> Doomed is whoever lies with [his] mother, sister, daughter or others like them. Even the people who dare to overstep one of the walls of the law, they remain protected by those [two walls] that remain. That is why doomed is Zarathustra who was armed with lustful desire due to which he became celebrated by many. He was encouraged through the action and the support of the demons which were rejoicing in [his] desire. He and his followers had the impudence to transgress [the boundaries] of these three walls of the law.[57]

We certainly should not ignore the polemic in these works, particularly in the case of Ishoᶜbokht, which may have led non-Zoroastrian writers to exag-

---

56 Helmut Schelsky, *Soziologie der Sexualität. Über die Beziehungen zwischen Geschlecht, Moral und Gesellschaft* (Hamburg: Rowohlt Taschenbuch Verlag, 1955), 88, my translation into English from German.

57 Ishoᶜbokht, *CorJ*, 34, l. 30–36, l. 6 (*Syr.*)/35 [ii, ii] (*Ger.*), my translation into English from Syriac.

gerate on what they considered to be despicable practice.[58] But, besides Ishoᶜbokht, the Armenian historian Eliše Vartabed (d. 475), in his remarks on the Sasanian conquests of Christian Armenia in the fifth century, states that the Zoroastrian priests demanded from the local population

> [...] to take many wives instead of one so that the Armenian nation expands, that the daughters unite with their fathers, the sisters with their brothers, the mothers with their sons, and the granddaughter with their grandfathers [...].[59]

In spite of the specific historical contexts these sources were written in, their different origins make it coceivable that next-of-kin marriage was, in fact, more or less common in Sasanian society or, at least, among the Sasanian elite.[60] In addition, other sources such as Mar Aba could be adduced to provide similar references to the practice of next-of-kin marriage.

It is rather important to note that the *Hazār Dādestān* illustrates that the sanctioning of these next-of-kin marriages was of utmost necessity to making sure that the offspring procured by an *ayōkēn* could be assigned to the lineage of the deceased *paterfamilias*.[61] Put differently, the functioning of the matrimonial institutions in Sasanian law was in many ways contingent on the sanctioning of next-of-kin marriage. To sum up, the doctrine of *ḫwēdōdah* was not only cosmologically sanctioned by the religious authorities, but was at its very heart necessary to ensure that the complicated legal institutions of the Sasanians were coherent and could at all come into effect.

5. *Sustaining elite households*

Regarding "women of high rank such as the queen and the mother of the king," Touraj Daryaee writes that they "were much freer [than women from lower classes] in the scope of their activity and decision making."[62] He then explains that the Sasanian seals, as well as the rock-reliefs which depict women of high rank attending the royal banquets (*bazm*) illustrate those women's importance. At this point, he quite clearly, in my view, confuses importance with freedom. Women of high rank were indeed considered in-

---

58 The *Corpus Juris* contains several polemics against Zoroastrians. See for instance, ibid., 98 (*Syr.*)/97– 99 [iv, i, §5] (*Ger.*).

59 Eliše Vartabed, *Collection des Historiens Anciens et Modernes de l'Arménie*, ed. Victor Langlois (Paris: Librairie de Firmin Didot Frères, 1869), 199, my translation into English from French.

60 However, the reality that the Sasanians entered marriages with next-of-kin relatives would not indicate an absence of a 'natural' aversion to incest. This point is well discussed by Maria Macuch; cf. Maria Macuch, "Inzest im vorislamischen Iran," 151–152.

61 Maria Macuch, "Incestuous Marriage in the Context of Sasanian Family Law," 143.

62 Touraj Daryaee, *Sasanian Persia*, 59.

dispensable in the Sasanian Empire in many regards, in particular, as regards producing male successors for the ruling class. However, we can argue that this responsibility, anchored legally in their obligation to serve as intermediary and substitute-successors, made them–to use the terminology of Daryaee–less "free" than women of lower rank.

The flexibility of marital unions in Sasanian law, accomplished in particular through the institution of auxiliary marriage and temporary alliances, could *de facto* result in women (and men) entering a number of marriages during their lifetime. The restrictions imposed concerning intermediary and substitute successors–the minimum property of 60 or 80 *satērs*–points towards the pressure to sexual reproduction these regulations exerted on members of elite households. Although we have few indicators about the lives of the elite in society, these legal stipulations illustrate that reproduction was not optional but rather an indispensable requirement to maintain the lineages of the Sasanian rulers. To augment opportunities for sexual reproduction, the authorities legitimized sexual relationships that, in other contemporary contexts, were usually prohibited. The sanctioning of next-of-kin marriage was accomplished by wrapping it in the idiom of Zoroastrian cosmology which proved to be the most obvious solution. Not only since Ohrmazd Himself had sexual intercourse with His daughter but because the Zoroastrian heritage provided abundant references that could be mobilized to sanction the practice. To sum up, the legal stipulations on Sasanian matrimony discussed in this chapter provide significant evidence in support of the first main argument of this thesis which is that matrimonial law was mediated between the cosmological imagery and the sociopolitical concerns of empire.

B. East Syrian law: challenging traditions of matrimony

1. On the nature of Christian marriage: marrying strangers (masbā d-nukrāyātā) and monogamy

The scriptural precepts of Christian religion largely conditioned the matrimonial legislation of the Church of the East. However, to argue that it was out of touch with the matrimonial realities of the majority populations in the Sasanian and Muslim Empires would be far from truth. This chapter sheds light on the interwoven nature of lawmaking in the Church of the East with the Sasanian polity while arguing that East Syrian law was subject to certain relaxations resulting in a notion of Christian matrimony which was probably more acceptable to the Sasanian authorities. Marriage, as ruled by the Church of the East, was dominated by two principles both outlined by the eighth-century author Isho^cbokht. The first is the conviction that there is a benefit in marrying strangers (*masbā d-nukrāyātā*), that is, individuals with whom one is not related through kinship.[63] In the opinion of Isho^cbokht:

ܢܨܝܚܐ [ܗܢܝܢܐ] ܡܢ ܡܣܒܐ ܕܢܘܟܪ̈ܝܬܐ [ܕܢܘܟܪܝܬܐ]. ܒܙܢܝ̈ܐ ܣܓܝ̈ܐܐ ܡܬܚܙܐ. ܩܕܡܝܬ ܡܢ
ܒܬܘܣܦܬܐ ܕܚܘܒܐ ܘܥܘܕܪܢܐ ܘܢܝܚܐ: ܘܝܘܬܪܢܐ ܕܗܘܐ ܠܒܢܝ̈ܢܫܐ ܡܢ ܚܘܒܐ ܕܚܕ ܚܕ̈ܕܐ.
ܒܬܪܟܢ ܕܝܢ ܡܢ [ܗܘ ܕܠܝܬ ܒܗ] ܡܘܡܐ ܐ̄ܚܪ̈ܢܐ ܐܝܠܝܢ ܕܒܬܪܟܢ ܡܬܚܘܝܢ.

> The benefit of marrying strangers becomes apparent in various ways: first, an increase of love, succor, satisfaction and virtue which arises among people through their mutual love. Also, [marrying strangers] is devoid of other blemishes to be presented later.[64]

Marrying strangers (*masbā d-nukrāyātā*), as opposed to marrying close-kin (*masbā d-qaribātā*), leads to the proliferation of love (*tawseptā d-ḥubā*), succor (*^cudrānā*), satisfaction (*nyāḥā*), and the virtue (*yutrānā*) of man.[65] To illustrate, the author asserts that a man who gives his daughter and his son in marriage to a man and a woman, respectively, from another place (*duktā (ʾ)ḥritā*) extends into two new families. He contrasts this with the case of a close-kin marriage arguing that it neither results in an extension of the family nor in the proliferation of love among mankind. What is more, Isho^cbokht visualizes the more intricate problems associated with close-kin marriage (*masbā d-qaribātā*). For instance, a man whose daughter is concomitantly his wife suffers two losses (*treyn mawte*) in the case that his wife dies; whereas someone whose daughter is not his wife, may find solace with and the support of the daughter.[66] It is most likely that, apart from the anguish that could be triggered through next-of-kin marriages, such alliances were especially disliked among the jurists due to the significant problems they caused with regard to inheritance. At any rate, in his narrative strategy, Isho^cbokht frames Christian marriage as directly integrated into the larger cosmological realm arguing that evil (*b^celdbābā*) became aware of the benefits that marrying strangers (*masbā d-nukrāyātā*) brought to mankind and therefore began to counteract it.[67] Whereas in the Mazdaean tradition evil is associated with anal inter-

---

63 Isho^cbokht, *CorJ*, 30, ll. 4–10 (*Syr.*)/31 [ii, ii] (*Ger.*).

64 Ibid., 30, ll. 6–9 (*Syr.*)/31 [ii, ii] (*Ger.*), my translation into English from Syriac.

65 Ibid., 30, ll. 7–8 (*Syr.*)/31 [ii, ii] (*Ger.*).

66 Ibid., 30, l. 28–32, l. 3 (*Syr.*)/33 [ii, ii] (*Ger.*):

ܬܘܒ ܕܝܢ ܟܕ ܐܝܬ ܠܓܒܪܐ ܐܢܬܬܐ ܘܒܪܬܐ. ܐܢ ܗܝ ܡܝܬܐ ܐܢ̈ܬܬܗ. ܗ̄ܘܐ ܠܗ ܒܘܝܐܐ
ܘܬܫܡܫܬܐ ܡܢ ܒܪܬܗ. ܐܢ ܕܝܢ ܒܪܬܗ ܡܝܬܐ. ܗ̄ܘܐ ܠܗ ܒܘܝܐܐ ܘܬܫܡܫܬܐ ܡܢ
ܐܢ̈ܬܬܗ. ܐܠܐ ܐܢ ܐܢ̈ܬܬܗ ܗܝ ܗ̄ܝ ܒܪܬܗ. ܐܢ ܡܝܬܐ ܠܗ ܠܐ ܒܪܬܐ ܐܝܬ ܠܗ ܡܕܡ. ܐܦܠܐ
ܐܢܬܬܐ. ܘܗ̄ܘܐ ܡܬܘܚܕ ܡܢ ܬܪ̈ܬܝܗܝܢ. ܘܠܒܝܬܝܢ ܠܗ ܠܝܬ ܡܢܘܬܐ. ܚܣܝܪܐ ܚܕܐ.

67 Ibid., 30, ll. 24–27 (*Syr.*)/33 [ii, ii] (*Ger.*):

course (*kunmarz*), Ishoᶜbokht, most ironically, equates it with close-kin marriage (*masbā d-qaribātā*).

Ishoᶜbokht precisely defines close-kin marriage (*masbā d-qaribātā*). He stakes out its boundaries by listing all family members a Christian ought not to marry. Based on a command in the *Old Testament*, he thus states:

> ܡܢ ܗܠܝܢ ܕܡܬܐܡܪܢ ܒܥܬܝܩܬܐ ܠܡܣܒ. ܐܡܐ. ܒܪܬܐ. ܐܢܬܬ ܐܒܐ. ܚܬܐ. ܒܪܬ ܐܒܐ. ܐܘ ܒܪܬ ܐܡܐ. ܚܬܐ ܕܐܒܐ. ܚܬܐ ܕܐܡܐ. ܐܢ̈ܬܬ ܐܚܐ. ܐܢܬܬ ܕܕܐ. ܚܡܬܐ. ܟܠܬܐ. ܒܪܬ ܐܢ̈ܬܬܐ. ܒܪܬ ܒܪܐ. ܒܪܬ ܒܪܬܐ.
>
> Among those mentioned in the Old Testament [who you are forbidden to marry] are: the *mother*, the *daughter*, the *wife of the father* [stepmother], the *sister*, the *daughter of the father* [sister] or the *daughter of the mother* [half-sister], the *sister of the father* [aunt], the *sister of the mother* [aunt], the *wife of the brother* [sister-in-law], the *wife of the uncle* [aunt], the *mother-in-law*, the *daughter-in-law*, the *daughter of the wife* [stepdaughter], the *daughter of the son* [granddaughter], and the *daughter of the daughter* [granddaughter].[68]

The *Corpus Juris* further stipulates that the term 'mother' incorporates the mother of the mother, 'daughter' the daughter of the daughter and the daughter of the son, and 'wife of the father' her daughter and daughter's daughter.[69] The law is not only careful to explicitly define the core of kinship from which a man may not, under any circumstances, marry but also specifies that someone ought not to enter a marriage with a divorcee (*attā da-šbiqtā*), pagan (*ḥanptā*), an unbeliever (*kāpurtā*), or a magician (*ḥarāštā*).[70]

ܘܟܕ ܚܙܐ ܘܐܬܬܟܠ ܗܘ ܒܡܠܠܕܒܒܘ ܕܝܠܗܘܢ. ܒܡܬܪܬܐ ܘܡܘܠܐ ܘܡܬܕܒܪܢܐ ܕܪ̈ܘܡܝܐ ܠܒܢ̈ܝܢܐ ܡܢ ܩܕܝܡ. ܐܬܚܙܝ ܡܢ ܟܠܗ ܚܝܠܗ ܠܡܣܬܪܘ ܟܠܗܘܢ ܗܠܝܢ ܕܠܡܬܪܢܐ ܘܚܢܐ ܘܡܕܘܬܐ ܕܒܢ̈ܝܢܐ ܚ̈ܝܠܝ ܦ̈ܘܩܕ.

68 Ibid., 28, ll. 19–22 (*Syr.*)/29 [ii, i, §1] (*Ger.*). The passage of the *Old Testament* which Ishoᶜbokht is referring to is most probably *Leviticus* 18, 6–16: "None of you shall approach anyone near of kin to uncover nakedness: […] You shall not uncover […] the nakedness of your *mother*[,] […] the nakedness of your *father's wife*[,] […] the nakedness of your *sister*, your *father's daughter* or your *mother's daughter*, […] the nakedness of your *son's daughter* or of your *daughter's daughter*, […] the nakedness of your *father's wife's daughter*, begotten by your father, […] the nakedness of your *father's sister*[,] […] the nakedness of your *mother's sister*, […] the nakedness of your father's brother, that is, you shall not approach his wife [*father's brother's wife*] […]. You shall not uncover the nakedness of your *daughter-in-law*[,] […] the nakedness of your *brother's wife* […]," *The New Oxford Annotated Bible. New Revised Standard Version with the Apocrypha. An Ecumenical Study Bible*, eds. Michael D. Coogan, Marc Z. Brettler, Carol A. Newsom, and Pheme Perkins (Oxford: Oxford University Press, 2010), 169 (*Lev* 18, 6–16).

69 Ishoᶜbokht, *CorJ*, 28, ll. 22–25 (*Syr.*)/29 [ii, I, §1] (*Ger.*).

70 Ibid., 30, ll. 1–3 (*Syr.*)/31 [ii, i, §4] (*Ger.*).

In addition, matrimonial alliances are, more largely, restricted to Christian women (*ba(r)t haymnutā*).[71]

The second principle is monogamy. The *Corpus Juris* states different reasons for its necessity. These, Ishoᶜbokht asserts, become manifest "through the act and the word of God" (*men ᶜabādā w-men meltēh d-alāhā*).[72] The "act" manifests itself in the initial creation of merely a single woman (*ḥdā a(n)ttā balḥud*) for one man.[73] Put differently, Ishoᶜbokht interprets the monogamous cohabitation of Adam and Eve as a precedent that justifies the Christian ideal of monogamy. With respect to the "word," he invokes a passage from the *Old Testament* which states:

> Therefore a man leaves his father and his mother and clings to his wife, and they become one flesh.[74]

The unification of husband and wife, manifest in the conflation of their bodies into one flesh during the sexual act as well as perpetual wedlock, is at the heart of the notion of Christian matrimony. The symbol of the flesh more broadly implies that both bodies enter a state in which they relinquish authority over themselves becoming subsumed under the physical and mental control of the united flesh. This is corroborated by another reference to the *Gospel*:

> For the wife does not have authority over her own body, but the husband does; likewise the husband does not have authority over his own body, but the wife does.[75]

---

71 Ibid., 30, l. 4 (*Syr.*)/31 [ii, i, §4] (*Ger.*).

72 Ibid., 52, l. 18 (*Syr.*)/53 [ii, ix] (*Ger.*).

73 Ibid., 52, ll. 19–20 (*Syr.*)/53 [ii, ix] (*Ger.*):
ܡܢ ܥܒܕܐ ܗܟܝܠ: ܒܗܿܝ ܕܒܪܐ ܐ̈ܢܬܬܐ ܒܠܚܘܕ ܚܕܐ ܠܓܒܪܐ ܚܕ ܠܚܕܐ.

74 *The New Oxford Annotated Bible*, 14–15 (*Gen* 2, 24). He then adduces another passage from the Gospels (*Matthew* 19, 6), *The New Oxford Annotated Bible*, 1774: "So they are no longer two, but one flesh. Therefore what God has joined together, let no one separate." The full passage as quoted by Ishoᶜbokht, *CorJ*, 52, ll. 20–29 (*Syr.*)/53 [ii, ix] (*Ger.*):
ܘܡܢ ܡܠܬܐ ܕܝܢ: ܒܗܿܝ ܕܐܡܪ. ܕܡܛܠ ܗܢܐ ܢܫܒܘܩ ܓܒܪܐ ܠܐܒܘܗܝ ܘܠܐܡܗ. ܘܢܩܦ
ܠܐܢܬܬܗ. ܘܢܗܘܘܢ ܬܪ̈ܝܗܘܢ ܚܕ ܒܣܪ. ܘܠܬܠܡ̈ܝܕܐ ܐܡܪ. ܘܠܐ ܩܪ̈ܝܬܘܢ. ܘܬܪ̈ܝܗܘܢ ܘܠܐ
ܡܫܪܐ. ܘܐܦ ܗܢܘ ܒܗ ܡܫܝܚܐ ܡܫܪܪ ܠܗܢܐ ܢܡܘܣܐ. ܐܡܪ. ܠܐ ܩܪ̈ܝܬܘܢ ܕܗܘ ܕܥܒܕ ܡܢ
ܒܪܫܝܬ: ܕܟܪܐ ܘܢܩܒܬܐ ܥܒܕ ܐܢܘܢ. ܘܐܡܪ. ܡܛܠ ܗܢܐ ܢܫܒܘܩ ܓܒܪܐ ܠܐܒܘܗܝ
ܘܠܐܡܗ. ܘܢܩܦ ܠܐܢܬܬܗ. ܘܢܗܘܘܢ ܬܪ̈ܝܗܘܢ. ܚܕ ܒܣܪ. ܘܡܢ ܡܫܝܚܐ ܠܗܿ ܠܡܠܬܐ
ܡܫܪܪ. ܘܐܡܪ. ܡܟܝܠ. ܠܐ ܗܘܘ ܬܪ̈ܝܢ. ܐܠܐ ܚܕ ܦܓܪ. ܘܡܘܣܦ ܐܦ ܦܘܩܕܢܐ. ܡܕܡ
ܗܟܝܠ ܕܐܠܗܐ ܙܘܓ. ܒܪܢܫܐ. ܠܐ ܢܦܪܫ.

75 *The New Oxford Annotated Bible*, 2008 (1 *Cor* 7, 4). For the reference by Ishoᶜbokht, see Ishoᶜbokht, *CorJ*, 52, ll. 29–32 (*Syr.*)/53 [ii, ix] (*Ger.*).

In brief, the reasons for monogamy proposed by our author are twofold, one resulting from the life of Adam and Eve as a monogamous couple, the other from God's verbal utterance concerning the unified flesh. Also, I would like to suggest that the monogamous type of marriage hailed in the Eastern Church may be thought of as a wordly reproduction of the strict monotheism laid claim to by Christianity. The personal relation of man to God, particularly, the requirement not to associate shareholders to the divine being, clearly reverberates in the realm of Christian matrimony. In other words, God's demand to exclusivity in the religious pantheon can be thought of as epitomized in the relationship between husband and wife. The prohibition not to have more than a single partner attests to this. In brief, the commitment of husband and wife to perennial fleshly unity in the material realm somewhat symbolizes the exclusive spiritual merger of the human mind with the truths of divine knowledge.

The hermeneutics of the *Corpus Juris* take on shape through two main strategies. On the one hand, Ishoᶜbokht relentlessly polemicizes the adherents of Zarathustra dismissing the practice of next-of-kin marriage (*masbā d-qaribātā*). His staging of Christian matrimony extensively relies on contrasting it with Zoroastrian law. This, more largely, illustrates how strongly the debates with the Zoroastrians reverberated within Christian matrimonial law. Related to this, Sebastian Brock argues that the narrow dimensions of matrimony, particularly, the Christian ideal of virginity, were rather sensitive issues in interactions with the Zoroastrian authorities.[76] On the other hand, the metropolitan frequently adduces Biblical passages which not only provide him with the conceptual tools to justify his views but which he simultaneously employs to establish textual authority. More broadly, this inquiry will show that while Ishoᶜbokht's ideal of matrimony is principally based on a literalist interpretation of scripture, his precursors had advocated a notion that was considerably in line with concurrent societal norms which were largely dictated by a Zoroastrian majority.

2. Filing for divorce (purshānā)–the impossible?

Divorcing a wife or husband is perhaps among the most cumbersome, if not impossible, undertakings for adherents of Eastern Christianity. Moreover, the law, as exhibited in Ishoᶜbokht, sets meticulous restrictions geared at preventing the dissolution of a marriage. Noteworthy, the conditions to divorce a spouse are gendered and depend on whether the husband or the wife instigate it. The *Corpus Juris* mentions three circumstances under which a

[76] Sebastian Brock, "Christians in the Sasanian Empire," 14.

husband may divorce his wife: if she renounces God (*kpurāyā db-alāhā*), commits adultery (*gawrā*), or murder (*qeṭlā*).[77] Ishoʿbokht specifies that performing magic (*ḥarāšutā*) belongs to the category of renouncing God.[78] We are further informed about the reasons why separations under the above circumstances are considered permissible. Apostasy (*kpurāyā db-alāhā*) is considered a legitimate ground for divorce due to the individual's abandonment of the community of believers.[79] This applies to men and women equally. As concerns adultery (*gawrā*), it constitutes a reason for divorce because the woman who commits it, destroys the fleshly union with her husband.[80] Murder, on the other hand, results in divorce because it leads to "the separation of the coherence and natural composition of the soul and the body"[81] of the one who commits it. Other than for the above reasons, a man may divorce his wife in order to reach perfection (*b-ʿelat myatrutā*). In other words, if he decides to become an ascetic, the divorce is sanctioned by God with the justification that the love to God is always superior to the love of other people (*Matthew* 10, 37).[82]

The leverage of women to divorce their husbands is minimal at best. That is, women can make claims based on apostasy and murder, but not adultery.[83] The *Corpus Juris* makes this unmistakably clear laying out the proper procedure to be adhered to in the case of a husband's infidelity:

> ܠܓܒܪܐ ܕܝܢ ܡܐ ܕܡܬܚܫܕ ܒܗ ܠܐܢܬܬܗ. ܒܟܠܗܬܐ ܒܗ ܘܒܡܚܫܒܬܐ ܘܒܐܘܪܚܐ ܘܒܡܠܬܐ
> ܡܬܚܢܢܝܢ ܥܡ ܠܗܘܢ. ܘܠܐ ܡܦܪܫ ܠܡܫܒܩܗ̇ ܕܬܬܦܪܫ ܡܢܗ.

77 Ishoʿbokht, *CorJ*, 56, ll. 26–29. (*Syr.*)/57 [ii, xi] (*Ger.*).

78 Ibid., 56, ll. 29–30. (*Syr.*)/57 [ii, xi] (*Ger.*):

ܕܐܦ ܚܪܫܘܬܐ. ܒܟܘܦܪܐ ܐܬܝܐ ܕܒܐܠܗܐ.

79 Ibid., 56, l. 31–58, l. 3 (*Syr.*)/57 [ii, xi] (*Ger.*):

ܘܒܐܢܬܬܐ ܠܓܒܪܐ ܡܗܝܡܢܐ ܚܠܦ ܒܐܢܬܬܗ. ܒܗ̇ܝ ܕܟܦܪܬ ܒܐܠܗܐ. ܐܝܟ ܕܐܬܦܪܫܬ ܡܢ ܐܠܗܐ. ܘܐܦ ܗ̇ܝ ܒܫܘܬܦܘܬܐ: ܒܗܝ ܕܢܦܠܬ ܐܠܗܐ.

80 Ibid., 58, ll. 3–4 (*Syr.*)/59 [ii, xi] (*Ger.*):

ܠܗܕܐ ܕܝܢ ܡܛܠ ܕܚܒܠܬܗ̇ ܫܠܛܐ ܠܡܫܒܩܘܬܐ ܕܫܘܬܦܘܬܗ̇. ܒܗ ܕܫܘܬܦܘܬܗ̇ ܕܠܓܒܪܐ ܐܚܪܢܐ.

81 Ibid., 58, ll. 4–8. (*Syr.*)/59 [ii, xi] (*Ger.*):

ܡܛܠܐ ܕܝܢ ܩܛܠ. ܡܛܠ ܕܦܪܫܗ ܠܚܝܘܬܐ ܘܪܘܚܐ ܥܡ ܦܓܪܐ ܕܢܦܫܐ ܥܡ ܦܓܪܐ: ܗܘ ܕܐܬܬܠܡܐ [ܐܬܬܠܡܐ؟] ܥܡ ܐܝܬܘܬܗ ܕܢܦܫܐ ܕܒܟܠ. ܘܐܦ ܕܐܦ ܗ̄ܝ ܬܬܦܪܫ ܡܢ ܫܘܬܦܘܬܐ ܕܠܓܒܪܐ: ܗܘ ܕܐܬܛܠܝܗ ܠܗ ܥܒܘܕܐ ܢܦܫܐ ܘܦܓܪܐ.

82 Ibid., 60, l. 10–62, l. 3(*Syr.*)/61–63 [ii, xiii] (*Ger.*).

83 Ibid., 58, l.13–60, l. 7 and 62, l. 24–64, l. 6 (*Syr.*)/59–61 and 63–65 [ii, xii and xiv] (*Ger.*).

> When the husband is witnessed committing adultery, then we must blame, reprimand, penalize, and hinder him from taking the sacrament. However, we do not command that the wife divorce him.[84]

In other words, even though he shall be "confronted, reprimanded, and penalized," the wife will have to bear with the reality of her husband committing adultery and cannot rely on the assistance of the bishops. More importantly, we need to ask why a wife whose husband committed adultery is not bestowed with the legal capacity to divorce him, whereas he–in the case that she is unfaithful to him–is. The justification expounded by Ishoᶜbokht is not only witty but attests to a more considerable concern that the law of matrimony is commonly regulated by: inheritance law. A wife, who delivers a child procreated in an illicit sexual relationship, necessarily brings the child into the wedlock with her deceived husband. The child, because of becoming affiliated with its unnatural father, would be entitled to the financial assistance and a share in the estate of its non-natural father.[85] To avoid liability inflicted through a wife's infidelity, the husband is legally protected through his capacity to dissolve a marriage with an unfaithful wife. On the other hand, if the husband commits adultery impregnating another woman, the child born from such an illicit encounter does not result in financial liability of the deceived wife because it is not affiliated with the lineage of her or the husband.[86] Ishoᶜbokht elucidates that the capacity given to husbands with regard to divorcing their wife is to account for two realities: that women are more trustworthy in matters of parentage and that husbands bear the costs of providing maintenance for their wives.[87] This is perhaps an example *par excellence* where it becomes apparent how the law creates room for and deals with doubt. Doubt, in this case, is counterbalanced by lawmakers by protecting the party it may compromise. In other words, providing husbands with the capacity to divorce their wives is *de facto* to balance out their legal position as opposed to their wives. Overall, we

---

84 Ibid., 60, ll. 1–3 (*Syr.*)/59–61 [ii, xii] (*Ger.*), my translation into English from Syriac.

85 Ibid., 58, ll. 24–27 (*Syr.*)/59 [ii, xii] (*Ger.*):
ܠܓܒܪܐ ܕܝܢ ܡܢ ܕܐܠܨܐ ܐܢܬܬܗ. ܦܪܘܩ ܕܡܫܬܠܛܝܢ ܡܢܗ̇. ܠܐ ܢܦܩ ܕܐܦ ܕܢܫܠܘ ܐܢܘܢ ܒܢ̈ܝܐ ܠܘ ܕܐ̄ܚܪ̈ܢܐ. ܘܡܦܣܩܘܬܐ ܒܓܒ̈ܪܐ ܕܫܘܠܛܐ ܕܒܢ̈ܝܐ ܘܡܘܙܢܐ ܕܝܘܒܠܐ ܢ̈ܫܐ ܗܘܐ ܡܬܝܗܒܝܢ ܡܢ ܓܒ̈ܪܐ.

86 Ibid., 58, ll. 17–19 (*Syr.*)/59 [ii, xii] (*Ger.*):
ܡܛܠ ܕܓܒܪܐ ܡܢ ܟܕ ܦܠܚ ܠܘܬܐ ܥܡ ܐܢܬܬܐ ܐ̄ܚܪܬܐ. ܒܢ̈ܝܐ ܕܡܫܬܠܛܝܢ ܡܢܗ̇. ܠܐ ܡܣܬ ܠܚܕܘܬܐ ܘܠܦܠܓܘܬܐ ܘܠܝܪܬܘܬܐ ܕܐܢܬܬܗ ܢܡܘܣܐ. ܘܐܦܠܐ ܒܚܝܢܐ ܕܬܘܪܣܝܐ ܘܡܬܪܒܝܢܘܬܐ ܕܐܢܬܬܗ. ܡܬܚܪܐ ܠܗܘܢ.

87 Ibid., 58, ll. 26–28 (*Syr.*)/59 [ii, xii] (*Ger.*):
ܘܡܦܣܩܘܬܐ ܒܓܒ̈ܪܐ ܕܫܘܠܛܐ ܕܒܢ̈ܝܐ ܘܡܘܙܢܐ ܕܝܘܒܠܐ ܢ̈ܫܐ ܗܘܐ ܡܬܝܗܒܝܢ ܡܢ ܓܒ̈ܪܐ.

need to note that husbands could mobilize claims for adultery, but not wives, who wished to separate from their spouses.

Other circumstances could lead to a divorce. For a wife keen on separating, perhaps the most blissful situation to arise is for her husband to develop a physical condition preventing him from sexual intercourse with her. In that case, she must not remain with him for more than a year.[88] Thus, matrimonial law seems to be concerned with safeguarding a fertile environment. If the husband or wife becomes a captive, the other party is allowed to dissolve the marriage after three years of waiting. However, it is clearly stated that keeping up the wait is highly appreciated and construed as a sign of chastity and marital love.[89] By far the worst thing that could happen to a wife is if her husband travels and he is not heard of. Even if he does not provide maintenance, she must keep up the wait for at least seven years before she may, under significant hardship, ask the authorities to separate from him. However, if the husband provides a living for her while traveling, she must wait for an additional three years to be capable of filing for divorce.[90] The significant constraints for women regarding the dissolution of a marriage may indicate that separations enforced by wives were rare. To get rid of her husband, the best a woman could do was to hope that he murders someone, becomes a pagan or develops an erectile dysfunction.

The many references to Biblical passages as well as the adoption of scriptural reasoning indicate that the *Corpus Juris* is profoundly grounded in the spirit of textuality. In other words, Ishoʿbokht's interpretation of matrimony has to be seen as following the cosmological and spiritual imagery of the Christian religion. More importantly, it evolved in reaction and conflict to a practice of lawmaking which, in its heydays at the end of the fifth century, had attempted to account for the changing realities of the Christian community under Sasanian rule.

---

88 Ibid., 82, ll. 10–16 (*Syr.*)/83 [iii, vi, §2] (*Ger.*):
ܥܠ ܐܢܬܬܐ ܕܓܒܪܗ̇ ܠܟܫܝܐ ܕܒܟܠܠܗ̇ ܘܠܐ ܡܫܟܚ ܕܢܫܡܫܝܗ̇ ܠܗ̇ ܡܛܠ ܟܠܠܬܐ ܕܡܘܡܐ ܡܫܢܝܐ. [...] ܐܦ ܕܝܢ ܠܐ ܫܦܝܪ ܫܠܝܛ ܠܗ̇ ܕܠܐ ܬܬܒ ܝܬܝܪ ܡܢ ܫܢܬܐ.

89 Ibid., 84, ll. 7–9 (*Syr.*)/ 85 [iii, viii] (*Ger.*):
ܥܠ ܫܒܝܐ ܗܢ ܕܫܒܝ ܢܛܪ ܠܬܠܬ ܫܢ̈ܝܢ. ܗܘ ܐܢܬܬܐ ܕܓܒܪܐ ܢܛܪܐ. ܐܬܐ ܢܟܦܘܬܐ ܕܪܚܡܬܐ. ܘܫܘܒܚܐ ܕܠܗ ܢܛܪܬܗ.

90 Ibid., 84, ll. 10–16 (*Syr.*)/85 [iii, ix] (*Ger.*):
ܥܠ ܐܢܬܬܐ ܕܓܒܪܗ̇ ܒܥܠܗ̇ ܠܐܬܪܐ ܐ̄ܚܪܢܐ ܕܥܡܕ ܙܒܢܐ ܠܗ̇ ܕܬܦܠܛ. ܐܦ ܗܢ ܡܬܡܛܝܐ ܠܡܛܪܝܢ: ܘܠܐ ܡܫܕܪ ܠܬܘܣܦܬܐ ܕܒܥܠܗ̇. ܘܟܕ ܕܬܬܠܐ ܫܢ̈ܝܢ ܢܬܡܣܟ ܕܬܦܠܛ. ܐܦ ܕܝܢ ܡܫܕܪ ܠܬܘܣܦܬܐ ܘܬܠܝܐ ܠܗ̇ ܦܢ ܡܘܢܐ ܘܬܘܪܨܐ ܡܢ ܒܥܠܗ̇. ܬܠܬ ܫܢ̈ܝܢ ܙܒܢ ܠܗ̇ ܕܬܦܠܛ ܘܬܬܦܠܛ. ܘܐܦ ܕܝܢ ܐܝܬ ܠܗ̇ ܡܘܢܐ ܡܢ ܒܥܠܗ̇. ܐܦ ܠܥܡܢܐ ܠܠܐܬܪ ܫܢ̈ܝܢ ܙܒܢ ܕܬܦܠܛ.

The minutes immediately following the Synod of 486, referred to as the Synod of Mar Aqaq, indicate it took place only two years after the Synod of Barṣawma (484). The latter, we are informed, is considered to have been illicit and is therefore not included in the *Synodion Orientale* with its synodical minutes.[91] The Patriarch Babowai, who assumed office between 457 and 484, was a Christian convert from Zoroastrianism. Supposedly, he strongly sympathized with the Chalcedonians to the frustration of Barṣawma, the metropolitan of Nisibis, who, as a pronounced advocate of diophysitism, fiercely opposed him. As the story has it, Babowai wrote a letter seeking assistance from the Roman Emperor Zeno, in which he condescendingly spoke of the Sasanian Empire. The letter made its way to Barṣawma who sent it to Shah Peroz I. In the illicit synod of 484, Barṣawma congregated with a multitude of supporters against Babowai. Babowai was eventually put to death by the order of the Shah.[92] As far as the *Synodicon Orientale* is concerned, the Patriarch Mar Aqaq made peace with Barṣawma who acknowledged him as patriarch and was pardoned for his reckless behavior.[93]

The preliminary minutes to the Synod of Mar Aqaq (486) begin by listing the bishops who participated in the congregation. Immediately after, the writer records the year and place the synod was held. Accordingly,

> ܒܝܪܚ ܐܝܠܘܠ ܕܫܢܬ ܬܪܬܝܢ ܕܫܝܢܐ ܘܡܫܝܢܐ ܘܠܓܫ ܡܠܟ ܡܠܟܐ܃ ܡܢ ܪܡܙܐ
> ܕܛܝܒܘܬܐ ܐܠܗܝܬܐ ܐܬܟܢܫܢ ܠܐܬܪܐ ܗܢܐ.

> in the month of September (*elul*) of the second year of the peaceful and amiable Walaš, Kings of Kings, we [the bishops] were gathered in *this place* by the will of the divine grace (*men remzā d-ṭaybutā alāhāytā*).[94]

From the minutes of the Synod of Mar Babai (497), we know that 'this place' corresponds to Beth ʿAdray.[95] In total, the Synod of Mar Aqaq issued

---

91 *SynO*, 61 (*Syr.*)/308–309 (*Fre.*).

92 William Young, *Patriarch, Shah and Caliph*, 54; also, cf. Jean B. Chabot, *SynO*, 308, footnote 1.

93 *SynO*, 61, ll. 10–13 (*Syr.*)/308 (*Fre.*):
ܘܐܢܝܚ ܐܠܗܐ ܘܫܝܢܐ ܕܥܕ̈ܬܐ ܗܟܝܠ ܗܘܐ ܡܬܬܘܠܝܐ ܦܪܨܘܡܐ ܡܛܠܗ ܠܐܒܪܘܡܐ
ܒܬܪ ܡܬܬܘܚܝܘܬܗ܃ ܘܟܬܒܐ ܘܫܠܡܐ ܠܗ ܚܕ̈ܬܐ ܠܟܠܗ܃ ܘܬܟܬܒܬܐ ܕܚܣܝܘܬܐ
ܘܡܡܟܝܢܘܬܐ ܕܠܐܝܬ ܡܛܝ̈ܒܐ ܠܬܝܒܘܬܗ ܬܘܠܝܬܐ.
Also, cf. Wilhelm Baum and Dietmar W. Winkler, *The Church of the East. A Concise History* (London and New York: RoutledgeCurzon, 2003), 28.

94 *SynO*, 53, ll. 13–14 (*Syr.*)/299–300 (*Fre.*), my translation into English from Syriac.

95 *SynO*, 63, ll. 18–23 (*Syr.*)/312 (*Fre.*):
ܟܕ ܟܢܝܫܝܢ ܒܝܘܡܐ ܗܢܐ ܘܐܦ ܠܟܢܘܫܝܐ ܗܘ ܕܗܘܐ ܒܐܬܪܐ ܕܒܝܬ ܥܕܪܝ ܒܝܪܚ
ܠܫܢܝܢ ܘܥܣܪ ܕܦܝܪܘܙ ܡܠܟ ܡܠܟܐ ܒܡܕܝܢܬܐ ܒܗ ܠܟܠܗ܃ ܘܠܟܢܘܫܝܐ ܗܘ ܕܒܝܬܐ

three canons. The first equates to a definition of the creed of the Church of the East. The second stipulates that ascetics ought not to live in townships or villages, among the people, where they could easily become a source of dissent but should preferably remain in places that accord to their habit.[96] The third and perhaps most sweeping canon states:

> ܗܢܐ ܬܚܘܡܐ ܢܗܘܐ ܠܢ: ܕܡܢ ܗܫܐ ܘܠܗܠ ܐܢܫ ܡܢ ܐܦܝܣܩܘܦܐ ܠܐ ܢܣܝܡ ܩܛܝܪܐ ܘܡܬܚܦܛܢܐ ܥܠ ܟܠܝܢܐ ܕܡܢ ܙܘܘܓܐ ܒܐܬܪܐ ܕܡܕܒܪ ܘܒܥܕܬܐ ܕܡܫܡܫ. [...] ܘܡܣܗܕܐ ܢܗܘܐ ܥܠ ܡܠܬܗ ܕܗܘ ܡܠܦܢܐ ܪܒܐ. ܕܫܪܝܪܐܝܬ ܦܩܕ ܠܡܣܒ ܐܢܬܬܐ ܛܒ ܡܢ ܕܠܡܬܝܩܕ ܒܪܓܬܐ. ܘܢܓܒܐ ܠܗ ܠܟܠܚܕ ܡܢܢ ܚܕܐ ܡܢ ܬܪܬܝܢ. ܕܐܘ ܢܬܪܚܩ ܓܡܝܪܐܝܬ ܐܘ ܢܬܩܪܒ ܬܩܢܐܝܬ [...]. ܕܐܢ ܐܢܫ ܪܓܝܓ ܐܦܝܣܩܘܦܘܬܐ: ܠܥܒܕܐ ܛܒܐ ܪܓܝܓ. ܘܠܐ ܠܗ ܗܟܝܠ ܠܐܦܝܣܩܘܦܐ ܠܡܗܘܐ ܠܐ ܥܕܝܠܐ: ܒܥܠ ܚܕܐ ܐܢܬܬܐ. [...] ܐܦ ܠܡܫܡ̈ܫܢܐ ܕܝܢ ܐܝܠܝܢ ܕܡܢ ܟܒܪ ܡܣܬܡܟ ܠܗܘܢ ܣܝܡ ܐܝܕܐ ܕܡܫܡܫܢܘܬܐ: ܫܠܝܛ ܠܗ ܠܟܠܚܕ ܡܢܗܘܢ ܠܡܬܢܣܒܘ ܠܚܕܐ ܐܢܬܬܐ ܒܙܘܘܓܐ ܬܩܢܐ ܘܢܡܘܣܝܐ [...]. ܗܕܐ ܡܠܦܝܢ ܚܢܢ ܕܐܢܫ ܕܒܨܒܝܢܗ ܓܒܐ ܠܗ ܦܪܝܫܘܬܐ ܕܡܢ ܙܘܘܓܐ: ܒܥܘܡܪܐ ܡܬܝܚܕܐ ܘܠܐ ܡܬܦܢܐ ܢܩܘܐ ܙܗܝܐܝܬ ܘܚܠܝܨܐܝܬ. [...] ܘܙܘܘܓܐ ܕܝܢ ܬܩܢܐ ܘܡܘܠܕܐ ܕܒܢ̈ܝܐ ܐܢ ܡܢ ܩܕܡ ܟܗܢܘܬܐ ܘܐܢ ܒܬܪ ܟܗܢܘܬܐ ܢܬܟܗܢ ܫܦܝܪ ܗܘ ܘܡܩܒܠ ܠܘܬ ܐܠܗܐ.

We [the bishops] are making the following resolution: that from now on and in future, no bishop shall create obstacles (*qṭirā*) or strive to interdict marriage in the country that he governs and in the church in which he exercises his functions (*b-ʿidtā da-mšameš*). [...] In fact, the Great Teacher (*malpānā rābā*) supports the command that truly it is better to take a wife than to be burned with desire (*dal-miqad b-regtā*). Everyone of us shall choose one of two things: *perfect abstinence* (*netraḥaq gmirāyit*) or *honest marriage* (*netqarab taqnāyit*) [...]. Whoever desires the episcopate should strive for good deeds. That is why the bishop should be without flaws, husband of a single woman. [...] Also, it is permissible to every single one of those deacons who have already been ordained to the diaconate to unite with a single woman in an honest and lawful marriage (*b-zuwāgā taqnā w-nāmusāyā*) [...]. Our teaching is that whoever chooses of one's own accord to stay away from marriage, should reside in a monastery in solitude, not be distracted [by other things], and live in chastity with determination (*neqwe zahyāyit w-ḥliṣāyit*). [...] Indeed, honest marriage and the procreation of children, whether before or after being ordained, is something beautiful that is acceptable to God.[97]

ܗܦܟܢ ܕܒܠܥ ܥܒܝܕ ܥܘܢܝܐ ܒܗ ܠܒܝܬ ܒܢܩܦ ܡܢܐ ܐܢܫ: ܘܐܬܟܢܫ ܒܐܬܪܐ ܕܒܝܬ ܐܪܡܝܐ: ܘܠܗܝܡܢܘܬܐ ܬܪܝܨܬܐ ܕܐܬܬܣܝܡܬ ܡܢ ܣܒ̈ܐ ܘܡܠܦܢܘܬܐ ܕܟܗܢ̈ܐ ܡܫܝ̈ܚܐ.
Also, cf. J. B. Chabot, *SynO*, 300, footnote 2. Baum and Winkler incorrectly state that the synod convened in Seleucia-Ctesiphon, *The Church of the East*, 28.

96 *SynO*, 55, l. 10–56, l. 4 (*Syr.*)/302–303 (*Fre.*).

97 Ibid., 56, ll. 6–8; 56, l. 31–57, l. 2; 57, ll. 4–5; 57, ll. 7–9; 57, ll. 31–32; 58, ll. 14–16 (*Syr.*)/303–305 (*Fre.*), my translation into English from Syriac.

Notably, the canon recognizes two distinct paths or lifestyles of man: the first being complete abstinence, the other being monogamous marriage. Most importantly, it expressly states that representatives of the clerical hierarchy may at any time, before or after their being ordained to the priesthood, decide to contract a marriage. This stipulation is confirmed by the Synod of Mar Babai (497) which, as is shown in the synodical text, was instigated by the Shahanshah.[98]

ܘܟܠܢ ܒܪܘܚܐ ܗܕܐ ܕܫܘܝܐ ܠܢܡܘܣܗ ܕܡܫܝܚܐ: ܚܢܢ ܐܝܠܝܢ ܕܚܬܡܢ
ܡܢ ܠܥܠ ܫܡܗܝܢ ܬܘܪܨܐ ܕܥܒܕܢ ܒܢܦܫܢ [ܠܟܠܢ] ܘܡܕܝܢܬܢ، ܒܕܘܒܪܐ ܕܙܘܘܓܐ
ܘܡܘܠܕܐ ܕܒܢܝܐ ܠܟܠܢ. ܘܝܗܒܢ ܡܦܣܢܘܬܐ: ܕܡܢ ܗܘ ܕܐܝܬܘܗܝ ܦܛܪܝܪܟܐ ܠܥܕܡܐ
ܠܐܚܪܝܐ ܕܐܝܬ ܒܛܟܣܐ: ܕܙܘܘܓܐ ܕܢܫܐ ܕܟܝܐ ܚܕܐ ܐܢܬܬܐ: ܕܐܝܬ ܒܗ ܡܘܠܕܐ
ܕܒܢܝܐ ܢܣܒ ܒܓܠܝܐ ܘܢܬܡܫܫ.

All of us, in the spirit that conforms with the law of Christ, we–those who have signed with their names above–approve of and have made reforms for ourselves and our dioceses with regard to marriage and the procreation of children. We, [therefore], give permission to [everyone], from whoever is patriarch down to the lowest one in the [clerical] hierarchy, to openly contract and attend to the duties of a pure marriage with a single woman, [a marriage] in which children may be procreated.[99]

It is, in fact, peculiar why the bishops would make such significant adjustments to Christian matrimonial law. Perhaps, most telling is the mentioning that the Shah not only called for the convention of the bishops in a synod but the remark that he explicitly demanded from them to

ܘܢܥܒܕܘܢ، ܬܘܪܨܐ ܒܕܘܒܪܐ ܕܙܘܘܓܐ ܐܚܝܕܐ ܘܡܘܠܕܐ ܕܒܢܝܐ ܠܟܠ ܚܕ ܐܢܫ ܡܢܗܘܢ،
ܕܒܟܠܗ ܐܬܪܐ.

[…] establish a reform with regard to legimitate marriage and the procreation of children concerning everyone who is part of the clergy in the entire country.[100]

I disagree with the observation of Baum and Winkler that the canons of the Synod of Mar Aqaq are tantamount to an abolishment of celibacy.[101]

---

98 Ibid., 63, ll. 9–13 (*Syr.*)/311–312 (*Fre.*):
ܘܐܦ ܠܗ ܗܢܐ ܗܘ ܕܡܢ ܩܕܡ ܚܝܠܐ ܘܦܘܩܕܢܐ ܕܡܠܟܘܬܐ ܕܢܨܚܢ ܡܠܟ ܡܠܟܐ ܐܬܟܢܫ
ܠܗ ܕܢܬܟܢܫܘܢ، ܠܘܬܗ ܐܦܝܣܩܘܦܐ ܕܐܬܪܐ ܒܟܠܗܘܢ: ܘܢܥܒܕܘܢ، ܬܘܪܨܐ ܒܕܘܒܪܐ
ܕܙܘܘܓܐ ܐܚܝܕܐ ܘܡܘܠܕܐ ܕܒܢܝܐ ܠܟܠ ܚܕ ܐܢܫ ܡܢܗܘܢ، ܕܒܟܠܗ ܐܬܪܐ.

99 Ibid., 63, ll. 13–18 (*Syr.*)/312 (*Fre.*), my translation into English from Syriac.

100 Ibid., 63, ll. 11–13 (*Syr.*)/312 (*Fre.*), my translation into English from Syriac.

101 Wilhelm Baum and Dietmar W. Winkler, *The Church of the East*, 32. Also cf. Yarshater, Ehsan (ed.), *The Cambridge History of Iran*, vol. 3 (2): *The Seleucid, Parthian and Sasanian* Periods (Cambridge: Cambridge University Press, 2008), 944; and Christopher Buck, *Paradise and Paradigm: Key Symbols in Persian Christianity and the Bahā'ī Faith* (Albany, NY: State University of New York, 1999), 79.

Looked at in conjunction with the Synod of Mar Babai, it was undoubtedly a setback for celibacy as well as the East Syrian monastic tradition both of which are circumscribed by the command that ascetics should live secluded among equals and because monogamy is contrived as the preferable lifestyle of bishops. We do, in fact, know that the marital reforms of these synods were not merely theoretical but effectuated in practice. To illustrate, while we have no evidence pointing towards the fact that any of the Patriarchs, who ruled before these changes occurred, were in wedlock, we know that already Mar Babai himself as well as Mar Shila, the patriarch superseding him, were both married men.[102]

Sebastian Brock expounds that Christian relations with the administration of *Ērānšahr* hinged on the state of affairs with the Roman Empire.[103] That is, the ability of the Church of the East to coexist as well as its political leverage significantly depended on keeping a low profile regarding its Western coreligionists. However, once the ties with the Roman Church were officially severed at the Council of Ephesus (431), the proliferation and integration of the Church of the East into the Sasanian imperial structure progressively had to depend on other factors. I suggest that two concerns are especially valid: restricting the missionary activities of the Church of the East and preventing the spillover of Christian matrimonial ideals on the Zoroastrian population. Other scholars have recently pointed out that conversions of Zoroastrians were momentous only when performed by members of the Sasanian elite.[104] With regard to matrimony, it seems that the Sasanian elite, represented by the Shah, had a keen interest in modifying East Syrian law to make it more acceptable to the Zoroastrian public. Keeping ascetics out of the public view as well as promoting monogamy among the episcopal hierarchy was certainly a way to go. Even though these reforms were not in line with the East Syrian tradition, they could be justified by references to scripture. More importantly, the adjustments stipulated at the Synods of Mar Aqaq and Mar Babai strongly point to the applicability of legal pluralism as a framework of inquiry. Rather than assuming the Sasanian elite imposed its idiosyncratic matrimonial laws on the Christian minority, monogamy, which was intrinsic to the Eastern Christian tradition, became the bargaining chip in interactions with the Sasanian rulers. The pattern that marks the relationship between East Syrian and Zoroastrian jurisprudence, in this case, was negotiation, rather than influence. To maintain its standing and leverage within *Ērānšahr*, the representatives of

102 William Young, *Patriarch, Shah and Caliph*, 54; also, Wilhelm Baum and Dietmar W. Winkler, *The Church of the East*, 32.

103 Sebastian Brock, "Christians in the Sasanian Empire," 7.

104 Richard E. Payne, *A State of Mixture*, 52.

the Church of the East had to sanction certain adjustments which proved more acceptable to the Zoroastrian authorities.[105] The latter, most probably, considered these changes necessary to prevent the spillover of Christian matrimonial ideals, particularly celibacy and monogamy, on the Zoroastrian population which could have undermined the authority of the Sasanian elite by threatening the reproductive machinery of the empire.

4. (Re)negotiating matrimony: the prohibitions of Mar Aba

With the juridical adjustments made at the Synods of Mar Aqaq (486) and Mar Babai (497), the East Syrian law on matrimony became subject to relaxations more admissible to the Zoroastrian authorities. However, these do not necessarily account for the increasing popularity of consanguineous marriages among Christians at the beginning of the sixth century. There *may or may not* be a causal connection with the synodical reforms. In other words, it is conceivable that the changes East Syrian law saw, its approximation to Sasanian standards, had more far-reaching repercussions on Christian matrimony. What I mean is that with the *de facto* undermining of celibacy and an episcopal hierarchy which increasingly contracted marriages, the Christian ideal of matrimony may have not survived unscathed. However, we lack evidence that would corroborate this assumption.

Whatever the reasons, the sixth-century treatise of Mar Aba attests to the fact that next-of-kin marriages posed an unwelcome reality the Christian elite could not control. More specifically, his writing constitutes a meticulous discussion of the taxonomy of close-kin matrimony and the reasons why it is prohibited.[106] Similarly to Ishoʿbokht, Mar Aba repeatedly adduces Biblical references to sanction a model of marriage that is more in line with the tenets of scripture. Whereas monogamous relations practiced by the clerical hierarchy were and could willingly be sanctioned through biblical references, the practice of marrying next-of-kin was, after all, deeply entrenched in the Zoroastrian tradition.[107] When viewed in conjunction with the *Corpus Juris*, the prohibitions of Mar Aba, more largely, seem to be

---

[105] Similarly, Manfred Hutter argues that the Church of the East molded a kind of "Zoroastrianized" Christianity recognized by the Zoroastrian authorities as properly Persian; cf. Manfred Hutter, "Impact of Zoroastrianism on Christianity in the 6th Century," 172.

[106] Mar Aba, *EheM*, 260, ll. 17–19 (*Syr.*)/ 261 (*Ger.*):
ܠܘ ܠܡܣܒ ܕܦܘܪܫܢܐ ܕܟܠ ܟܘܬܪܘܬܐ ܡܕܡܝܬܐ ܟܡܕܪܐ ܢܟܪܝܐ. ܘܟܠ ܚܕ ܠܟܠ ܚܕ ܚܕ
ܡܢܗܘܢ، ܚܡܐ ܕܡܬܚܙܝܐ ܡܫܠܡܝܢ [ܡܫܠܠܡܝܢ].

[107] Manfred Hutter, "Impact of Zoroastrianism on Christianity in the 6th Century," 171.

indicative of an attempt by the Christian elite to reclaim the legal space it had ceded to the Zoroastrian authorities. To be more precise, sanctioning the monogamy of the clerical elite was acceptable even to the bishops; however, the prevalence of next-of-kin marriage threatened to undermine the support base of the Church of the East because the practice was closely associated with Mazdaism. The relationship of East Syrian to Sasanian jurisprudence was once again not characterized by influence, but negotiation–this time to the effect of promoting an outlook on matrimony which was more permissible to the Christian elite.

5. *Reclaiming legal space?*

To theorize the boundaries of Christian matrimony, it is worthwhile resorting to the classification of sexual regimes suggested by Helmut Schelsky.[108] Based on the taxonomy Schelsky suggests, the 'sexual regime' pertaining to the Church of the East is aptly captured by what he refers to as '*absolute* monogamy' which he defines as:

> Monogamy [Einehe] in which the woman is sexually bound to her partner for a lifetime with the threat of severe punishment or other sanctions, whereas the same is expected from him to the degree that his wife complies with these social expectations [...].[109]

The severe restrictions regarding marriage, and, notably, the hardship of divorce, indicate that the East Syrian law on matrimony profoundly contrasts with Sasanian law which was aimed at assuring the cultivation of a multitude of marriages during the lifetime of a Zoroastrian. To sanction monogamy, the religious elite reverted to scriptural interpretations capitalizing on the notion of the husband and wife's conflation in one flesh. Most importantly, Biblical scripture provided the historical precedent of Adam and Eve which could be mobilized to approve of the righteousness of absolute monogamy against the backdrop of a Zoroastrian majority which adhered to conflicting standards. The ideal of monogamy was, on the microcosmic plane of the relationship between man and woman, a symbolic reflection of a Christian's putative relationship with God. Peculiarly, when the Christian elite was coerced to reform the laws on matrimony of the clerical hierarchy, the notion of monogamy seems to have functioned as a bargaining chip in negotiating adjustments. The changes adopted indicate that the integration and leverage of the Christian community in the Sasanian Empire were,

---

108 Schelsky divides matrimonial regimes into four different types: moderate polygamy, absolute polygamy, moderate monogamy, and absolute monogamy. Helmut Schelsky, *Soziologie der Sexualität*, 31, my translation into English from German.

109 Ibid.

while mostly a smooth process, dependent on complying with the orders of the Zoroastrian authorities. Although we have no indicators as to why next-of-kin marriages were more frequently practiced towards the beginning of the sixth century, I illustrated that the Christian elite, such as Mar Aba and Ishoʿbokht, was keen on reclaiming the legal space that had been ceded to the Sasanians, particularly, since this type of marriage could not be justified by reverting to Christian cosmology but was deeply entrenched in the Mazdaean tradition.

In this chapter, I invoked significant evidence in support of my main research arguments. First, the Christian bishops deployed cosmology interwoven in scriptural references for a variety of purposes. The synodical reforms showed that cosmological imagery could, in fact, be utilized to accommodate the interests of the Zoroastrian authorities. Meanwhile, the writings of Mar Aba and Ishoʿbokht indicate that it could also serve the promotion of a distinctive notion of a Christian community whose elite fashioned a vision of matrimony which was in conflict with that of the Zoroastrian majority it was accountable to. Secondly, the particular instances in which East Syrian and Sasanian jurisdiction were in close contact make apparent that their interaction was–at least in the case of the late fifth-century synods and the legal compilations of Mar Aba and Ishoʿbokht–a matter of negotiation, rather than influence.

C. Early Islamic law: fiscal emancipation of women?

1. The conditions of marriage (shurūṭ al-zawāj)

In this section, I carve out the legal nature of Islamic marriage, as regulated by al-Shāfiʿī and Saḥnūn b. Saʿīd al-Tanūkhī and attempt to situtate it in their society more broadly. Thus, I marshal evidence in support of my first main argument that matrimony is mediated through the triad of cosmology, lawmaking, and the sociopolitical concerns of the religious elite.

A close reading of the chapters "fī shurūṭ al-zawāj" and "shurūṭ al-nikāḥ ayḍan" in the *Mudawwana* indicates that Saḥnūn is dealing with conditions that can lawfully be stipulated in wedlock. His stipulations, more largely, provide important insights into the nature of Islamic matrimony as imagined and regulated by Mālikī jurists. Throughout his work, the format of Saḥnūn's inquiry is that of responsa. His first question asks:

أرأيت إن تزوج امرأة على أن لا يتزوج عليها ولا يتسرر أيفسخ هذا النكاح وفيه
هذا الشرط إن أدرك قبل البناء في قول مالك؟

If he [a man] marries a woman on the condition that he not marry a second wife and not take a concubine, is this marriage, with this condition, annulled if the condition is known before the consummation of the marriage according to the saying of Mālik?[110]

The question is answered by Mālik with the words: "the marriage is permissible, but the term is void."[111] Mālik then states that the marriage is allowed based on the authority of Saᶜīd b. al-Musayyab (d. 95/715) and others who ruled that the conditions stipulated for this marriage–not to marry a second wife and not to take a concubine–are not such that would annul the marriage.[112] Hereafter, Saḥnūn makes reference to the story of a man who lived in the time of ᶜUmar b. al-Khaṭṭāb. The man supposedly entered a marriage, which in its contract stated that: "he would not take her out of her country."[113] This condition, just like the above, was considered null, but did not corrupt the marriage contract.[114]

By asking his second question, Saḥnūn continues his inquiry attempting to put his finger on what contractual terms would result in the annulment of wedlock.[115] Based on the authority of Mālik, he presents a legally complicated and linguistically challenging case:

من تزوج امرأة على شروط تلزمه ثم إنه صالحها أو طلقها تطليقة فانقضت عدتها ثم تزوجها بعد ذلك بنكاح جديد قال: قال مالك: يلزمه تلك الشروط ما بقي من طلاق ذلك الملك شيء. قال: وإن شرط في نكاحه الثاني أنه إنما ينكح على أن لا يلزمه من تلك الشروط شيء. قال: وإن شرط في نكاحه الثاني فإن ذلك لا ينفعه، وتلك الشروط له لازمة ما بقي من طلاق ذلك الملك شيء.

Whoever marries a woman with conditions placed on himself and then reaches a compromise (settlement) with her or divorces her: if he waits until she has completed her waiting period [*ᶜiddatuhā*] and marries her in a new marriage, then,

---

110 Saḥnūn, *MudK*, vol. 2, 131, ll. 1–2 [fī shurūṭ al-nikāḥ], my translation into English from Arabic.

111 Ibid., ll. 2–3:

النكاح جائز والشرط باطل.

112 Ibid., ll. 3–4.

113 Ibid., ll. 6–7:

لا يخرجها من أرضها.

For an interpretation of this passage, see Kecia Ali, *Marriage and Slavery in Early Islam*, 73.

114 Saḥnūn, *MudK*, vol. 2, 131, ll. 8–9:

وليس هذا من الشروط التي يفسد بها النكاح.

115 Ibid., l. 13:

فأي شيء الشروط التي يفسد بها النكاح في قول مالك؟

Mālik said, those conditions remain incumbent on him so long as anything remains from that divorce (the divorce of that marriage) [*yalzamuhu tilka al-shurūṭu mā baqiya min ṭalāqi dhālika al-mulki shay'un*]. He said: and if he, in the second marriage, stipulates that he marries on the condition that it [the second marriage] is not accompanied by those conditions; he said: if he stipulated a condition in the second marriage, then that is of no use. And those conditions for it [the marriage] are obligatory so long as anything remains from that divorce.[116]

In the case described, a man enters the first marriage on certain conditions the nature of which we are not informed. The marriage is then divorced and the waiting period of the wife (*ʿidda*)–usually four lunar months and ten days–comes into effect. Once the waiting period expires, the couple remarries. As the above passage has it, the same terms stipulated in the first marriage come into effect in the second. Saḥnūn reinforces this point by stating that, even if the husband stipulates that the second marriage is based on the condition that the terms from the first marriage are void, it is not valid. What remains unclear here is whether the man's conditional stipulating of the second marriage invalidates only its terms or the entire marriage. This question is, indeed, not explicitly answered by the text. However, from the context of the passage, particularly, the question preceding it "what is the kind of condition upon which the marriage becomes void?", I conclude that the marriage, rather than its conditions, is annulled based on the man's attempt to stipulate it with the condition that the terms of the first marriage do not apply. In addition, it remains unclear what the expression "so long as anything remains from that divorce" (*mā baqiya min ṭalāqi dhālika al-mulki shay'un*) seeks to hint at. We do not precisely know if there is a point in time where nothing "remains of the divorce" and whether somebody would then be allowed to contract a marriage in defiance of the terms from the first marriage he entered with that woman. However, it may simply refer to the obligation of the husband to stick to the conditions stipulated in the first marriage contract.

The legal passages on the conditions of marriage are particularly instructive regarding the legal status of women, the way the law may protect, enforce, oppose, or infringe on their interests. For instance, the case below illustrates how the law on the one hand acknowledges the financial exposure of a wife in the case that she illicitly attempts to stipulate conditions to a marriage contract before it is concluded, whereas on the other it may act in accordance with her interests if placing such conditions on her husband, with his agreement, after the marriage contract has been concluded:

لو أن رجلاً تزوج امرأة وشرطت عليه شروطاً وحطت من مهرها لتلك الشروط،
أيكون لها ما حطت من ذلك أم لا؟ قال: ما حطت من ذلك في عقدة النكاح، فلا

[116] Ibid., ll. 14–18, my translation into English from Arabic.

يكون لها على الزوج شيء من ذلك وما شرطت على الزوج فهو باطل إلا أن يكون فيه عتق أو طلاق وهذا قول مالك. قلت: أرأيت إن كانت إنما حطت عنه بعد عقدة النكاح على أن شرطت عليه هذه الشروط؟ قال: يلزمه ذلك ويكون له المال، قال: فإن أتى شيئاً مما شرطت عليه رجعت في المال فأخذته مثل ما يشترط أن لا يخرجها من مصرها ولا يتسرر عليها ولا يتزوج قلت: فإن كانت أعطته المال على أن لا يتزوج عليها، فإن تزوج عليها فهي طالق ثلاثاً؟ قال: فإن فعل وقع الطلاق ولم يرجع في المال لأنها اشترت طلاقها بما وضعت عنه.

> If a man marries a woman and she demands conditions from him in exchange for renouncing a part of her dower, does she then have a right to the part of the dower she renounced or not? He said: What she renounced of the dower in the marriage contract is not hers, and she did not place a condition on him. And, in fact, the condition she made to the husband is invalid except if it is a manumission or a divorce (from another woman). This is the saying of Mālik. I said: What do you think if she renounced a portion of the dower after contracting the marriage in exchange for placing on him these conditions? He said: They (the conditions) are incumbent on him and the property is his (the portion of the dower she renounced). He said: And if he does not fulfill the conditions she placed on him, then the property goes back to her (*rajaʿat fi l-māli*) taking it as if he did not stipulate that he would not take her from her country, not take a concubine to his side, and not marry (in addition to her). I said: And if she gave him the property on the condition that he does not add another wife to her, then, if he marries another wife, is she (the first wife) divorced three times? He said: A divorce is instigated, and she does not receive back her property because she (the first wife) purchased her (own) divorce with what she set down for him.[117]

In the above case, a couple enters a marriage with the wife attempting to impose certain conditions on her husband. For him to abide by these, she offers to renounce a portion of her dower. Saḥnūn states that the part of the dower she renounces cannot be reclaimed by her (*mā ḥaṭṭat min dhālika fī ʿuqdati l-nikāḥi, fa-lā yakūnu lahā*). In this case, the law does not assume a protective function in terms of guaranteeing the financial integrity of the wife presumably because the wife is not supposed to ask for certain conditions before the conclusion of the marriage contract. Thus, the conditions she demanded are considered invalid (*bāṭil*). Importantly, whereas the conditions are annulled, the marriage is not. We are further informed that her condition is not considered annulled if it encompasses either a manumission, presumably her own if she was the slave girl (*jāriya*) of the man she is getting married to, or a divorce, possibly her husband's divorcing another wife before she enters wedlock with him. Saḥnūn continues his inquiry by clarifying whether she can place conditions on him after the marriage has been

---

[117] Ibid., 132, ll. 6–7 [shurūṭ al-nikāḥ ayḍan].

contracted. Accordingly, if she does so, the portion of the dower she revokes in return for these conditions is considered part of his property. However, should he fail to abide by these conditions after having agreed to them, the portion of the dower she renounced again becomes part of her property. If her condition was that the husband should not marry another woman in addition to her, and if he does not abide by it and takes another woman, then the first wife's marriage with her husband is divorced. In other words, the part of the dower she renounced is used to "purchase" the divorce from her husband, should he fail to abide by her condition not to take another wife. What becomes apparent from this case is that a wife may–in return for giving up a part of her dower–stipulate certain marriage conditions after the marriage has been contracted. Although we can see a clear infringement of her financial integrity as the law is accepting of the reduction of her dower, the wife also retains the possibility to advance her interests and have them, to some extent, legally protected. In that case, if the husband attempts to breach the conditions by marrying another wife, the law is keen on safeguarding the first wife's interest by providing her with the option of an immediate divorce.[118] Thus, a wife cannot stipulate monogamy; however, the law functions in accord with her interest, dissolving the marriage, in the case her husband does not keep his promise of not taking other wives in addition to her. Moreover, since this divorce necessarily activates her husband's obligation to pay her what is left of her dower, the husband's breaching of his promise would be financially costly. To some extent, thus, the interests of women who find themselves in marriages are legally protected.

This subchapter has led to important findings. First, whereas certain conditions stipulated in a marriage contract result in its annulment, others do not. For instance, when remarrying his wife, a husband is obliged to adhere to the same marriage conditions as in his first marriage with her, if not, the second marriage is (most likely) considered annulled. Having said that, other conditions, such as the promise not to take a wife out of her hometown, do not result in the invalidation of marriage but merely do not come into effect. Perhaps most strikingly, the law generally seems to allow that women exchange part of their dower in return for certain marriage conditions (after the marriage contract has been concluded). Thus, it appears to be accepting of the trade-off that comes by exchanging financial integrity with more favorable circumstances in wedlock. It would certainly be prema-

[118] Kecia Ali discusses this hypothetical, cf. Kecia Ali, *Marriage and Slavery in Early Islam,* 74–5. Also, cf. a more general reference in Kecia Ali, "Progressive Muslims and Islamic jurisprudence: the necessity for critical engagement with marriage and divorce law," in *Progressive Muslims on justice, gender and pluralism*, ed. Omid Safi (Oxford: Oneworld, 2003), 168 in which she states that this constituted a rather important issue for the Muslim legal schools on which their opinions differed substantially.

ture to engage in conclusions about the social ramifications of such legal stipulations. However, this small number of laws on the conditions of marriage shows the ambiguous tendencies of the law, on the one hand, allowing, to some extent, the infringement on women's financial integrity, while on the other, protecting their individual interests by enforcing the immediate termination of a marriage in case the husband acts counter to his promise not to take other wives.

2. Women forbidden to marry (muḥarramāt al-nisā᾿)

In his *Risāla*, al-Shāfiʿī provides an entire subchapter on which women somebody ought not to marry. He begins by quoting Q 4:23 and Q 4:24:

> [23] Forbidden to you are your mothers, daughters, sisters, aunts paternal and maternal, nieces on your brothers' or sisters' sides, milk-mothers who suckled you and milk-sisters, mothers of your wives, and step-daughters in your custody from wives with whom you have consummated marriage–unless you have not consummated marriage with them, in which case no blame attaches to you. Forbidden too are legal wives of your own sons, and marriage with two sisters–unless that act belongs to the past. God is All-Forgiving, Compassionate to each. Forbidden too are married women, unless they be your slaves. [24] The Book of God thus commands you. Licit for you is all that lies outside these limits, provided you use your wealth to contract legal marriage, not fornication. To those women among them whom you take pleasure in marrying, you must render their dowries, as a legal obligation. But no blame attaches to you regarding what you have willingly agreed upon, once the legal obligation is fulfilled. God is All-Knowing, All-Wise.[119]

Following this quotation, al-Shāfiʿī comments on how to interpret the stipulations in these Qur᾿ānic verses. To begin with, he points out that the

---

[119] *The Qur'an*, tr. Tarif Khalidi (London: Penguin Classics, 2008), 65 (Q 4:23–24). Original Qur'anic passage:

[23] حُرِّمَتْ عَلَيْكُمْ أُمَّهَاتُكُمْ وَبَنَاتُكُمْ وَأَخَوَاتُكُمْ وَعَمَّاتُكُمْ وَخَالَاتُكُمْ وَبَنَاتُ الْأَخِ وَبَنَاتُ الْأُخْتِ وَأُمَّهَاتُكُمُ اللَّاتِي أَرْضَعْنَكُمْ وَأَخَوَاتُكُم مِّنَ الرَّضَاعَةِ وَأُمَّهَاتُ نِسَائِكُمْ وَرَبَائِبُكُمُ اللَّاتِي فِي حُجُورِكُم مِّن نِّسَائِكُمُ اللَّاتِي دَخَلْتُم بِهِنَّ فَإِن لَّمْ تَكُونُوا دَخَلْتُم بِهِنَّ فَلَا جُنَاحَ عَلَيْكُمْ وَحَلَائِلُ أَبْنَائِكُمُ الَّذِينَ مِنْ أَصْلَابِكُمْ وَأَن تَجْمَعُوا بَيْنَ الْأُخْتَيْنِ إِلَّا مَا قَدْ سَلَفَ ۗ إِنَّ اللَّهَ كَانَ غَفُورًا رَّحِيمًا [24] وَالْمُحْصَنَاتُ مِنَ النِّسَاءِ إِلَّا مَا مَلَكَتْ أَيْمَانُكُمْ ۖ كِتَابَ اللَّهِ عَلَيْكُمْ ۚ وَأُحِلَّ لَكُم مَّا وَرَاءَ ذَٰلِكُمْ أَن تَبْتَغُوا بِأَمْوَالِكُم مُّحْصِنِينَ غَيْرَ مُسَافِحِينَ ۚ فَمَا اسْتَمْتَعْتُم بِهِ مِنْهُنَّ فَآتُوهُنَّ أُجُورَهُنَّ فَرِيضَةً ۚ وَلَا جُنَاحَ عَلَيْكُمْ فِيمَا تَرَاضَيْتُم بِهِ مِن بَعْدِ الْفَرِيضَةِ ۚ إِنَّ اللَّهَ كَانَ عَلِيمًا حَكِيمًا.

The Qur᾿ān, Q 4:23-24, https://quran.com/4/23-33. For the quotation by al-Shāfiʿī, see *RisF*, 146, ll. 2–9.

verse could have two meanings. The first, he states, is the apparent meaning (*al-maʿnā huwa al-ẓāhir*) of the verse.[120] Reinforcing that all women the verse explicitly mentions as prohibited are indeed prohibited (*mā sammā Allāh min nisāʾi muḥarraman muḥarramun*), al-Shāfiʿī expounds that, by inference, all those it is silent on are lawful because of the verse's silence on them (*bi-l-ṣamti ʿanhu*). By mentioning everything that is not allowed, it becomes clear to the reader/listener what is. Silence creates permissibility.

He then expands on the rationale underlying the explicit designation of pairs in Q 4:23 such as the "two sisters." Accordingly, the purpose of such combinations (*jamʿ*) is different from that of the interdiction not to marry (one's) mothers, daughters, maternal, or paternal aunts.[121] Whereas the latter ought not to be married because the relationship with them is not subject to change, it is not prohibited to marry two sisters *per se* because one's relationship with them can be altered. However, rather than one's own relationship with the two sisters, it is the sister's relationality to each other triggering the interdiction. That is, their relationship as sisters provides the legal cause (*ʿilla*) for this marriage to be considered despicable. In line with this reasoning, al-Shāfiʿī states that each sister alone is presumptively permissible (*ḥalāl fī l-aṣl*).[122] Effectively, a man can marry two sisters, but simply, not be married to them simultaneously.[123] Most importantly, we can gauge that the prohibition not to marry mothers (as well as daughters, maternal, or paternal aunts) is more unyielding–because the relationship with a mother cannot be modified–than the prohibition to marry sisters, who only in their relationality to each other as sisters, are forbidden.

The purpose behind such legal reasoning must be understood in the context of the formation of the Muslim legal schools in the ninth century, more precisely, the transformation of the circles of jurisprudence centered on individual figures into authoritative doctrinal complexes.[124] While I do not claim that applied legal practice had not yet internalized the prohibition not to marry two sisters, I would suggest that in the time of al-Shāfiʿī such legal judgements still had to be made legible and justified through the

---

120 Al-Shāfiʿī, *RisF*, 146, ll. 11–12.

121 Ibid., l. 12:

وكان بيناً في الآية أن تحريم الجمع بمعنى غير تحريم الأمهات.

122 Ibid., ll. 14–15:

وكان في نهيه عن الجمع بينهما دليل على أنه إنما حرم الجمع وأن كل واحدة منهما على الانفراد حلال في الأصل [...].

123 Ibid., ll. 13–14.

124 Cf. Wael Hallaq, *An Introduction to Islamic Law* (Cambridge: Cambridge University Press, 2009), 33–34.

elaboration of hermeneutics and legal reasoning. The hermeneutic method of al-Shāfiʿī, besides other jurists, was probably crucial as to providing the guidelines to interpreting Qurʾānic commandments.

To elucidate the concept of "relational prohibitions" in the Qurʾān, al-Shāfiʿī comes up with another example reverting to the command that a man must not marry more than four women. He first explains that each woman must be lawful for the husband to marry (*al-nisāʾ al-mubāḥāt*).[125] Similar to the previous example, he argues that the fifth woman is not unlawful as such, meaning as a single wife (*qad kānat al-khāmisat min al-ḥalāl bi-wajhin*), but only in her relationality to the other four. He reinforces this stating that the Qurʾānic stipulation of "lawful are those other than the ones mentioned" indicates the permissibility of marriage in the sense that marriage is always generally encouraged. However, not absolutely (*lā muṭlaqan*), but based on the condition that a marriage is entered lawfully (*ʿalā al-sharṭ alladhī aḥallahu bihi*).[126] In consequence, a man who is married to four women can–as regards his fifth marriage–only comply with the conditions of lawfully entering a marriage, if he first divorces one of the other wives.

The account of al-Shāfiʿī is useful for two reasons, one content-wise and one methodological. First, the verses he construes set out the realm of women who are considered unlawful to marry. Most of those forbidden are next-of-kin relatives. In a fashion similar to Ishoʿbokht, those women considered unlawful to marry are listed explicitly. While a meticulous comparison might be out of place, it should be noted that al-Shāfiʿī's inferred restriction extends to a smaller number of next-of-kin relatives than Ishoʿbokht's. To the women mentioned by al-Shāfiʿī when referring to Q 4:23 and 4:24, Ishoʿbokht would add the stepmother, the half-sister, the sister-in-law, and granddaughters, while not concerned with milkmothers. Of course, one could argue that the stepmother and the half-sister are contained in the Islamic terminology of "mother" and "sister." However, it is instead conceivable that one could marry one's maternal half-sisters and sisters-in-law in the Islamic context because they do not constitute paternal blood relatives.

Second, the hermeneutic method used by al-Shāfiʿī unmistakably illustrates the flexibility of legal reasoning based on which Qurʾānic stipulations could be interpreted. This may point to the validity of the thesis suggested, implying that the laws on matrimony were being negotiated with a view to scriptural commands as well as the sociopolitical concerns of the elite, in this case, jurists. In the case of al-Shāfiʿī, it can be seen with relative clarity

---

125 Ibid., 148, ll. 3–4:

فإن النساء المباحات لا يحل أن ينكح منهن أكثر من أربع.

126 Ibid., 148, ll. 5–7.

that the scriptural prohibitions of certain women–which others could have potentially read as absolute prohibitions–needed to be clarified through sophisticated argument and legal reasoning. More importantly, such legal reasoning constituted a strategy through which the prohibitive character of Qurʾānic verses could be captured while simultaneously circumventing *strictly* prohibitive constructions of such stipulations. In other words, while the jurist had to come to terms with the essence of prohibition innate to such passages, he could macerate their strictly prohibitive character by creating contingencies that would minimize the purview of applicability of such prohibitions.

3. Saḥnūn's types of marriage

a. Unprotected (exchange) marriage (nikāḥ al-shighār)

Saḥnūn discusses a multitude of legal opinions as to the concept of *nikāḥ al-shighār*. To begin with, he states that, based on an *isnād* leading back to ʿAbdallāh b. ʿUmar, the authorities of al-Qāsim, Ibn Wahb (d. 196/812), and ʿAlī b. Ziyād (d. 183/799) transmit

وقد روى القاسم وابن وهب وعلي بن زياد عن مالك عن نافع عن عبد الله بن عمر أن رسول الله صلعم نهى عن الشغار، والشغار أن يزوج الرجل ابنته لرجل على أن يزوجه الآخر ابنته وليس بينهما صداق.

> […] that the Messenger of God prohibited the *shighār*. The *shighār* is when [a] man gives his daughter into marriage with a man on the condition that the other man gives his daughter into marriage with him while no dower (*ṣadāq*) is being stipulated between them.[127]

Given the possibilities for variation in the *nikāḥ al-shighār*, it is difficult to circumscribe the least common denominator of this type of marriage. It usually seems to be an agreement between two men who contract marriages for at least two other persons of whom they have guardianship without stipulating the appropriate dowers.

Other hypotheticals help elucidate the boundaries of the *shighār* with more clarity. The probably most common variety of the *nikāḥ al-shighār* is stipulated as an exchange between two men, in which a family relative of each man is given in marriage to the other:

زوجني مولاتك وأزوجك مولاتي ولا مهر بينهما، أهذا من الشغار عند مالك؟ قال: نعم.

[127] Saḥnūn b. Saʿīd al-Tanūkhī, *MudK*, vol. 2, 98, ll. 19–20 [nikāḥ al-shighār].

> Give your lady in marriage to me and I [in return] give my lady in marriage to you; and there will be no dower (*mahr*) between them. Is this [then] a *shighār* in the opinion of Mālik? He said: Yes.[128]

It should be noted that both marriages in the hypothetical are contracted without a dower (*mahr*). Saḥnūn tells us that the classification as *nikāḥ al-shighār*, however, is not contingent on these marriages being stipulated as an exchange of female blood relatives, but can similarly be contracted as marriages with or between slaves owned by the contracting parties.[129] That is, regardless of whether the exchange encompasses free people or slaves, there is no legal differentiation with respect to classifying these marriages as *shighār*.[130] In addition, it is laid out that the *shighār* does not necessarily entail a marriage in which one of the stipulating parties is involved, but may be contracted by them solely for the purpose of marrying off their respective male and female slaves with one another.[131]

Regardless of who is being married as the result of a *shighār*-exchange, there is a relative consensus among the jurists that the *nikāḥ al-shighār* is not sanctioned by Muslim authorities. This is commonly justified by reference to a saying of the Prophet. The reason for interdicting the *shighār*, as stated by Kecia Ali, seems to be the lack of stipulating a dower (*mahr/ṣadāq*).[132] In other words, what makes this marriage so repulsive to jurists is the mitigation of a wife's financial protection resulting from the absence of a dower (rather than her lack of consent in contracting the marriage). This is made evident by Saḥnūn:

وأرى أن يفرض لكل واحدة صداق مثلها لأن هذين قد فرضا والشغار الذي نهى عنه هو الذي لا صداق فيه.

> I opine that an equal dower must be given to each one [woman] because both of them require it and the *shighār*, in which no dower is stipulated, is prohibited.[133]

---

128 Ibid, 98, ll. 4–5.

129 Ibid., ll. 8–12.

130 Ibid., ll. 9–10.

الشغار بين العبيد مثل الشغار بين الأحرار وأرى أن يفسخ وإن دخل بها، فهذا يدلك على أن مسألتك شغار.

131 Ibid., ll. 11–12:

زوج عبدي أمتك بلا مهر على أن أزوج عبدك أمتي بلا مهر أن هذا كله سواء وهو شغار كله.

132 Kecia Ali, *Marriage and Slavery in Early Islam*, 57–58.

133 Saḥnūn, *MudK*, vol. 2, 99, ll. 13–14 [nikāḥ al-shighār].

More specifically, in consequence of the lack of dowers, the bodies of the women such marriages are contracted for, particularly their vulvas (*buḍʿ*), become impermissible to husbands:

والشغار أن ينكح الرجل امرأة وينكحه الآخر امرأة بضع إحداهما ببضع الأخرى بغير صداق وما يشبه ذلك.

> The *shighār* is when [a] man gives a woman into marriage and the other gives a woman into a marriage with him while the vulva (*buḍʿ*) of one of them, like that of the other, is not made permissible through a dower.[134]

In the absence of a dower, sexual intercourse with *shighār*-women is considered illegitimate. Kecia Ali points to the complicated relationship between the financial and bodily integrity of women in the Islamic legal context. Although, she states, women could be and were likely often married off by their guardians without their consent, infringing on their financial integrity was considered something more serious.[135] The above passage supports the notion of the direct link created by jurists between the financial and bodily integrity of women. In other words, it is precisely due to the lack of the dower that the body of a woman is not made permissible. Thus, the financial protection of a wife is, following the opinion of Saḥnūn, at the heart of legal reasoning allowing a husband access to her body.

b. Marriage of the daughter without her consent (bi-ghayr riḍāhā)

Saḥnūn begins by clarifying that, according to Mālik, it is not permissible to force someone into marriage.[136] He instantly restricts this provision stating that a father may compel his virgin daughter (*ibnatihi al-bikr*), young son (*ibnihi al-ṣaghīr*), slave girl (*amatihi*) or slave (*ʿabdihi*) and a guardian his orphan child (*yatīmihi*) into marriage.[137] While the subsequent cases discussed by Saḥnūn illustrate that forced marriage is permissible, they also elucidate that it is not generally desired. For instance, a virgin (*bikr*) girl who is incompetent (*safīha*) should not be given in marriage to someone without her approval (*riḍāhā*).[138]

---

134 Ibid., 99, ll. 3–4.

135 Kecia Ali, *Marriage and Slavery in Early Islam*, 57–58.

136 Saḥnūn, *MudK*, vol. 2, 100, ll. 15–16 [inkāḥ al-ab ibnatahu bi-ghayr riḍāhā]:

لا تجبر على النكاح ولا يجبر أحد أحداً على النكاح عند مالك [...].

137 Ibid., ll. 16–17.

138 Ibid., l. 19:

لا تزوج إلا برضاها.

Should the legal rationale, then, be construed as trying to ensure that marriages are contracted in respect of a daughter's right of approval? Even though Saḥnūn signifies the importance of such approval, he does not tie a marriage's legal validity to it, probably aware that this may result in an infringement of the father's authority over his daughter guaranteed through his guardianship. The juristic discussion, then, is seemingly juggling between the daughter's right of approval (*riḍāhā*)–her self-determination–and the authority the father has over her. This conceptual struggle is perhaps most clearly presented in the opinion of Ibn al-Qāsim:

فأرى أن إنكاح الأب إياها جائز عليها إلا أن يأتي من ذلك ضرر فيمنع من ذلك.

I opine that it is allowed for the father to give her in marriage except if there is harm from it, then it is forbidden.[139]

Based on this, the ultimate say is with the father.[140] He may marry off his daughter without her consent, but it is not desirable. The law, therefore, is seemingly resolving the dilemma between paternal authority and the integrity of the daughter by placing on the father the moral imperative not to give her into marriage against her will,

c. Marrying without a legal guardian (bi-ghayr walī)

The paramount position of the legal guardian is reflected in the discussion on the consequences of getting married without giving notice to the guardian. Kecia Ali claims that the term *walī* is understood, in this regard, to exclude fathers in the capacity of guardians.[141] A footnote, in which she refers to a number of chapters from the *Mudawwana* in support of her claim, does not explicitly clarify how she reaches this conclusion. At any rate, marriages contracted without the support of the legal guardian may result in dreadful consequences:

قلت: أرأيت إذا تزوج الرجل المرأة بغير أمر ولي بشهود، أيضرب في قول مالك الزوج والمرأة والشهود والذي زوجها أم لا؟ قال: سمعت مالكاً يسأل عنها فقال: أدخل بها؟ فقالوا: لا وأنكر الشهود أن يكونوا حضروا فقالوا: لم يدخل بها فقال: لا عقوبة عليهم إلا أني رأيت منه أن لو دخل عليها لعوقبوا المرأة والزوج والذي أنكح. قلت: والشهود؟ قال ابن القاسم: نعم، والشهود إن علموا.

---

139 Ibid., ll. 27–28.

140 Based on evidence from the *Mudawwana* and the *Umm* of al-Shāfiʿī, Kecia Ali concludes that the authority of the father over his daughter is legally constructed as inclusive of decisions with respect to her virginity but not necessarily the daughter's maturity or age; Kecia Ali, *Marriage and Slavery in Early Islam*, 35.

141 Kecia Ali, *Marriage and Slavery in Early Islam*, 35.

> I said: Do you opine that when [a] man marries [a] woman in the presence of witnesses without notice to the guardian, [then], according to the saying of Mālik, are they, the husband, the wife, the witnesses, and whoever married them, to be smitten or not? He said: I heard Mālik being asked about this and he asked: did he penetrate her? He answered: no, the witnesses denied they were present and said: He did not penetrate her. He [Mālik] then said: There is no punishment incumbent on them, but I opine that if he penetrated her, the wife, husband, and whoever married them would be subject to punishment. I said: and the witnesses? Ibn al-Qāsim said: yes, the witnesses too if they knew about it.[142]

The pertinent question therefore when getting married without the support of a legal guardian is whether or not sexual intercourse between the married parties took place before the guardian came to know of the marriage contract. If it did, the married parties as well as the witnesses, and the officiant who sanctioned the marriage are to be punished. It should be noted that the notion of punishment for adultery (*zinā'*) is seemingly inferred from the *Qur'ān*.[143]

Saḥnūn also justifies his opinion that getting married without the permission of a guardian is tantamount to adultery by adducing two *aḥādīth*, both of which are contained in the *Ṣaḥīḥ*-collection of al-Bukhārī in similar versions. The first states:

لا يزني الزاني حين يزني وهو مؤمن ولا يسرق وقد أنزل الله حده على الإيمان وقطعه على الإيمان.

> The adulterer who commits adultery is not a believer at the time of committing adultery and a thief is not a believer at the time of committing theft, and Allāh revealed the boundaries of the faith and the limits (?) of the faith.[144]

The second *ḥadīth* he quotes is a direct moral imperative directed towards men:

لا تزوج المرأة إلا بولي.

> Do not marry the woman without a guardian.[145]

More importantly, the understanding of illicit sexual intercourse resulting in the punishment designated for adultery is closely connected to the notion that legitimate sexual intercourse requires the possession of authority over a woman. Such possession may only be granted by a woman's guardian who, when agreeing to a marriage contract, can transfer his guardianship to the husband. Kecia Ali puts this in a nutshell:

---

142 Saḥnūn, *MudK*, vol. 2, 117, ll. 14–18 [fī al-tazwīj bi-ghayr walī].
143 Q 4:25, 24:2, 25:68.
144 Saḥnūn, *MudK*, vol. 2, 118, ll. 5–6.
145 Ibid., l. 11.

> The connection between *milk* and lawful sexuality stands at the core of all regulation of marriage and divorce and by its absence marks discussions over punishment for illicit sex. [146]

Thus, based on the legal cases featured by Saḥnūn and the secondary literature, we may confidently state that the intertwined nature of authority and the legitimacy of sexual relationships is central to the laws on Islamic marriage as regulated by the Mālikī school.

d. Fixed-term marriage (al-nikāḥ ilā ajal)

The fixed-term marriage (*al-nikāḥ ilā ajal*) must not necessarily be equated with the pleasure marriage (*mutʿa*) which is practiced particularly within the contemporary Shīʿa and is often rendered as "temporary marriage."[147] Despite Saḥnūn's referring to *al-nikāḥ ilā ajal* as *mutʿa* at least once, one should take into consideration the distinct historical development the *mutʿa* has undergone. For that reason and to avoid confusion, I do not employ the term *mutʿa* except where expressly referred to as such by Saḥnūn.

It is relatively clear that the *nikāḥ ilā ajal* cannot generally be tantamount to the *mutʿa*. Saḥnūn begins by claiming that a marriage, which is contracted with the permission of the guardian (*bi-idhni walī*), a dower (*bi-ṣadāqin qad sammāhu*), and stipulated to expire after months (*ashhur*), a year (*sana*), or two years (*sanatayn*), is void (*bāṭil*).[148] Further into his inquiry, he reiterates and expands the hypothetical arguing that somebody cannot contract a valid marriage by declaring: "I marry you for a month" because that would correspond to stipulating a *mutʿa*.[149] The author, therefore, elucidates the first meaning of *ilā ajal*, which is the designation of a temporal limit to a marriage.

He then discusses a more complex hypothetical, presumably to illustrate that *nikāḥ ilā ajal* carries other meanings which do not necessarily overlap

---

146 Kecia Ali, *Marriage and Slavery in Early Islam*, 12.

147 For a brilliant article on the pleasure-marriage (*mutʿa*), see Dietrich von Denffer, "Mutʿa – Ehe oder Prostitution," 299–325.

148 Saḥnūn, *MudK*, vol. 2, 130, ll. 8–9 [al-nikāḥ ilā ajal]:

إذا تزوج امرأة بإذن ولي بصداق قد سماه تزوجها إلى أشهر أو سنة، أو سنتين أيصلح هذا النكاح؟ قال: قال مالك: هذا النكاح باطل إذا تزوجها إلى أجل من الآجال فهذا النكاح باطل.

149 Ibid., ll. 18–19:

إن قال أتزوجك شهراً يبطل النكاح أم يجعل النكاح صحيحاً ويبطل الشرط؟ قال: قال مالك: النكاح باطل يفسخ وهذه المتعة وقد ثبت عن رسول الله.

with the concept of the *mutʿa*. Unfortunately, however, its translation and interpretation remain relatively uncertain in some places. The hypothetical is as follows:

قلت: أرأيت إن قال لها إن مضى هذا الشهر فأنا أتزوجك ورضي بذلك وليها ورضيت؟ قال: هذا النكاح باطل ولا يقام عليه. قلت: أرأيت لو أن رجلاً تزوج امرأة بثلاثين ديناراً نقداً أو ثلاثين نسيئة إلى سنة؟ قال: قال مالك: لا يعجبني هذا النكاح ولم يقل لنا فيه أكثر من هذا. قال مالك: ليس هذا من نكاح من أدركت، قلت: فما يعجبك من هذا النكاح إن نزل؟ قال: أجيزه وأجعل للزوج إذا أتى بالمعجل أن يدخل عليها وليس لها أن تمنعه نفسها وتكون الثلاثون المؤخرة إلى أجلها. قلت: فإن طال الأجل أو قال في الثلاثين المؤخرة إنها إلى موت أو فراق؟ قال: أما إذا كان إلى موت أو فراق فهو مفسوخ ما لم يدخل بها وكذلك قال مالك وأما إذا كان إلى أجل بعيد فأراه جائزاً ما لم يتفاحش بعد ذلك.

I asked: What do you think if he tells her, after the expiration of one month, I will marry you and her guardian and she herself are satisfied with this? He said: This marriage is invalid and it must not be contracted. I asked: Did you consider [the case of] a man marrying a woman for 30 dīnārs in cash and [or?] 30 dīnārs on credit to be paid after a year? He said that Mālik said: I do not like this marriage and he said no more. Mālik said: This is not the (kind of) marriage I have encountered. I said: So, what do you prefer if this occurs? He (Mālik) said: I allow it and grant the husband to consummate the marriage if he brings it (the money) immediately. She must not keep herself from him. The 30 promised for later are due with the appointed time. I asked: So, if the duration is prolonged or if he says: the 30 are hers upon (his) death or (their) separation? He said: As concerns his saying (that it is hers) upon (his) death or (their) separation, it is invalid. He should not consummate the marriage. Mālik also said: If he postpones it (the payment of the 30 dīnārs) to a significantly later point, then I opine it is allowed. He should not postpone (the payment) after that.[150]

At first glance, it may not be obvious how Saḥnūn is suggesting a second semantic layer of *nikāḥ ilā ajal* here. In the hypothetical, a man attempts to stipulate a marriage with a woman telling her that he will marry her after a specified period of one month. Accordingly, this marriage does not come into effect. Subsequently, Saḥnūn inquires about whether a man may contract a marriage with a woman in exchange for 30 dīnārs in cash and the same amount on credit to be paid by him after a year. Somewhat reluctantly Mālik opines that husband and wife can consummate such a marriage, with the wife being incapable of refusing her husband if he pays the 30 dīnārs immediately (*bi-l-muʿajjali*) after the marriage was contracted. The second part of the stipulation states that the husband may pay the remaining 30

150 Ibid., ll. 20–28.

dīnārs (*al-thalāthuna al-muʾakhkhara*) after a stipulated time but must certainly do so before his death or the dissolution of the marriage. What this case seems to be hinting at is that a man may contract a marriage with a wife, even though he cannot pay her the full amount of the dower she is entitled to instantaneously. The 30 dīnārs paid up front are, therefore, given to the wife as a security ensuring she does not end up entirely dower*less*. The hypothetical makes evident that the underlying rationale is the protection of the financial integrity of the wife. By looking at the stipulation in conjunction with the first question of the above case–the promise of a man to marry a woman after a certain period–it should become clear that a man's promise alone is insufficient for a marriage contract to come into effect; rather, he needs to come up with at least part of her dower to symbolically reinforce his intent to marry her. The second meaning of the term *ilā ajal* thus hints at a marriage in which payment of the dower is deferred. In other words, *ajal* in this context would seem to refer to postponing the payment of the dower. This type of marriage is, according to Saḥnūn, generally prohibited, except if the husband pays at least a portion of the dower upon contracting the marriage.

In this subchapter, I argued that *nikāḥ ilā ajal* has two meanings: the first being a marriage with a stipulated time limit; the second being a marriage in which the payment of the dower is deferred. Both types are, except under special circumstances, prohibited. It should have become evident by now that although the basic concepts of the law are based on and correspond to the scriptural commands such as the prohibition not to stipulate marriages with an expiry date (*mutʿa*), the Muslim jurists of the ninth century were in the process of laying down the hermeneutical tools in order to establish guidelines for interpreting the stipulations in the *Qurʾān* and *Sunna*.

4. Stipulating the bridal dower (ṣadāq/mahr)

The previous subchapters already emphasized that the stipulation of a bridal dower (*ṣadāq/mahr*) constituted a frequently recurring theme in the regulations on Islamic marriage. The inquiry has shown that, according to the law, it is generally desirable to stipulate a dower–an appropriate one at the best. In the *Risāla*, al-Shāfiʿī enumerates the necessary requirements for a marriage contract to be considered valid:

فإذا جمع النكاح أربعا رضا المزوجة الثيب والمزوج وأن يزوج المرأة وليها بشهود حل النكاح [...].

> The marriage is composed of four things: the approval of the deflowered bride, [approval of] the bridegroom, that the guardian of the woman marries her [off], and the presence of witnesses when the marriage is contracted […][151]

The bridal dower is not among the conditions mentioned. This overlaps with the evidence marshaled in this chapter. The stipulations on the fixed-term marriage (*al-nikāḥ ilā ajal*) showed that the financial integrity of a wife could not be neglected entirely. Al Shāfiʿī puts the jurisprudential view on the bridal dower (at least the Shāfiʿī one) in a nutshell:

ولا يفسد النكاح بترك تسمية الصداق لأنّ الله أثبت النكاح في كتابه بغير مهر وهذا مكتوب في غير هذا الموضع.

> Marriage should not be annulled because the dower [*ṣadāq*] is omitted since God confirmed in his scripture [the validity] of marrying without a dower and this is written in other places than this.[152]

Even though the bridal dower is not a mandatory condition for a marriage to come into effect, the law's inclination is obviously towards stipulating it. Our inquiry has produced evidence in support of this. The perspicuous prohibition of the exchange marriage (*nikāḥ al-shighār*) and the regulations pertaining to the fixed-term marriage (*nikāḥ ilā ajal*) are cases in point. The very rationale behind the proscription of such matrimonial arrangements is based on the complicated link between the financial and bodily integrity of women. By ensuring women's financial security through a bridal dower, sexual relationships with women are made permissible to men. Having said that, the stipulations on the terms of marriage (*shurūṭ al-zawāj*) made plain that women could forfeit a portion of their dower in return for more favorable marriage conditions for as long as such an exchange occurred after the marriage was contracted.

While the law operated as a safeguard of women's interests particularly in cases where such interests were guaranteed through a promise or oath made by the husband, it was also complicit in mitigating the financial integrity of a wife by sanctioning practices such as the wife's giving up a portion of the dower. Nevertheless, even though the dower is neither legally mandatory nor stably installed, the recurring recommendation to stipulate one, more largely, indicates that the matter occupied a legal spot that was noticeably saturated by the ethical concerns of the jurists. Externalizing their interests into the language of ethics, then, constituted a way of dealing with the dilemma between the husband's authority over his wife and ensuring her financial integrity.

151 Al-Shāfiʿī, *RisF*, 250, ll. 11–12 [ṣifat nahy Allāh wa-nahy rasūlihi].
152 Ibid., ll. 14–15.

In this chapter, I marshaled evidence in support of the first main argument of this thesis. In the treatises of Saḥnūn and al-Shāfiʿī, matrimonial law is, first and foremost, dealt with by circumscribing the boundaries between the permitted and the prohibited in addition to being crosscut by a variety of moral categorizations such as preferred and disliked. In other words, the nature of Islamic matrimony is carved out by both authors by reverting to the hermeneutic method of "definition by default." By elucidating what is forbidden, legal subjects become cognizant that everything which is not, is allowed. More broadly, the overtone is: what is not expressly forbidden, is allowed even if to varying moral degrees.

This chapter showed that the Muslim jurists reverted to scriptural commands to sanction or prohibit specific marital practices. When strictly prohibiting, the consequences of such commands could be mitigated by suggesting that they apply only under certain conditions. In other words, coating legal provisions in scriptural references, the jurist could, through sophisticated legal reasoning and hermeneutics, macerate strict prohibitions and create room for making permissible such things as taking a fifth wife (after divorcing one of the others) or marrying two sisters (after divorcing the first). That is, by tying certain decrees of the *Qurʾān* and *Sunna*, which could potentially be interpreted as strictly forbidden, to specific conditions, the jurists created frameworks within which they could interpret such prohibitions more leniently. The degree to which these frameworks allowed for lenient interpretations of prohibitions is, at least to some extent, representative of the ethical concerns of the Muslim jurists. Thus, matrimonial jurisprudence as suggested by al-Shāfiʿī and Saḥnūn could not be detached from the personal concerns of the juristic elite–rather, they seemed to be very much situated at its heart.

D. Preliminary conclusion

This chapter was geared towards responding to the three main research questions from the perspective of matrimonial law: What legal forms do the laws of matrimony cultivate? How are these legal forms related to the cosmological imagery and the sociopolitical concerns of the community/empire which engenders and enables them? What patterns mark the interactions between Sasanian, East Syrian, and Islamic law?

I first focused on Sasanian law. To that end, I carved out the types of matrimony discussed in the *Hazār Dādestān*. Most importantly, it became clear that Sasanian jurisprudence knew a variety of marriage types reaching from full (*pādiḫšāy*), auxiliary (*čagar*) to consensus marriage (*ḫwasrāyēn*). In addition, each of these types could be contracted temporarily (*nē az ān ī hamēig*). The numerous variations of matrimonial agreements bestowed the legal system with a significant amount of flexibility.

Secondly, I looked at how these matrimonial forms were mediated through the triangle of cosmology, lawmaking, and the concerns of the elite. By mobilizing references to Mazdaean cosmology–creating direct benefit in the larger cosmos through sexual reproduction and following the example of Ohrmazd to procreate with next-of-kin–the Sasanian authorities could effectively sanction forms of matrimony that were more broadly conducive to sustaining elite households. The presence of sociopolitical concerns in marriage law is most evident in the institutions of the intermediary (*ayōkēn*) and substitute-successors (*stūr*), both of which served the particular historical conjuncture of Sasanian rule. By interweaving the maintenance of elite households with the law of matrimony the rulers made sure the sun on the Sasanian Empire would not set all too soon.

I then examined the laws of matrimony of the Church of the East. The unmistakable hallmark of the laws on Christian matrimony is absolute monogamy. The law rigorously set the terms for curbing the presence of next-of-kin marriage (*masbā d-qaribātā*) and promoting marriages with strangers (*masbā d-nukrāyātā*). As illustrated by the prohibitions of Mar Aba and the *Corpus Juris* of Ishoᶜbokht, the prohibition of next-of-kin marriages loomed large in the jurisprudential writings from the mid-sixth century onwards.

Subsequently, I illustrated how East Syrian matrimony was mediated between Christian cosmological imagery, lawmaking, and the sociopolitical concerns of the Christian elite. The treatises of Ishoᶜbokht and Mar Aba indicate that scripture, particularly references to the inseparable union of husband and wife decreed by God were mobilized to sanction monogamy and foster a distinct sense of community. Perplexingly, the monogamous vision of matrimony, which was closely knit to Christian ideas of cosmology, also served as the bargaining chip when the Sasanian elite demanded adjustments to the East Syrian laws on matrimony of the clerical hierarchy. The inquiry on East Syrian matrimony more broadly exemplified how adamantly the bishops tied matrimonial laws to Christian cosmological imagery in order to establish a communal sense of identity, which was deliberately made distinct from that of the Sasanians.

The last part of this chapter dealt with matrimony in Islamic law. I used the *Mudawwana* of Saḥnūn and the *Risālā* of al-Shāfiᶜī as case studies to explicate a limited number of the types of matrimony known to Islamic law. Notably, the most characteristic feature was that most of the matrimonial forms discussed by these two jurists were prohibited. The nature of matrimony, therefore, seems to be overwhelmingly defined by default. Marriage exchanges (*nikāḥ al-shighār*), marrying without a guardian (*bi-ghayr walī*), and fixed-term marriages (*nikāḥ ilā ajal*) were, for the most part, interdicted. Marrying from the core of next-of-kin relatives was interdicted. Conditions stipulated before contracting a marriage (*shurūṭ al-zawāj*) were not interdicted but did simply not come into effect.

In the following, I discussed how Islamic matrimony was seemingly negotiated within the triangle of scriptural references, lawmaking, and the sociopolitical concerns of the Muslim elite. Saḥnūn and al-Shāfiʿī arguably based their legal opinions on scriptural commands, particularly such of a prohibiting nature. That is, Qurʾānic decrees and prophetic practices did not only constitute archetypes and entry points to their discussions but served as larger interpretative frameworks for determining what is permissible and what is not. While their legal reasoning and hermeneutics were coated in the language of scripture, the jurists could macerate divine interdictions–which may have otherwise been read as strictly prohibiting–by tying them to certain conditions resulting in a smaller purview of applicability of such prohibitions. Thus, Islamic jurisprudence, as advanced by al-Shāfiʿī and Saḥnūn, was saturated by the ethical concerns of the jurists to the extent that juristic ethics ultimately determined to what extent divine prohibitions were mitigated or not.

The findings of this chapter indicate the applicability of my first thesis statement. For all three legal systems, it became evident that there is significant value in scrutinizing the laws on matrimony in conjunction with the cosmological imagery and the sociopolitical and ethical aspirations of the elite which more often than not seems to have had significant stakes in encouraging or prohibiting specific forms of matrimony. Notably, scriptural references were not employed consistently and could be utilized to include and undergird, but also to curb and prevent certain matrimonial practices of the Sasanian and Islamic Empires.

Regarding the question of what patterns marked the interactions between Sasanian, East Syrian, and Islamic law, this chapter marshaled some evidence. Two junctures are especially noteworthy: first, the convocation of the East Syrian bishops in the Synod of 497 which was instigated by the King of Kings to reform the matrimonial laws of the clerical hierarchy; and secondly, Mar Aba's list of prohibitions from the mid-sixth century. Both historical moments complicate our understanding of the interaction of legal systems, showing that the underlying pattern was a matter of negotiation, rather than influence. To support the second argument of this thesis of *varying* patterns of interaction, more evidence will have to be adduced. I shall now revisit my two thesis statements by once again examining Sasanian, East Syrian, and Islamic jurisprudence from the perspective of slavery laws.

Chapter VII
Slaves

A. Sasanian law: slave trade–a risky financial venture

1. Prelude: basic legal concepts in Sasanian property law

a. Substance (bun) and fruit/increase (bar)

Maria Macuch has theorized the critical concepts in Sasanian property law. Considering that slaves are deemed to constitute a type of property, it is useful to outline these concepts. Every legal object (*ẖwāstag*) is composed of a substance (*bun*) and a fruit/increase (*bar*) or income/interest (*windišn/ wa*ẖ*š/wa*ẖ*t*).[1] The distinction can be exemplified by considering an orange tree. The tree itself, including the roots, stem, branches, twigs, and leaves, are the substance (*bun*). The oranges that are yet to grow constitute the fruits/increase (*bar*). This distinction is essential to many principles and institutions of Sasanian law, particularly, the law of inheritance and endowments. As for the slave, the substance (*bun*) is her body. The fruit/increase (*bar*) encompasses everything that cannot be fully anticipated but creates value such as the slave's labor and, supposedly, pregnancies.

b. Ownership (ẖwēšīh) and possession (dārišn)

The second important distinction is made between ownership (*ẖwēšīh*) and possession (*dārišn*). To own an object (*ẖwāstag*) is to have full authority over it, including the right to use, transfer, bequeath, sell, or even destroy it. On the contrary, the right to possession (*dārišn*) implies only the physical control of an object (*ẖwāstag*) but not necessarily ownership.[2] For example, someone leasing a plot of land possesses it, but does not have ownership of it. Selling or transferring it is not permissible. But if she buys the plot, she acquires ownership of it, which implies that she does not merely have physical control over it but can transfer, resell, bequeath, or even destroy it. As a legal object (*ẖwāstag*), the slave is capable of and usually ought to be owned by another party. It is more intricate, however, whether a slave herself is authorized to ownership and/or possession of property. The *Hazār Dādestān*,

1 Maria Macuch, "Substance and Fruit in the Sasanian Law of Property and the Babylonian Talmud," in *Proceedings of the Conference on "Talmudic Archeology," University College London, June 22–24, 2009* (Leiden: Brill, 2015), 248.

2 Ibid., 248–249.

in fact, illustrates that a slave, by rule, does not have the capacity to acquire property.[3] Property transferred to her thus comes to be owned by the slave's master. Even so, a master may bestow on her slave limited legal capacity. In that case, the slave is authorized to dispose over her own income (*pad windišn pādiḫšāykard*) and is thus entitled to acquire property from third parties.[4]

2. *Transacting slaves*

a. *Selling and pledging slaves*

We have multiple cases in the law book in which slaves are part of a transaction, particularly, as sold commodities or pledges. First of all, it is important to note that slaves owned by Zoroastrians ought not to be sold to non-Zoroastrians:

> A slave may not be sold to a non-Zoroastrian. If, however he is sold, (then) both of them (the buyer and the seller) shall be considered thieves by the Zoroastrian *rat* [priest] on account of the slave (i.e. the action shall be equated with theft - A.P.) and they shall be branded [...].[5]

The stipulation, in fact, indicates that selling slaves to non-Zoroastrians is not only undesirable but punished by the law. Thus, both contracting parties, the vendor as well the non-Zoroastrian purchaser, are to be convicted of theft. We can reasonably assume that the prohibition strives to prevent the transfer of slaves who have been living in Zoroastrian households to environments in which they would be exposed to the Bad Religion (*agdēnīh*).

Even though slaves are legally considered objects (*ḫwāstag*), they possess qualities, which even the law cannot deny as being human. Interestingly, such human qualities result in a multitude of legal problems in cases where slaves are stipulated as commodities in transactions:

> When he sells a pregnant female-slave–if the pregnancy is visible–then the pregnancy is also sold (i.e. the fruit is included in the transaction - A.P.).[6]

Accordingly, if the pregnancy of a slave-woman is visible when contracting the sale, the child is included in the deal. As a logical consequence thereof, a pregnant slave, whose pregnancy is not yet apparent, is sold without the child. More generally, the vendor only conveys to the contracting party

---

3 It appears that the slave in terms of his incapacity to acquire property matches the legal status of women and minors; Farroḫmard, *HazDP*, 151 (58, 16–59, 1): "In addition to a woman, a slave, and a minor, others from the same category are also to be considered insolvent unless it is evident that they are solvent [...]."

4 Maria Macuch, "Barda and Barda-Dāri."

5 Farroḫmard, *HazDP*, 29 (1, 13–15).

6 Ibid., 111 (40, 17–85, 2).

what she intends to sell, rather than what the legal object (*ẖwāstag*) might be. Since the pregnancy cannot be anticipated at the time of the contracting parties' stipulating the transfer, the law works in favour of the vendor following the maxim of *ignorantia facti excusat*–the facts of which she is ignorant, she cannot be held responsible for. More importantly, it seems that the time a child is conceived is critical. If conceived while a slave-woman is owned by her vendor, then the vendor has a legal right to profit from the fruit (*bar*), meaning the child. However, if conceived after the sale, the child comes to be owned by the purchaser. This is corroborated by another stipulation:

> It is also said, that if Farraxv concluded (the following) agreement concerning a slave-woman with Mihrēn: "(she shall belong (?)) to you after my death," Pērož ī Veh-Ohrmizdān and Pusānveh ī Burzātur Farnbaγan (… … … … … …) (if) a child is born (to the slave-woman) in Farraxv's lifetime, then he should not be conveyed (to Mihrēn).[7]

Similarly, in this case, a slave-woman who is stipulated to be transferred at the time of Farroẖ's death, is merely conveyed within the scope of her substance (*bun*) excluding the fruits (*bar*) she generates in the lifetime of Farroẖ. To sum up, the legal maxim in transactions of pregnant slaves seems to be determined by two factors: the intent of the vendor and the time the child is conceived.

In Sasanian law, slave trade constitutes a relatively volatile financial venture that entails significant risks for the contracting parties. Such threats were not limited to the fruits (*bar*) of a slave, which we discussed, but also encompass her substance (*bun*). In the following, more complicated legal case, this becomes quite evident:

> If Farraxv makes the following contract with Mihrēn: 'whatever you choose ('name') that has a value of 200 (*drahms*) (from) the estate belonging to me, shall belong to you'. And if Mihrēn declares his agreement to the receipt (= the transfer to him) of several slaves who were minors at that time and valued at 200 (*drahms*) altogether and who now are valued each separately at 200 *drahms*, then–since their value has grown because of their (= the slave's) bodily improvement (i. e. the minors are now fully grown - A.P.) and not because of a conjunction of prices in the town/*šahr*–the transfer shall be made in accordance with their present value and not with what they were worth at the time of the drawing up of the contract. And the declaration (made by Mihrēn regarding his agreement to receive several slaves - A.P.) is not in force.[8]

In the above case, Farroẖ and Mihrēn stipulate the transaction of multiple slaves, who at the conclusion of the contract have a total value of 200

7 Ibid., 241 (108,8–11); also, see Farroẖmard, *HazDM*, 650–651. Perikhanian's and Macuch's translations are identical in spite of the lacunae in the passage.

8 Farroẖmard, *HazDP*, 141 (54, 11–15).

drahms. The increase in the value of the slaves, resulting from their bodily improvement, to 200 *drahms* each, voids the stipulated contract causing Mihrēn to receive only one slave. It would be useful to know, whether the same logic applies to cases where the slaves' value decreases. Would the seller have to add more slaves? We cannot answer this question here. Likewise, certain insecurities prevail in transactions in which slaves are pledged to a creditor. If a slave is manumitted by a debtor after having been put in pledge, then, unless the debtor is insolvent, that slave is instantly free. To compensate for the loss of the creditor, the debtor is obliged to pay an equivalent sum of money to her, or, otherwise, the creditor may hold the slave in pledge until the money is settled.[9] This more broadly indicates that transactions with slaves bore significant risks for the parties involved. Similar to animals and other living property, the law book probably had to account for the fact that slaves were less consistent in their market value than other things, and subject to the human experience of disease, pregnancy, and death.

Most peculiarly, Sasanian slave law does not protect Zoroastrian believers from becoming enslaved. Unlike in other legal systems, being an adherent of the Good Religion (*wehdēn*) was not a safeguard against being enslaved. In fact, the law book stipulates that a contracting party may herself end up enslaved as a result of stipulating a slave trade with someone else:

> If Farraxv receives Mihrēn from Āturfarnbay, as a slave (= *loco servi*) once again, then–if Āturfarnbay makes a claim–Farraxv must hand Mihrēn over, otherwise (Āturfarnbay) shall be entitled to seize Farraxv (himself) in compensation ('exchange') for Mihrēn [...].[10]

In this case, the debtor (Farroẖ) becomes enslaved in case he fails to comply with the creditor's (Ādufarrbay) demand to return the slave (Mihrēn). The stipulation indicates that the property of the creditor ought to be maintained against all odds, even if that results in the enslavement of a fellow Zoroastrian. So far, our inquiry has shown that slave trade was associated with significant risks for the contracting parties. These risks were not limited to the *de facto* loss or transmutation of slaves into other forms of property but could be as significant as a contracting party becoming herself enslaved as a result of transacting with a slave.

9 Ibid., 107 (39, 2–5). For another stipulation with similar outcome, cf. ibid., 107 (38, 13–17).

10 Ibid., 149 (58, 9–14).

b. Selling children into slavery

Selling children into slavery is generally not allowed. However, under extenuating circumstances, the *paterfamilias* may sell a child for its own sake and the protection of other family members. Maria Macuch has well researched this hypothetical.[11] The law book is clear that transactions of children or other family members under the guardianship of the *paterfamilias*, are only permissible under two circumstances as indicated by the following stipulation:

> Only the father is authorized to sell the child into slavery. And he is authorized to sell (the child) in the case of (impending) death and injury (*margīh ud rēštagīh*), (but) he (=the father) is only authorized to sell it (= the child) for its (own) sake (*pad ān ī ōy*). In the case of an *adwadād* ("inability to maintain") the father is authorized to sell it (= the child) for the sake of his (= the father's) own (needs) (*pad ān ī xwēš*) and for its (= the child's) sake (*pad-iz ān ī ōy*) and that of the mother (*ud mād*), for himself (*pad ān ī xwad*) and for the sake of him, who has been affected (by the *adwadād*) (*pad ān ī ōy kē abar mad ēstēd*). And the other guardians are authorized to sell it (= the child) for the sake of themselves (*pad ān ī xwad*) (and) of him, who has been affected (by the *adwadād*) (*pad ān ī . . . ōy kē abar mad ēstēd*).[12]

The first features a situation of general emergency in which the child would be exposed to imminent harm resulting in its injury or death. It is important to highlight that the rationale behind the selling of the child, in this case, is the well-being of the child itself, rather than that of other parties. The second circumstance noted in the hypothetical is referred to as *adwadād*. By conflating the stipulations in the *Hazār Dādestān* with the usage of the term in other sources, Macuch concludes four meanings of the term, only one of which is relevant to the above hypothetical. It presumably implies a shortage of supplies or a lack of food.[13] Unlike the first section of the hypothetical, the child may be sold in order to protect not only its own well-being but also that of other family members. Another stipulation illustrates that the selling of family members by the *paterfamilias* is not restricted to children but may also apply to the wife, the adopted son or daughter as well as the substitute-successorship (*stūrīh*) or legal guardianship (*sālārīh*) over a woman.[14] From these stipulations, it becomes clear that selling children (and other family members) was only an option in rare instances. In such destitute situations were it was, the rationale behind such transactions was, first and foremost, the safeguarding of the child itself, and only, in the second place, the protection of other family members.

---

11 See Maria Macuch, "The adwadād Offence in Zoroastrian Law," 247–269.

12 Farroḫmard, *HazD*, (33, 6–9), quoted in Maria Macuch, "The adwadād Offence in Zoroastrian Law," 260.

13 Maria Macuch, "The adwadād Offence in Zoroastrian Law," 260.

14 Farroḫmard, *HazDP*, 95 (33, 6–9).

3. *Manumitting slaves*

a. *Full and partial manumission*

Manumission is the act of freeing a slave. Some legal systems, at least in theory, are based on the notion that being a slave is mutually exclusive with being an adherent of a specific religion. The stipulations previously discussed, in which Zoroastrians may end up being enslaved as the result of a transaction, imminent harm or a shortage of supplies, have shown that Sasanian law does not protect Zoroastrians from servitude. However, it seems that in order to acquire new adherents to the Good Religion (*wehdēn*), the legal system developed certain incentives that mainly applied to slaves. First, it is written that if a slave owned by a Christian master converts to Zoroastrianism, she is manumitted and must remunerate the former master with her market value.[15] Therefore, a slave belonging to a Christian could, at least in theory, escape slavery by converting to Zoroastrianism. The benefit of manumission that comes with conversion is only effectuated, however, if the slave's master does not simultaneously convert to Zoroastrianism. In other words, should both, master and slave, convert, then the slave is not subject to manumission.[16] The following is a rather elusive hypothetical:

> It is written in one place that if a slave belonging to a Christian converts to Zoroastrianism ('the Good Religion') and (enters the service) of a Zoroastrian, (the latter) must return the value ('price') of the slave to (his former master) and free the slave, and the latter (= the slave) must compensate him for this loss [...].[17]

Macuch suggests that the passage probably operates to make obligatory to the Zoroastrian community the financial support of a slave-convert to help her pay the release money to her former master.[18] This makes sense against the background that, with the manumission of the slave, her financial responsibilities towards the non-Zoroastrian community would be immediately settled. Perhaps a bit too far-fetched, but an interesting alternative reading would be that the slave enters a kind of contractual relationship with someone from the Good Religion (*wehdēn*) who–in the Zoroastrian version of the Muslim *mawālī*–would oversee her integration into the community while provisionally covering the costs of the slave's release.

The stipulations in Sasanian law make clear that manumissions could be partial. What I mean is that, rather than entirely freeing the slave, only a

15 Ibid., 29 (1, 10–13).

16 Farroḫmard, *HazDM*, 25 (1, 16–17). Note that the translation of Perikhanian is entirely different in this case; cf. Farroḫmard, *HazDP*, 29 (1, 16–17).

17 Ibid., 29 (1, 10–13).

18 Maria Macuch, *HazDM*, 34–35.

portion of her may be manumitted. For instance, if she is owned by shareholders each of whom owns one-half of the slave, then, if one shareholder manumits her half, the slave is one-half free and one-half enslaved. Manifold hypotheticals are conceivable, meaning a slave might be released to even the tiniest portion of her substance (*bun*). This procedure is similarly attested to in other systems of jurisprudence. More importantly, we ought to ask what the practical implications of a partial manumission were. The law book features a rather unusual case which Perikhanian and Macuch translate quite differently. According to Perikhanian:

> Alongside it is written that if he makes the following declaration: 'I have conveyed this slave to Mihrēn for one year out of every two', then this slave cannot be manumitted without mutual consent. And if one of them frees his share (= his share of the real right on the slave–A. P.) with the consent of the other, then note should be taken (that the slave) is entirely free (one year out of every two).[19]

Based on the translation, the right to dispose of the slave is owned by two persons. Their shares in the slave's substance are equal, allowing them to each make use of him at intervals of one year. Besides, the stipulation states that the other party needs approval if a shareholder wants to manumit his share in the slave. Once approval is given, the slave transforms into a hybrid that oscillates between the status of freedom and slavery in intervals. That is, he is free for one year and is again fully enslaved in the year following. The translation of Macuch leads to an entirely different result:

> And along with the (sentences), which are written down, it must be kept in mind: When someone declares: 'This slave is given by me to Mihrēn every two years for (a) year', (then) nobody is authorized to manumit the slave, except by mutual agreement. And if one [shareholder] releases his share with the agreement of the other [shareholder], (then) he (= the slave) (is considered) free to equal shares (*hamēwēn*).[20]

In her commentary, Macuch explains that the hypothetical stages a situation in which two shareholders hold the right of disposal over a slave. To manumit a share in the slave, the approval of the other shareholder is needed. If the other shareholder approves, the slave is transmuted back and forth into the property of each shareholder. That is, the slave enters the property of one shareholder for one year and the property of the other shareholder in the following year. The partial manumission causes each shareholder to profit only half of what they used to from the slave's labor since he now benefits from his labor to one-half, the other half going to both shareholders jointly.[21] What is peculiar about Macuch's version is that

19 Farroḫmard, *HazDP*, 171 (69, 3–6).

20 Farroḫmard, *HazDM*, 467 (69, 3–6), my translation into English from German.

21 Maria Macuch, *HazDM*, 470.

it seems incomprehensible why the shareholder, who manumits his share in the slave, should be allowed to further profit from the substance and fruit of the slave. From a contextual–not philological–perspective, the translation of Perikhanian would appear more plausible.

Before continuing, it is important to note that the fruits (*bar*) of slaves are always as free as their substance (*bun*). In other words, if a female slave is manumitted to one tenth, then children born to her, are deemed free to the same degree.[22] We can reckon that this equally applies to slave labor and other "fruits" produced by a slave.

b. Reclaiming former slaves into slavery

The law book is relatively clear about protecting manumitted slaves from being reclaimed into slavery by their former masters or others. For instance, if a slave is part of a transaction of a father with his wife and children, in which the father stipulates that the estate he *will* acquire shall be conveyed to them, then, in the case that he subsequently manumits the slave, the slave cannot be claimed by the wife or children as the following legal passage indicates:

> Vahrām has said that if a father transmits to his wife and children (the estate which) he will receive and he subsequently frees a slave (from servitude), then, according to the opinion of Syāvaxš, the (former) slave cannot ('may not') be brought back from his (acquired status of) a 'subject of the King of Kings,' and I express the same opinion, but Rāt-Ōhrmizd had rendered a different judgement on this question […].[23]

In the opinions of Farroḫmard and Siyāvaḫš, this is also the case if the father promises to them his current estate of which the slave is a part of. Again, if he subsequently manumits the slave, the latter cannot be reclaimed by the wife or children.[24] More broadly, we can gauge that a slave's manumission is given priority over property claims. In other words, once a slave acquires freedom, she may only with difficulty be reclaimed into slavery.[25]

4. Locating the slave in Ērānšahr

In spite of the various stipulations extant in the *Hazār Dādestān*, it remains rather arduous to situate slaves and their societal role within the larger context of the Sasanian Empire. What is certainly peculiar is that being en-

22 Farroḫmard, *HazDP*, 27 (1, 6–7).

23 Ibid., 67 (20, 7–10).

24 Ibid., 91 (15–32,1).

25 More stipulations exist on cases in which slaves are claimed by someone in spite of having been manumitted; ibid, 305 (A31, 15–32, 2).

slaved is not mutually exclusive with being an adherent of the Good Religion (*wehdēn*). It may at first glance seem that cosmological imagery did not play a role in the configuration of the law on slavery. But the incentive of manumission set for non-Zoroastrian slaves owned by Christian masters indicates that slave law was not entirely isolated from the precepts of Mazdaism. By buying into Mazdaean religion, a slave could be rewarded with manumission. The law therefore made use of an interesting tool which was to offer to slaves an exchange: rejecting the Bad Religion in exchange for a more desirable societal position in the realm of the Good Religion and attaining freedom. In that case, Mazdaean imagery functioned as a persuasive argument through which slavery could be overcome. It can be assumed that the law book's note that such exchange deals were available to slaves owned by *Christian* masters is rather significant. In other words, at stake for the Sasanian authorities was to make sure that slaves owned by Christians would convert to Zoroastrianism, rather than Christianity. This would indicate that my first argument holds true, in spite of uncertainties remaining. Thus, the Sasanian practices of slavery were at least to some extent mediated through the triangle of cosmological imagery, lawmaking, and the sociopolitical concerns of the elite. Furthermore, the express stipulation about the manumission of slaves owned by Christians in case they convert to Mazdaism evidently presents a matter in which Sasanian laws were geared to compete with East Syrian laws. Therefore, the pattern of legal interaction in this case–in support of my second main argument–was probably competition rather than influence.

B. East Syrian law: rather enslaved than manumitted?

1. Slavery–a corollary of the original sin?

Although more than 30 stipulations about slavery can be found in the *Corpus Juris*, it remains a challenge to conceptualize the legal status of slaves. In the second chapter of his useful *Das Islamische Sklavenrecht*, Rainer Oßwald contrasts justifications of slavery in the Christian and Islamic tradition.[26] Given the lack of research on slavery in the East Syrian tradition, it is useful to begin our inquiry by looking more closely at the argument by Augustine (d. 430) who is considered to be among the most influential of Western Christian theologians and philosophers:

[26] See Rainer Oßwald, *Das islamische Sklavenrecht*, 19–28.

> The prime cause of slavery, then, is sin, so that man was put under man in a state of bondage; and this can be only by a judgement of God, in whom there is no unrighteousness, and who knows how to assign divers punishments according to the deserts of the sinners.[27]

Of course, we do not know whether Eastern Christianity functioned based on the same assumption about managing its slaves. But considering the shared historical development and textual legacy of the Eastern Church with its Western counterpart until the mid-fifth century and even beyond, it is not unlikely that East Syrian writers had internalized similar rationales about slavery. Most importantly, contriving slavery as a corollary of the original sin (*peccatum originale*) would have significant implications for its reception in the legal realm.[28] Theologically speaking, because the original sin constitutes an irreversible mundane reality, slavery, in turn, remains a perpetually sanctioned practice. In other words, the individual cannot overcome the legacy of the original sin. The justification of Augustine, therefore, implies that there is no expiration to slavery.[29] This premise can be thought of as more broadly regulating the dimensions of East Syrian law in terms of limiting incentives to overcome such limited legal status or even abolish the institution of slavery *per se*. I am aware that most of this is speculative. To improve our understanding of slavery in East Syrian law and make a more nuanced judgment, we must, therefore, attempt to make sense of the legal stipulations that have come down to us.

2. *Sketching the legal status of the slave*

a. *Root (ʿeqārā) and fruit (pirā)*

East Syrian law, similar to Sasanian, conceptually distinguishes between the root (*ʿeqārā*) and fruit (*pirā*) of property. The following stipulation makes this evident:

> ܐܢ ܡܫܟܚܝܢ ܬܪ̈ܝܢ ܠܗܘܢ ܫܘܬܦܘ: ܐܡܬܐ ܐܘ ܥܒܕܐ ܐܘ ܒܥܝܪܐ ܐܘ ܩܢܝܢܐ ܕܐܝܬܝܗܘܢ ܠܬܪ̈ܝܗܘܢ
> ܘܠܐ ܥܒܕ ܗܘܐ ܐܢܫ ܦܠܓܘܬܐ: ܘܝܠܕܐ ܗ̄ܝ ܐܡܬܐ ܐܘ ܒܥܝܪܐ ܐܘ ܩܢܝܢܐ: ܡܛܠ ܕܝܠܕܐ ܠܗ

---

27 Augustine, *De civitate Dei*, 19.15, quoted in Peter Garnsey, *Ideas of slavery from Aristotle to Augustine* (Cambridge: Cambridge University Press, 1996), 47.

28 Garnsey convincingly argues that for Augustine slavery is rooted in the original sin, rather than merely individual sin. For the entire argument see Peter Garnsey, *Ideas of slavery*, 219; also, Rainer Oßwald, *Das islamische Sklavenrecht*, 20.

29 In his comparison, Oßwald hints at this pointing out that in Islam unbelief–which constitutes the Muslim justification for slavery–can, at least in theory, be overcome by conversion whereas the original sin cannot; cf. Rainer Oßwald, *Das islamische Sklavenrecht*, 26.

ܦܐܪܐ ܗܘ̇ ܐܠܐ ܥܩܪܐ: ܘܗܘ̇ ܕܡܬܝܠܕ ܡܫܬܠܛ ܒܗܿܝ ܡܫܟܢܘܬܐ [ܡܢ] ܗܿܝ ܐܡܬܐ: ܐܘ
ܓܡܠܬܐ ܐܘ ܢܩܝܐ: ܕܗܘ̇ ܕܡܫܟܢ: ܗܿܝ ܐܡܬܐ ܐܘ ܓܡܠܬܐ ܐܘ ܢܩܝܐ. ܐܝܬܘܗܝ.

> If someone pledges, without making any stipulation, to someone else a female slave (*amtā*), female camel, goats, or a sheep which subsequently give birth, then, what is born to the female slave (*amtā*), female camel, or sheep is not [considered] fruit (*pīrā*) because it is brought forth, but instead, root (*ʿeqārā*). Therefore, what is born to the female slave, the female camel, or the sheep while in the state of being pledged belongs to the pledger [or: debtor].[30]

The hypothetical features a situation in which a female slave or animals are made part of a pledge. Accordingly, if the female slave, while in possession of the pledgee, gives birth to a child, that child does not belong to the pledgee but instead to the pledger. The reason given is that the child is not considered the fruit (*pīrā*) but the root (*ʿeqārā*). This hints at the fact that the pledgee is allowed to make use of the fruit (*pīrā*) of the slave, whereas the right to profit from the root (*ʿeqārā*) remains with the pledger. By reason thereof, the pledgee, in the case she nourishes and rears the slave child at her expense, is entitled to reclaim the costs she incurred from the pledger.[31] In another stipulation featuring the birth of children to a female slave, it is stated that, if she is manumitted by her master, and the latter does not declare that the yet unborn are also free, they are nevertheless manumitted together with her.[32] Theorizing both stipulations, it seems that the fruit (*pīrā*)–root (*ʿeqārā*) distinction does, at least in the case of slave children, not come into effect until they are born, since in both stipulations the yet unborn is conceptually considered one unit with the mother who is equated with the root (*ʿeqārā*) of the property.

b. The *peculium* of the slave

The *Corpus Juris* elucidates that slaves are, by nature of their status, granted a *peculium*. In other words, they may freely acquire and dispose of property as becomes evident in a passage stating:

ܐܢ ܝܗ̇ܒ ܡܪܐ ܠܥܒܕܗ ܐܘ ܠܐܡܬܗ ܩܢܝܢܐ ܐܘ ܫܘܠܛܢܐ: ܐܘ ܡܕܡ ܐ̄ܚܪܢ. ܫܠܝܛ ܗܘ
ܗܘ̇ ܥܒܕܐ ܐܘ ܐܡܬܐ ܒܗܘ̇ ܡܕܡ ܠܡܥܒܕ ܐܝܟ ܕܨܒܐ ܒܙܒܢܐ ܘܐܦ ܒܡܘܬܒܗ ܒܕܝܬܩܐ.

---

30 Ishoʿbokht, *CorJ*, 158, l. 30–160, l. 3 (*Syr.*)/159–161 [v, vii, § 10] (*Ger.*), my translation into English from Syriac.

31 Ibid, 160, ll. 3–7 (*Syr.*)/161 [v, vii, § 10] (*Ger.*).

32 Ibid., 178, ll. 3–6 (*Syr.*)/179 [v, xiii, § 4] (*Ger.*):
ܡܢ ܕܡܚܪܪ ܠܐܡܬܗ: ܟܕ ܒܟܪܣܐ ܐܘ ܟܕ ܠܐ ܒܟܪܣܐ: ܐܦ ܠܐ ܐܡܪ ܡܦܪܫܐܝܬ: ܕܐܦ ܒܢܝܗ̇
ܕܡܬܝܠܕܝܢ ܡܢܗ̇ ܡܚܪܪܝܢ: ܐܠܐ ܐܦ ܒܢܝܗ̇ ܕܡܬܝܠܕܝܢ ܡܢ ܗܿܝ ܐܡܬܐ ܚܐܪܐ ܐܢܘܢ.

ܐܢ ܕܝܢ ܠܐ ܡܘܨܝ ܐܘ ܚܕ ܡܢܗܘܢ ܘܡܝܬ. ܗܦܟ ܗܘ ܡܕܡ ܟܠ ܡܕܡ ܕܠܗ ܕܝܠܗ ܐܬܝܗܒ ܠܡܪܗ ܕܝܗܒܗ ܠܗ.

> If a man endows his male (*ʿabdēh*) or female slave (*amtēh*) with a house, a field, or something else, the male or female slave can do with it whatever he or she wants during life, and even dispose of it in death by means of testation.[33]

Accordingly, a slave does not only have the right to property in the actual sense but is capable of bequeathing it to whomever she wishes provided she die testate. If she fails to make a will, her property is returned to its donator (here: the master). This provision is restricted, however, by the following paragraph, in which Ishoʿbokht states that if the slave was given property by her first master, then transfered to another master, meanwhile failing to make a will, her property stays with the second master.[34] At any rate, Ishoʿbokht informs us that a slave is allowed to acquire property, to dispose of it, and bequeath it to who she wants.[35] As a result, upon the slave's death, her property is not necessarily allocated to her Christian master, and therefore slave property not bound to be transmuted into Christian ownership.

Although a slave may have her own property, she does not necessarily have the legal right to maintain the property acquired in bondage when manumitted. The following stipulation makes this evident:

ܘܐܢ ܐ̄ܢܫ ܡܚܪܪ ܠܥܒܕܗ ܐܘ ܠܐܡܬܗ: ܘܠܐ ܡܚܪܪ ܥܡܗ ܡܕܡ ܕܐܝܬ ܠܗ: ܠܐ ܡܚܪܪ ܡܢ ܩܢܝܢܗ.

> If someone manumits his male or female slave and does not together with him manumit the things he possesses, then [the things] are not released from his [the master's?] property.[36]

That is, a slave may be freed with her property remaining in bondage. This situation arises when a master manumits her slave without the explicit mention that the slave's assets are also released. In that case, the slave's possessions are transmuted into the property of her master. This provision is, in fact, bizarre. Whereas the slave while being in the state of bondage is capable

---

33 Ibid., 138, l. 27–140, l. 1 (*Syr.*)/139 [v, iii, §16] (*Ger.*), my translation into English from Syriac.

34 Ibid., 140, ll. 4–7 (*Syr.*)/141 [v, iii, § 18] (*Ger.*):
ܐܢ ܝܗܒ ܡܪܐ ܠܥܒܕܗ ܚܩܠܐ: ܐܘ ܒܝܬܐ: ܐܘ ܡܕܡ ܐ̄ܚܪܢ: ܘܒܬܪܟܢ ܡܘܨܝ ܠܗ ܠܗܘ ܠܐܚܪܢܐ ܥܡ ܟܠ ܡܕܡ ܕܐܝܬ ܠܗ: ܗܘ ܡܕܡ ܕܝܗܒ ܠܗ ܡܪܐ ܩܕܡܝܐ ܠܥܒܕܗ. ܫܠܝܛ ܗܘ ܥܒܕܐ ܒܢܟܣܘܗܝ ܐܘ ܒܩܢܝܢܗ ܠܡܥܒܕ ܟܠ ܕܨܒܐ. ܘܐܢ ܠܐ ܢܦܩ ܘܠܐ ܡܘܨܝ ܘܡܝܬ. ܕܡܪܗ ܐ̄ܚܪܢܐ ܐܬܝܗܒ.

35 Likewise, cf. Maria Macuch, "Barda and Barda-Dāri."

36 Ibid., 178, ll. 2–3 (*Syr.*)/179 [v, xiii, § 3] (*Ger.*), my translation into English from Syriac.

of freely disposing of her property, upon her manumission she ought not to. Put differently, the slave acquires freedom but loses the entirety of her acquired property upon manumission. The trade-off seems quite simple: freedom for loss of assets. This is perhaps telling about the function East Syrian law assigns to slaves. Given that upon manumission a slave loses the entirety of her property, the incentive to become manumitted is rather small. From a strictly economic perspective, a slave may find enslavement more expedient because she can acquire and preserve property, whereas, when she is manumitted, she incurs a complete loss of goods.

3. *Manumitting slaves*

Bearing a resemblance to Sasanian law, the *Corpus Juris* states the possibility of manumitting slaves partially. To begin with, the degree to which a slave is free is handed down to her offspring. The law book features an example in which a female slave is owned by shareholders with one of them holding a tenth of her. In the case that shareholder manumits her share in the female slave, then, we are informed, the children born to the slave-woman are, in turn, free to the extent of one-tenth.[37] Furthermore, the labor performed by a slave is deemed to be free as much as the slave herself:

> ܥܒܕܐ ܐܘ ܐܡܬܐ ܟܕ ܚܕܐ ܡܢ ܟܡܐ ܡܢܘ̈ܗܝ ܡܚܪܪ. ܒܗܿܝ ܡܢܬܐ ܫܠܝܛ ܠܗ ܠܡܥܒܕ
> ܥܒܕܐ ܠܢܦܫܗ ܘܠܡܩܢܐ ܩܢܝܢܐ ܠܢܦܫܗ ܡܚܪܪܐ [ܕܡܚܪܪܐ] ܗ̄ܘ.
>
> It is lawful for a male or female slave, who was partially manumitted, to perform labor for himself or buy property for himself to the degree of his manumission [lit.: in that part in which he is manumitted].[38]

Together with the above, it is relatively certain that the fruit (*pīrā*) of the slave corresponds, in its degree of freedom, to that of the slave herself. In another, rather interesting case, several slaves are owned by multiple shareholders. Accordingly, if one of the shareholders manumits the share she owns in the entirety of slaves without explicitly specifying which slaves are to be manumitted, then the slaves to be manumitted are determined by lot.[39] The law, therefore, seems to recognize a certain amount of random-

---

37 Ibid., 178, ll. 6–9 (*Syr.*)/179 [v, xiii, § 5] (*Ger.*):
ܘܐܦ ܕܐܡܬܐ ܕܒܥܣܪܐ ܡܢܘ̈ܢ. ܡܢܗܝܢ ܚܕܐ ܕܝܠܗ ܐܢܬܬ ܡܚܪܪܐ: ܘܡܬܝܠܕܝܢ ܡܢ ܗܿܝ
ܐܡܬܐ ܒܢ̈ܝܐ ܘܒܢ̈ܬܐ: ܒܠܚܘܕ ܡܢ ܒܢ̈ܝܗ̇ ܐܘ ܡܢ ܒܢ̈ܬܗ̇ ܚܕܐ ܡܢ ܥܣܪ ܡܢܘ̈ܢ ܡܚܪܪܐ.

38 Ibid., 178, ll. 14–17 (*Syr.*)/179 [v, xiii, § 7, a] (*Ger.*), my translation into English from Syriac.

39 Ibid., 178, ll. 12–14 (*Syr.*)/179 [v, xiii, § 6, b] (*Ger.*):
ܐܘ ܗ̄ܟܢܐ ܐܢܫ ܕܟܠ ܥܒ̈ܕܐ ܘܐܡ̈ܗܬܐ ܕܫܘܬܦܝܢ ܠܗ ܒܡܢܘܬܐ. ܚܪܪ ܐܢܘܢ: ܢܦܠܘܢ
ܘܢܪܡܘܢ ܦܣ̈ܐ. ܘܐܝܢܐ ܕܢܦܠ ܒܡܢܘܬܐ ܘܦܣܬܐ ܠܗܘ ܠܚܪܪܐ ܚܪܝܪܐ ܗ̄ܘ.

ness when it comes to the manumission of slaves. In addition, the *Corpus Juris* makes clear that slaves, once manumitted, for no reason ought to be reclaimed into slavery.[40]

4. Eternal slavery?

We have been able to sketch some of the features of slavery practices in East Syrian jurisprudence. Most importantly, slaves are, by nature of their legal status, bestowed with the capacity to own property. This practice significantly diverges from Sasanian slavery practices. Peculiarly, while a slave can acquire, sell, and even bequeath property while being enslaved, she most likely loses her assets entirely upon manumission. From the economic perspective of the slave, the effect is that manumission is discouraged.

Nevertheless, a lucid picture of the slavery practices and their precise function in the communities of the Church of the East remains to be drawn. Perhaps unlike matrimony, one ought to assume that lawmakers lacked a consistent policy towards slavery laws. That is, many of the judgments on slavery may have been produced negligently and as ad-hoc stipulations rather than being systematically dovetailed with the rationales and the corpus of East Syrian jurisprudence. Nevertheless, it remains noteworthy that Augustine's justification for slavery, his reference to the original sin, with the consequence that slavery constitutes a legal status that ought to be endured and is eternal, may be construed as significantly concurring with the few incentives East Syrian jurisprudence creates for slaves to be manumitted. In order to enhance our understanding of slavery in the Church of the East, scholarship may want to identify the justifications Eastern Christianity mobilized for slavery practices, some of which may not be found in jurisprudential, but rather theological treatises.

Should Augustine's justification for slavery hold true in the context of Eastern Christianity, the first argument of this thesis would be substantiated. Taking into consideration the shared historical and textual legacy of the Church of the East with Western Christianity, this would not seem unlikely. If that is the case, one could more easily draw a connection between cosmology and the legal configuration of slavery. That is, because slavery is a corollary of the original sin, with no end in sight, the social institution of slavery would have arguably been contrived with no incentives for enslaved

40 Ibid., 176, l. 27–178, l. 2 (*Syr.*)/177–179 [v, xiii, § 2] (*Ger.*):
ܘܡܛܠ ܕܐܬܚܪܪܘ. ܠܐ ܫܠܝܛ ܥܒܕܐ ܡܢ ܟܠܠ: ܠܡܫܥܒܕܘܬܗܘܢ. ܐܝܟ ܕܝܢ ܐܬܦܪܫܬ
ܕܒܟܬܒܐ ܗܘܐ ܐܣܝܪ. ܕܐܦ ܐܬܚܪܪܘ. ܐܠܐ ܐܝܟ ܠܡܫܥܒܕܘܬܗܘܢ ܡܬܗܦܟܝܢ: ܐܠܐ ܐܢܫܝܢ ܕܡܬܚܪܪܝܢ
ܐܬܚܪܪܘ. ܐܠܐ ܠܗ ܒܥܠ ܕܒܪ ܗܘ. ܘܐܦܠܐ ܕܝܢ ܒܥܠܬܐ ܚܕܐ ܗܘܬ ܗܕܐ.

subjects to overcome bondage. This, however, at least for now, remains speculative.

C. Early Islamic law: from slaves to clients

1. Islamic justifications for slavery

In his recent *Das islamische Sklavenrecht*, Rainer Oßwald notes that the Islamic attitude towards slavery principally matches that of Christianity.[41] Notably, Oßwald points to the fact that the later rationale of the Muslim jurists, according to which the natural state of man corresponds to freedom (*aṣl al-nās al-ḥurrīya*), together with the notion that slavery is rooted in unbelief (*aṣl al-riqq huwa al-kufr*), does not appear in the legal writings of the Mālikīya before Ibn Abī Zaid (d. 386/996).[42] Tying in with this, Irene Schneider argues that the *Adab al-qāḍī*, the legal manual of a certain al-Khaṣṣāf (d. 261/847), makes the first express reference to the idea that the natural state of man is freedom (*al-aṣl huwa al-ḥurrīya*).[43]

Most importantly, we must discuss how the Muslim jurists conceptually interwove slavery (*riqq*) with unbelief (*kufr*). By causally situating unbelief before slavery, the jurists could arguably create fictive ties between bondage and the realm of Islamic cosmological imagery, expressed in the punishment for disbelief. Despite such imagery, it seems, however, that one of the purposes behind slavery practices was to account for an increasing number of people who had been captured with the spread of Islam. Bernard Lewis mentions that capturing constituted, at least during the early centuries of Islam, the most critical source of slavery.[44] It seems that reverting to such macro-justifications for slavery served the purpose of dealing with and sanctioning the reality of an abundance of newcomers to the Islamic Empire by denying them the privileges enjoyed by Muslims.

With slavery practices conceptually tied to unbelief, the question arises whether somebody may overcome bondage by converting from unbelief. The following passage showcases a hypothetical from al-Shāfiʿī's *Risāla*:

أخبرنا مالك عن هلال بن أسامة عن عطاء بن يسار عن عمر بن الحكم قال أتيت رسول الله بجارية فقلت يا رسول الله عليّ رقبة أفأعتقها؟ فقال لها رسول الله (أين الله؟) فقالت في السماء فقال (ومن أنا؟) قالت أنت رسول الله قال فأعتقها.

41 Rainer Oßwald, *Das islamische Sklavenrecht*, 22.
42 Ibid.
43 Irene Schneider, *Kinderverkauf und Schuldknechtschaft. Untersuchungen zur frühen Phase des islamischen Rechts* (Stuttgart: Steiner, 1999), 24.
44 Bernard Lewis, *Race and Slavery in the Middle East*, 9.

Mālik reported to us from Hilāl b. Usāma from ʿAṭā ʾ b. Yasār from ʿUmar b. al-Ḥakam, who said: I came to the Messenger of God with a slave girl. I asked him: Oh, Messenger of God, must I manumit her? The Messenger of God spoke to her: Where is God? She answered: In heaven. He then asked: Who am I? She said: You are the Messenger of God. He said: Free her.[45]

I suggest interpreting the anecdote as an incident of testing. That is, the slave girl is tacitly questioned about her religious conviction. Given that she metaphorically affirms that God is in the heavens and identifies Muḥammad as the Messenger of God–probably measuring up to the standards of what al-Shāfiʿī considered to be a decent Muslim–the Messenger of God commands to her master that she should be manumitted. This case may suggest that conversion to Islam is sufficient a condition for a slave to be manumitted. Nevertheless, my inquiry will show that the practical side to the equation was quite different.

2. The legal (in)capacity of the slave to property

Al-Shāfiʿī conceptually distinguishes between ownership (*mulk*) and possession (*iḍāfa ilayhi*). This distinction is noteworthy, particularly concerning the question of a slave's *peculium*. Thus, a slave by reason of lacking ownership of herself, cannot but possess property. That is, property is only attributed to (*iḍāfa ilayhi*) but not owned by the slave (*lā annahu mālikun lahu*). This distinction seems so self-evident to al-Shāfiʿī that he states in jovial wordplay:

فلمّا كان بيّناً في سنّة رسول الله أنّ العبد لا يملك مالاً وأنّ ما ملك العبد فإنّما يملكه لسيّده وأنّ اسم المال له إنّما هو إضافة إليه لأنّه في يديه لا أنّه مالك له ولا يكون مالكاً له وهو لا يملك نفسه وكيف يملك نفسه وهو مملوك يباع ويوهب ويورث [...].

[...] it is evident from the Practice [*sunna*] of the Messenger of God that the slave does not own property, that what he owns is, in fact, owned by his master, that the name of the property is with him. However, it is only attributed to him [*huwa iḍāfatun ilayhi*] because it is in his (two) hands. (However,) he is not the owner of it [*lā annahu mālikun lahu*], will not be the owner of it, and he does not (even) own himself. How can he himself own, when he is (in fact) owned [*wa-kayfa yamliku nafsahu, wa-huwa mamlūkun*], may be sold, donated, and inherited [...].[46]

The passage is invoked after a report by Ibn ʿUyayna according to which the property owned by a slave is transmuted into ownership of the seller if the slave ends up being sold. Disagreeing with the report of Ibn ʿUyayna,

---

45 Al-Shāfiʿī, *RisF*, 62, ll. 10–12 [bayān farḍ Allāh fī kitābihi ittibāʿ sunnat nabīhi].

46 Ibid., 124, ll. 16–19 [al-farḍ al-manṣūṣ alladhī dallat al-sunna ʿalā annahu innamā arāda al-khāṣṣ].

al-Shāfiʿī argues that the incapacity of a slave to *own* property manifests itself in the fact that, like other forms of property, she is owned by someone else, may be sold, donated, or inherited. Thus, it seems that–as was the case in Sasanian and East Syrian law–the legal configuration of a slave, in the opinion of al-Shāfiʿī, is predicated on the conceptual distinction between ownership (*mulk*) and possession (*iḍāfa ilayhi*). Precisely because they are being owned, slaves themselves may only *possess* assets but not claim ownership to them.

He goes on explaining that a slave's incapacity to own property affects her capacity to inherit. Theoretically, if a slave were to inherit a share in somebody's estate, her master would acquire the property bequeathed to the slave. This becomes clear from the following stipulation:

وإن كان العبد أباً أو غيره ممّن سمّيت له فريضة فكان لو أُعْطِيَها ملكها سيّده عليه لم يكن السيّد بأبي الميت ولا وارثاً سميّت له فريضة فكنّا لو أعطينا العبد بأنّه أب إنّما أعطينا السيد الذي لا فريضة له فورّثنا غير من ورّثه الله فلم نورّث عبداً لما وصفت ولا أحداً لم تجتمع فيه الحرّيّة والإسلام والبراءة من القتل حتّى لا يكون قاتلاً.

> And if the slave is the father or someone else for whom a share of inheritance is allocated, then if it is given to him, the property (of the inheritance) is his master's, [even though] the master is not the father of the deceased and not an heir to the estate of the deceased. Therefore, if we were to give [a share of the estate] to the slave because he is the father, then what we give, we would, in fact, give to the master for whom no inheritance share is allocated, so that [in effect] we bequeath [our property] to someone God did not make an heir. Therefore, we do not bequeath [our property] to the slave, as it was described, and not to anyone who does not combine in himself freedom, submission [*Islām*], and innocence of murder so that he is not a murderer.[47]

Notably, the rationale for denying slaves the capacity to inherit property is that, because of their incapacity of owning property, the share in the estate allocated to them would not be acquired by them, but rather their masters. Such an outcome would, according to al-Shāfiʿī, be in contradiction with God's will. That is, God would not sanction a share in the estate of someone to effectively pass to someone other than the person intended by the deceased. Therefore, al-Shāfiʿī commands that slaves, like unbelievers and murderers, ought, by nature of their status and as a rule, not to be assigned a share in anyone's estate.

Other sources contradict with al-Shāfiʿī's unreserved opinion that slaves, because of their legal status, lack the capacity to own property. The argument made by Oßwald is most persuasive in this regard. He expounds that

47 Ibid., 126, ll. 1–4.

the *peculium* of the slave interferes with her master's right to requisition her property (*intizāʿ*). That is, the concept of *intizāʿ* seems to directly conflict with the notion of the slave's capacity to property. Oßwald keenly points out that, in practice, this issue was resolved with a master's tacit acceptance that a slave had her own property while such property could be requisitioned.[48] At any rate, the *Mudawwana* of Saḥnūn illustrates that the opinion of al-Shāfiʿī concerning the *peculium* was not consistently applied throughout the Islamic legal schools and was perhaps idiosyncratic to him. This becomes more apparent in the following section on slave manumission, in which the hypotheticals discussed indicate that Saḥnūn wrote his legal treatise based on the assumption that slaves may not only possess but also own property.

3. Manumitting slaves

The idea of slave manumission is, in spite of sociopolitical concerns, interwoven in the cosmological imagery of Islam. Aside from stipulating that masters should be kind towards "who[m] your right hands possess" (Q 4:36, Q 24:58), the *Qurʾān* generally considers slave manumission a beneficent act recommended in instances where believers are compelled to atone for their sins (*kaffāra*). This is made evident in Q 4:92:

وَمَا كَانَ لِمُؤْمِنٍ أَن يَقْتُلَ مُؤْمِنًا إِلَّا خَطَأً ۚ وَمَن قَتَلَ مُؤْمِنًا خَطَأً فَتَحْرِيرُ رَقَبَةٍ مُّؤْمِنَةٍ وَدِيَةٌ مُّسَلَّمَةٌ إِلَىٰ أَهْلِهِ إِلَّا أَن يَصَّدَّقُوا ۚ فَإِن كَانَ مِن قَوْمٍ عَدُوٍّ لَّكُمْ وَهُوَ مُؤْمِنٌ فَتَحْرِيرُ رَقَبَةٍ مُّؤْمِنَةٍ ۖ وَإِن كَانَ مِن قَوْمٍ بَيْنَكُمْ وَبَيْنَهُم مِّيثَاقٌ فَدِيَةٌ مُّسَلَّمَةٌ إِلَىٰ أَهْلِهِ وَتَحْرِيرُ رَقَبَةٍ مُّؤْمِنَةٍ ۖ فَمَن لَّمْ يَجِدْ فَصِيَامُ شَهْرَيْنِ مُتَتَابِعَيْنِ تَوْبَةً مِّنَ اللَّهِ ۗ وَكَانَ اللَّهُ عَلِيمًا حَكِيمًا.[49]

> No believer is to kill another save in error. Whoever kills a believer in error, the freeing of a believing slave is decreed and blood-money handed over to his kin, unless the latter forgo this as an act of charity. If he belongs to a clan which is your enemy while he is a believer, the freeing of a believing slave is decreed. If he belongs to a clan with whom you have a compact, then blood-money is handed over to his kin and the freeing of a believing slave. He who finds not the means, then fasting for two consecutive months is decreed, as penance from God. God is All-Knowing, All-Wise.[50]

48 Rainer Oßwald dedicates an entire chapter to the question of the *peculium* based on his research of Mālikī legal texts; see Rainer Oßwald, *Das islamische Sklavenrecht*, 71.

49 *The Qurʾān*, Q 4:92, https://quran.com/4/92-102.

50 *The Qur'an*, tr. Tarif Khalidi (London: Penguin Classics, 2008), 73 (Q 4:92).

This shows that the *Qur'ān* has some more or less clear-cut ethical standards about slavery which arguably permeated the realm of slavery laws as reflected in the complex regulations pertaining to manumission.

Saḥnūn's *Mudawwana* includes a lengthy chapter entitled *Kitāb al-mukātab* in which he focuses on the formalities and procedures of what is known as the manumission contract (*kitāba*). Legally speaking, the *kitāba* constitutes a contractual agreement as the result of which a slave is manumitted by her master in exchange for paying off her value in installments. Indeed, such contractual arrangements are highly interesting with respect to what I discussed in the previous section on the capacity of slaves to own property. Saḥnūn, who advocates the position that slaves may own property, points to a noteworthy legal problem which arises when a manumission contract is stipulated:

قال: وقال مالك: إذا كاتب الرجل عبده فإن جميع مال العبد للعبد ديناً كان أو غير ذلك عرضاً كان أو فرضاً إلا أن يشترطه السيد حين يكاتبه، فيكون ذلك للسيد، فإن لم يشترطه فليس للسيد أن يأخذه بعد عقد الكتابة. قال: وقال مالك: إذا كاتب الرجل عبده تبعه ماله بمنزلة العتق.

> He said: Mālik said: if a man stipulates a manumission contract with his slave [*ʿabdahu*], then the property of the slave [*māl al-ʿabd*] (stays with) the slave, if as debt [*dainan*] or something similar, a loan [*ʿarḍan*] or by religious duty [*farḍan*]; except if the master conditions something else when he stipulates it [the manumission contract]. Then, (in that case) it [the property] stays with the master. But if he did not condition it, then the master must not seize the property after the manumission contract [*ʿaqd al-kitāba*]. He said that Mālik said: if a man stipulates a manumission contract with his slave, then his [the slave's] property follows the conduct of manumission [*bi-manzilat al-ʿitq*].[51]

In line with this stipulation, a master can only invoke his right to requisition a slave's property (*intizāʿ*) up until contracting his manumission. To be more precise, a slave is, except if stipulated in the *kitāba* to the contrary, permitted to take away the property she acquired in bondage in exchange for remunerating her former master. Most importantly, Saḥnūn emphasizes that a master ought not to reclaim, whatever the circumstances, the property of the manumitted slave (*mukātab*), in the case he omitted requisitioning her property before the slave's manumission.

Elsewhere Saḥnūn elucidates this regulation arguing that such is not the case concerning the children which a slave procreated with another female slave. The author, more specifically, states:

---

[51] Saḥnūn, *MudK*, vol. 2, 472, ll. 17–20 [li-man yakūn māl al-mukātab idhā kātabahu sayyiduhu].

ابن وهب، قال مالك: في كتمان المكاتب ولده من أمته عن سيده حتى يعتق قال: ليس مال العبد والمكاتب بمنزلة أولادهما لأن أولادهما ليسوا بأموال لهما إذا عتق العبد تبعه ماله في السنة، وليس يتبعه أولاده فيكونون أحراراً مثله، وإذا أفلس بأموال الناس أخذ جميع ماله ولم يؤخذ ولده، فإذا بيع واشترط ماله لم يدخل في ذلك ولده وإنما أولادهما بمنزلة رقابهما [...].

> Ibn Wahb on what Mālik said about the slave's hiding of his child, conceived with his slave girl, from his master until he is manumitted: there is no property of the slave and the manumitted slave when it comes to their children. They [the children] are not part of the property belonging to them. If the slave is manumitted, his property follows him [into freedom] according to the custom [*sunna*]. But the children do not follow him [into freedom] [...]. Indeed, their [the slave's and the manumitted slave's] children are in the state of slavery.[52]

The case makes clear that when a male slave knowingly and intentionally conceals the pregnancy of his slave girl hoping that the children born to her will together with her be manumitted, he can, by no means, claim ownership of the children. Instead, the children born belong to the master and do not follow their mother into freedom. Thus, children born to a slave girl are bound to remain in bondage, no matter if conceived before or after stipulating a manumission contract.

4. From slaves to clients (mawālī)

In his useful article on the state of emancipated slaves in Islam, Daniel Pipes informs us about the prevailing uncertainties about this peculiar legal status.[53] Scholars agree that particularly after the first century of the Islamic conquests, manumitted slaves, rather than being fully released, obtained the position of *mawālī*. That is, freed slaves acquired a fictitious affiliation of kinship to Arab Muslims by means of stipulating a contractual relationship (*walāʾ al-islām*) with a Muslim sponsor (*mawlāʾ*).[54] This would, in the long term, assure their integration into the genealogies of the rulers. However, it is clear that clientage (*walāʾ al-islām*) became a historical necessity in the early Islamic Empire to prevent the privileges of Arab-Muslims from watering down. In other words, due to the increased attraction to convert to Islam for its social and financial benefits–in conjunction with the notion

52 Ibid., 472, l. 24–473, l. 2.

53 Daniel Pipes, "Mawlas," 133.

54 For a concise article on the origins, development, and different types of clientage, see Ulrike Mitter, "Origins and Development of the Islamic Patronate," in *Patronate and Patronage in early and classical Islam*, eds. Monique Bernards and John Nawas (Leiden and Boston: Brill, 2005), 70–133.

that Muslims should, in theory, not be enslaved–the Empire's elite had to find loopholes to impede the process of large numbers of new Muslim converts making their privileges less exclusive. The institution of *walāʾ* should, in my opinion, be understood based on this assumption.

This chapter elucidated that the early Islamic legal stipulations about slaves are intimately tied to Qurʾanic imagery and the political needs of the Arab-Muslim elite. While the *Qurʾān* sanctions and justifies slavery practices by linking them to the notion of unbelief, it simultaneously urges leniency and kindness towards slaves. Moreover, slave manumission is construed as a beneficent act through which the individual believer can atone for previous sins such as murder. This results in an interesting equation: on the one hand, scripture provides the cosmological sanctioning for enslaving subjects that have not subscribed to Islam, on the other, it lays out the ethical guidelines for treating them kindly and, if possible, manumit them. Whereas scriptural justifications for slavery cannot be neglected, slavery laws and practices were nevertheless subjected to modifications in line with the political needs of the Arab-Muslim elite. The social reality of the early Islamic Empire, which in its conquest period experienced the influx of a significant number of people who were captured as slaves, most likely induced the Muslim jurists to deal with and find viable solutions to accommodating new people. The complexity of slavery law and the multitude of legal opinions, which even diverge on simple questions such as whether a slave is entitled to property, attest to the fact that carving out legal mechanisms to deal with slaves was of utmost importance. Invoking the institution of *walāʾ*–which we are, in fact, quite little informed about–show that the legal stipulations pertaining to slaves were largely shaped by the concerns of an Arab-Muslim elite which presumptively had a keen interest to protect and possibly expand its own privileges.

D. Preliminary conclusion

In this chapter, I attempted to answer the three main questions of this thesis from the perspective of slavery laws: How were slaves legally configured? How were slavery practices justified through cosmological imagery and interwoven with the sociopolitical needs of the community/empire which engendered and enabled them? By what patterns were interactions between Sasanian, East Syrian, and Islamic law characterized?

I first focused on Sasanian jurisprudence. Whether Zoroastrian or not, slavery could reach any person. For instance, a Zoroastrian subject could become enslaved following an unsuccessful transaction involving a slave or by merely being sold by the *paterfamilias*. By nature of their legal status, slaves were not entitled to own property but granted limited legal capacity which allowed them to acquire property. Once emancipated, slaves were protected by the law in order not to be reclaimed into slavery.

Secondly, I discussed how Sasanian slavery practices incorporated cosmological imagery and may have served the sociopolitical aspirations of the Sasanian elite. As to cosmology, it is notable that the law was keen to reward slaves owned by Christian masters with manumission if they convert to Zoroastrianism. Conversion was, therefore, constructed as a means by which slavery could be overcome. The creation of the incentive to convert to Zoroastrianism was arguably tied to the rationale that slaves owned by *Christians* should convert to Zoroastrianism, rather than Christianity. The Sasanian laws on slavery, then, were undergirded with a scriptural rationale that was mobilized by the Sasanian elite to gain new adherents to the Good Religion.

In the second part, I dealt with slavery practices in the Church of the East. The *Corpus Juris* is relatively clear that a slave was granted a *peculium* by nature of her status. Thus, she would have been capable of owning, acquiring, and bequeathing property. Most notably, when being manumitted, a slave was subjected to having her entire estate confiscated. This practice, from a purely economic perspective of the slave, created significant discouragement for her to become emancipated.

In the following step, I tentatively looked at how the slavery practices of the Church of the East were saturated with cosmological references and shaped by the elite's interests. In the absence of knowing how precisely the bishops justified and accounted for slaves, a lucid picture of how bondage and cosmological imagery are intertwined, remains to be drawn. Augustine's justification for slavery may hold true in the Eastern Christian context. That is, slavery could arguably have been construed by the Church as consequential to the original sin with the outcome that there existed no reasonable need for its abolishment. If that is so, the connection between the law and the Christian elite's interests would seem rather obvious. That is, it is precisely the absence of legal incentives for slaves to terminate bondage which would indicate that the practical rationale of the law may have indeed rested on the implied idea of eternal slavery. The subchapter on the slavery practices of the Church of the East indicated that more concrete evidence would have to be adduced to support the validity of my main thesis in the context of Eastern Christianity.

In the last section, I dealt with slavery in Islamic law. The jurists' legal opinions seem to have differed significantly on whether a slave may be granted a *peculium*. In practice, the capacity of a slave to own property was recognized with the restriction that her master could make use of her right to requisition her possessions any time. As concerns a slave's emancipation, she could stipulate a manumission contract (*kitāba*) with her master effectuating her manumission in return for paying off her own and the value of her possessions in installments. Such manumission agreements, by rule, did not extend to children conceived with a female slave.

Finally, I explained how the slavery practices of the early Islamic Empire were interspersed with cosmological imagery and seemingly served the needs of an Arab-Muslim elite. In terms of their justification, such practices were predicated on the notion of punishment for unbelief. Meanwhile, the *Qurʾān* stipulates a critical code of ethics with respect to the treatment of slaves. For instance, behaving kindly towards slaves is recommended and their manumission is even made compulsory (with alternative options) in the case of grave sins for which a believer ought to repent. Muslim jurists seemingly employed the scriptural justifications for enslaving people to account for the significant number of subjects held in bondage in the early Muslim Empire. Moreover, the complex regulations and institutions pertaining to slavery may indicate that viable solutions had to be found to the problem of large numbers of newcomers to Islam. Once the storm of the conquests had settled, the Muslim Emperors witnessed an increasing amount of slave converts trying to overcome their restricted legal status through conversion to Islam. Preventing Arab-Muslim privileges from watering down, the Muslim jurists invoked the institution of *walāʾ al-islām* which was conducive to slowing down the process of privilege being made moribund all too soon.

This chapter led to moderate findings in support of my first thesis statement. The link between cosmological imagery, lawmaking, and the elites' sociopolitical interests was made obivious in the case of Sasanian and Islamic slavery laws and potentially–if more evidence can be found–East Syrian. My impression is that, although the slavery laws in these three legal systems are to some degree interspersed with the language of cosmology, other factors may have perhaps been more critical. This could be related to the reality that slavery law, in contrast to matrimony, ought and was expected to be more flexible, due to unexpected influxes of slave populations into society, and was perhaps more often established through ad-hoc provisions.

The other main question of this thesis–what patterns of interaction marked the relationship of Sasanian, East Syrian, and Islamic law–could be answered to a satisfying degree. The express stipulation in Sasanian law that slave-converts to Zoroastrianism owned by *Christian* masters were to be rewarded with manumission illustrates that, on this matter, Sasanian with East Syrian law's interaction was a matter of competition. By offering to slaves owned by Christians the opportunity to be released in exchange for giving up their previous religion, Sasanian law set a significant incentive for them to convert. However, the question is whether this opportunity would have been grabbed by a slave who was owned by a Christian, since–as I discussed in the section on the East Syrian laws on slavery–that slave would have lost all her property upon manumission/conversion. But perhaps the very rationale of setting negative incentives for slaves to be manumitted, propelled through the loss of assets, should be seen as a response by the Church elite to prevent slaves from converting to Zoroastrianism. Thus, to contain the problem of Christian converts to Zoroastrianism, the East Syrian bishops were likely compelled to find a resolution to the problem: consfiscating the estate of slaves in case they were manumitted. This arguably indicates that the relationship between Sasanian and East Syrian law was more complex than mere influence, and, in fact, also characterized by competitive dynamics.

Chapter VIII
Conclusion:

Towards a shared framework of Late Antique legal epistemes?

This thesis was designed as a comparative inquiry into Sasanian, East Syrian, and Islamic laws through the themes of matrimony and slavery. The period investigated reached from the fifth to the ninth century. The findings in support of my main arguments were made by following the lead of three main questions: What legal forms were known to Sasanian, East Syrian, and Islamic law? That is, what was the taxonomy of matrimonial relations in these laws and what were their slavery practices? Second, how were their legal forms related to cosmological imagery and the sociopolitical interests of the elite? Third, what patterns marked the interactions between those legal systems?

To respond to these questions, I used a tripartite methodological approach. The first part was descriptive. Based on my primary sources, I extracted the types of matrimony and how slavery was configured in these legal traditions. The second step relied on legal culture which served as an analytical lens to situate primary sources at the nexus of cosmological imagery and elite concerns. In the third step, I reverted to legal pluralism which provided the theoretical assumptions of how coexisting legal systems can be thought of as interacting with one another.

In this thesis, I made two main arguments: First, I argued that the matrimony and slavery practices of Sasanian, East Syrian, and Islamic law were negotiated within the triangle of cosmology, lawmaking, and the sociopolitical interests of elites. Second, I argued that the relationship between Sasanian, East Syrian, and Islamic law cannot be construed as restricted to influence but was characterized by more complex, unstable, and varying patterns of interaction.

In the chapter on matrimony, I made significant findings in support of my first argument. The subchapter on Sasanian law illustrated that Zoroastrian authorities were keen to mobilize cosmological imagery in order to sanction matrimonial institutions such as next-of-kin marriage (*ẖwēdōdah*), intermediary (*ayōkēn*), and substitute-successors (*stūr*). That is, the cosmic benefit that comes with sexual reproduction and the precedent of Ohrmazd who engaged in sexual intercourse with his relatives were used to undergird the specific needs of the Sasanian elite: maintaining royal lineages and increasing sexual reproduction. Thus, the first main argument holds true regarding Sasanian law.

In the ensuing subchapter, I dealt with the matrimonial practices of the Church of the East. Notably, the Christian elite, in similar fashion to the Zoroastrian authorities, employed scriptural references to cosmology to justify its notion of matrimony which was deeply ingrained in "absolute" monogamy. However, mobilizing scriptural ideas fulfilled different purposes: on the one hand, it proved to be the bargaining chip in negotiations with the Zoroastrian authorities when the Christian elite was compelled to reform the laws on matrimony of its clerical hierarchy. On the other, it became a distinct feature in the process of symbolically defining the community of the Church of the East after the practice of next-of-kin marriage seems to have gained some popularity among Christians. Hence, the argument of matrimony being situated at the nexus of cosmology, lawmaking, and the sociopolitical concerns of the elite appears equally valid in the case of East Syrian law.

Subsequently, I examined matrimony in Islamic law. The subchapter showed that al-Shāfiʿī and Saḥnūn used commands concerned with matrimony from the *Qurʾān* and *Sunna* and tied them to certain conditions through which their sometimes strictly prohibiting character could be toned down. Most importantly, this illustrated how flexibly scriptural and cosmological notions could be mobilized depending on what matrimonial practices were considered desirable at a specific historical conjuncture. Besides Islamic ethics, we do not precisely know for what sociopolitical purposes such references to cosmology were mobilized. Nevertheless, the Islamic taxonomy of matrimonial forms was arguably mediated through cosmology, lawmaking, and the ethical concerns of the jurists, the latter being reflected in the creation of legal frameworks within which the prohibiting character of certain divine commandments could be macerated.

To sum up, the chapter on matrimony strongly indicated the applicability of my first thesis statement. Thus, the jurisprudential writings on marriage, produced in the Sasanian and early Islamic Empires, should be scrutinized in conjunction with the cosmological imagery and elite's sociopolitical interests in the communities that engendered and enabled them. Most importantly, it seems that scriptural cosmology provided a useful idiom to jurists to legitimize such matrimonial practices which could serve the agendas and sociopolitical aspirations of the community's leadership.

In the chapter on slavery, I made moderate findings in support of my first thesis statement. Inquiring into Sasanian law showed that cosmology was utilized by the Sasanian elite to attract slaves who were owned by Christian masters to convert to Mazdaism. The Sasanian slavery laws, then, were interspersed with cosmological justifications in order to gain new adherents to the Good Religion. Meanwhile, our lack of knowledge concerning a justification for slavery practices in the context of the Church of the East made it difficult to ascertain how precisely cosmological imagery was intertwined with the legal stipulations on bondage. The notion of slavery being consequential to the original sin, as argued by Augustine, may have prevented the bishops from creating incentives for slavery to be overcome because it remained bound to the idea that mundane slavery is perpetually sanctioned. The section on Islamic law illustrated that al-Shāfiʿī and Saḥnūn were keen to justify slave practices by reference to unbelief. Meanwhile, sinful believers were encouraged to atone for their sins by manumitting slaves. It is important to note that Islamic slavery laws were arguably influenced by the sociopolitical reality of the Islamic Empire which compelled the jurists' creativeness as to establishing new institutions through which the increasing number of newcomers to Islam could be controlled effectively, and Arab-Muslim privilege be prevented from watering down too quickly.

The chapter on slaves, more broadly, adduced reasonable evidence concerning my first thesis statement. It seems that, in all three legal systems covered, an intricate link is, to a greater or lesser extent, established between cosmological imagery, lawmaking, and the elite's interests in slave matters. However, it appears that to justify slavery practices, cosmology was not as abundantly mobilized as in the case of matrimony. This may be related to the reality that slavery practices, in contradistinction to marriage, were more often shaped by ad-hoc regulations and less consistent policies.

Important evidence was marshaled in support of the second thesis statement concerning the more complex patterns of interactions between Sasanian, East Syrian, and Islamic law. While such patterns have not yet become evident in the case of Islamic law and its interaction with Sasanian and East Syrian laws, they can certainly be found by taking into consideration other fields of law such as property, obligations, or inheritance. In Sasanian and East Syrian law, some critical moments, which were conclusive towards *varying* and unstable patterns of interaction, could be identified. Three are noteworthy: first, the convocation of the East Syrian bishops in the Synod of 497, instigated by the King of Kings for them to reform the law on matrimony of the clerical hierarchy, was an instance of *negotiation*. Second, Mar Aba's prohibitions from the sixth century, geared towards containing next-of-kin marriage which had gained increased popularity among the Christian flock, can again be construed as a matter of *negotiation*. Thirdly, the explicit Sasanian practice of slave-converts to Zoroastrianism, if owned by *Christian* masters, being rewarded with manumission constitutes an example of *competition* with East Syrian law. It is important to note that the problem with recognizing patterns of interaction is mostly a practical one. They do not seem to emerge except in the rare cases in which the historian is fortunate enough to come across such unique references and their implications about other legal systems. Despite more research to be done, *negotiation* and *competition* could be singled out as patterns marking the relationship between Sasanian and East Syrian laws.

How are these findings relevant more broadly? The triangular relationship of cosmological imagery, lawmaking, and the elite's interests is critical for future scholarly inquiries. That is, it shows that matrimony and slavery practices in these Late Antique legal traditions should not be scrutinized in isolation from the cosmological imagery employed to sanction an elite's political interests. More broadly, the argument indicates that matrimony and slavery are not simply based on religious precepts and value systems but, instead, are significantly shaped by the mundane realities of community, empire, and politics.

Sasanian and East Syrian laws being characterized by *varying* and unstable patterns of interaction such as negotiation and competition is significant methodologically. Previous studies have approached comparative law particularly with a view to pinpointing influences between legal systems, with many problematic assumptions underlying such a method. This thesis has shown that we can significantly scale up how we think of interactions between Late Antique legal systems. That is, the methodological approach of legal pluralism was conducive to illustrating that varying patterns are arguably underlying such legal interactions. More importantly, if we strive to move towards non-Orientalist arguments and produce findings which are *not* based on the assumption that Roman and Judaic law alone provided the legal tools for most of the societies and legal systems that came after, then legal pluralism can provide a valuable methodological tool for future studies.

In addition, the theoretical insights gained from legal culture illustrated that jurisprudence in Late Antiquity was not merely in line with the precepts of religion. Instead, the jurists modeled and molded laws by relying on and continuously revisiting the societal and political needs of their respective communities/empires. This finding is significant, if we are keen to dismantle the scholarly assumption that the law of Late Antique societies was relatively static and is best examined by focusing on scriptural writings. My research indicated that scriptural rationales were throughout mobilized by the jurists. But which explanations were activated and how they would be integrated into legal writings strongly depended on what was at stake for the elite or, more broadly speaking, the specific historical conjuncture of the community/empire.

This thesis highlighted that meaningful conversations and intellectual exchanges appear to have existed between the legal cultures of the Sasanian and early Islamic Empires. Rather than functioning in isolation from one another, their relationship was marked by varying patterns of interaction—not restricted to the absorption of foreign elements. This, more largely, points to the reality of a Late Antique legal and conceptual space in which varying epistemes coexisted, while being simultaneously integrated into a shared legal framework of interaction in which jurists referenced and conversed with one another beyond confessional boundaries and, if necessary, modified their legal stipulations–in other words, a legal space comprised of shared Late Antique legal epistemes.

Bibliography

For the convenience of the reader, the bibliography is arranged according to the main lines of inquiry in this thesis. Thus, it is divided into three sections: Sasanian law, East Syrian law, and early Islamic law.

A. Sasanian law

Primary sources

[Dēnkart] Le Troisième Livre du Dēnkart, ed. Jean de Menasce (Paris: Librairie C. Klincksieck, 1973).

Farroḫmard i Wahrāmān, *Das Sasanidische Rechtsbuch Mātakdān i Hazār Dātistān (Teil II)*, ed., tr., and ct. Maria Macuch (Wiesbaden: Deutsche Morgenländische Gesellschaft, 1981).

–, *Rechtskasuistik und Gerichtspraxis zu Beginn des siebenten Jahrhunderts in Iran. Die Rechtssammlung des Farroḫmard i Wahrāmān*, ed., tr., and ct. Maria Macuch (Wiesbaden: Harrassowitz Verlag, 1993).

–, *The Book of a Thousand Judgements (A Sasanian Law-Book)*, ed. and tr. Anahit Perikhanian (Costa Mesa, CA: Mazda Publishers, 1997).

The Sacred Books of the East, vol. 5, ed. F. Max Müller (Oxford: Clarendon Press, 1880), pp. 237–406.

[Vidēvdad] Wrestling with the Demons of the Pahlavi Widēwdād, ed., tr., and ct. Mahnaz Moazami (Leiden and Boston: Brill, 2014).

Secondary literature

Assmann, Jan and Guy Stroumsa (eds.), *Transformations of the Inner Self in Religious Traditions* (Leiden: Brill, 1999).

Bartholomae, Christian, *Über ein sasanidisches Rechtsbuch* (Heidelberg: Carl Winter's Universitätsbuchhandlung, 1910).

Boyce, Mary, "On the Orthodoxy of Sasanian Zoroastrianism," in *Bulletin of the School of Oriental and African Studies, University of London* 59/1 (1996), pp. 11–28.

–, "Origins of Zoroastrian Philosophy," in *Companion Encyclopedia to Asian Philosophy*, eds. Brian Carr and Indira Mahalingam (London and New York: Routledge, 1997), pp. 4–23.

– (ed.), *Textual Sources for the Study of Zoroastrianism* (Chicago: The University of Chicago Press, 1984).

–, *Zoroastrians. Their Religious Beliefs and Practices* (London, Boston and Henley: Routledge & Kegan Paul, 1979).

Carr, Brian and Indira Mahalingam (eds.), *Companion Encyclopedia to Asian Philosophy* (London and New York: Routledge, 1997).

Choksy, Jamsheed K., *Conflict and Cooperation. Zoroastrian Subalterns and Muslim Elites in Medieval Iranian Society* (New York, NY: Columbia University Press, 1997).

–, *Evil, Good, and Gender. Facets of the Feminine in Zoroastrian Religious History* (New York, NY: Peter Lang, 2002).

–, *Purity and Pollution in Zoroastrianism. Triumph over Evil* (Austin, TX: University of Texas Press, 1989).

Coakley, Sarah (ed.), *Religion and the Body* (Cambridge: Cambridge University Press, 1997).

Crone, Patricia, "Zoroastrian Communism," in *Comparative Studies in Society and History* 36/3 (Jul. 1994), pp. 447–62.

Curtis, Vesta S. and Sarah Stewart (eds.), *Birth of the Persian Empire* (London and New York: I.B. Tauris, 2005).

– (eds.), *The Sasanian Era. The Idea of Iran*, vol. III (London: I.B. Tauris, 2008).

Daryaee, Touraj, "Zoroastrianism under Islamic Rule," in *The Wiley Blackwell Companion to Zoroastrianism*, eds. Michael Strausberg Yuhan S.-D. Vevaina, (Chichester: Wiley Blackwell, 2015), pp. 103–118.

–, *Sasanian Persia. The Rise and Fall of an Empire* (London. I.B. Tauris, 2009).

Floor, Willem, "Judicial and Legal Systems. iv. Judicial System from the Advent of Islam through the 19th Century," in *Encyclopædia Iranica.*

Frenchkowski, Marco, "Christianity," in *The Wiley Blackwell Companion to Zoroastrianism*, eds. Michael Strausberg Yuhan S.-D. Vevaina, (Chichester: Wiley Blackwell, 2015), pp. 457–75.

Gould, Ketayun H., "Outside the Discipline, Inside the Experience: Women in Zoroastrianism," in *Religion and Women*, ed. Arvind Sharma (Albany, NY: SUNY Press, 1994), pp. 139–82.

Grenet, Frantz, "Religious Diversity among Sogdian Merchants in Six-Century China: Zoroastrianism, Buddhism, Manichaeism, and Hinduism," in *Comparative Studies of South Asia, Africa and the Middle East* 27/2 (2007), pp. 463–78.

Haug, Martin, *Essays on the Sacred Language, Writings, and Religion of the Parsis* (London: Kegan Paul, Trench, Trübner & Co. Ltd., 1907).

Herrenschmidt, Clarisse, "Once Upon a Time, Zoroaster," in *History and Anthropology* 3 (1987), pp. 209–37.

Hinnells, John R., "Ancient Persian Mythology," in *Persian Mythology* (London: Hamlyn, 1973), pp. 27–47.

–, *Persian Mythology* (London: Hamlyn, 1973).

Howard-Johnston, James, "State and Society in Late Antique Iran," in *The Sasanian Era. The Idea of Iran*, vol. III, eds. Vesta S. Curtis and Sarah Stewart (London: I.B. Tauris, 2008), pp. 118–31.

Hutter, Manfred, "Manichaeism in Iran," in *The Wiley Blackwell Companion to Zoroastrianism*, eds. Michael Strausberg Yuhan S.-D. Vevaina, (Chichester: Wiley Blackwell, 2015), pp. 477–89.

Huyse, Philip, "Late Sasanian Society between Orality and Literacy," in *The Sasanian Era. The Idea of Iran*, vol. III, eds. Vesta S. Curtis and Sarah Stewart (London: I.B. Tauris, 2008), pp. 140–55.

János, Jany, "The Four Sources of Law in Zoroastrian and Islamic Jurisprudence," in *Islamic Law and Society* 12/3 (2005), pp. 291–332.

–, *Judging in the Islamic, Jewish and Zoroastrian Legal Traditions. A Comparison of Theory and Practice* (Farnham: Ashgate, 2012).

de Jong, Albert, "Women and Ritual in Medieval Zoroastrianism," in *The Fire Within. Jamshid Soroush Soroushian Commemorative Volume.* Vol II: *(Ātaš-e Dorun) The Fire Within–in English & French*, eds. Carlo G. Cereti and Farrokh Vajifdar (New York: 1stbooks, 2003), pp. 147–61.

–, "Religion and Politics in Pre-Islamic Iran," in *The Wiley Blackwell Companion to Zoroastrianism*, eds. Michael Strausberg Yuhan S.-D. Vevaina, (Chichester: Wiley Blackwell, 2015), pp. 85–101.

–, "Purification in Absentia: On the Development of Zoroastrian Ritual Practice," in *Transformations of the Inner Self in Religious Traditions*, eds. Jan Assmann and Guy Stroumsa (Leiden: Brill, 1999), pp. 301–29.

Kiel, Yishai, *Sexuality in the Babylonian Talmud. Christian and Sasanian Contexts in Late Antiquity* (Cambridge: Cambridge University Press, 2016).

Kotwal, Dastur F. M. and James W. Boyd, *A Persian Offering. The Yasna: A Zoroastrian High Liturgy* (Paris: Association pour l'Avancement des Études Iraniennes, 1991).

Kreyenbroek, Philip G., "The Zoroastrian Priesthood After the Fall of the Sasanian Empire," in *Transition Periods in Iranian History: Actes du Symposium de Fribourg-en-Brisgau (22–24 mai 1985)*, ed. Philippe Gignoux (Leuven: Peeters, 1987), pp. 151–66.

–, "Cosmogony and Cosmology i. In Zoroastrianism/Mazdaism," in *Encyclopedia Iranica* (1993).

Lincoln, Bruce, "'The Earth Becomes Flat'–A Study of Apocalyptic Imagery," in *Comparative Studies in Society and History* 25/1 (Jan. 1983), pp. 136–53.

Maas, Michael, *Readings in Late Antiquity. A Sourcebook* (London and New York, NY: Routledge, 2000).

Macuch, Maria, Weber, Dieter and Desmond Durkin-Meisterernst (eds.), *Ancient and Middle Iranian Studies: Proceedings of the 6th European Conference of Iranian Studies* (Iranica, 19, Wiesbaden: Harrassowitz Verlag, 2010).

Macuch, Maria, "Incestuous Marriage in the Context of Sasanian Family Law," in *Ancient and Middle Iranian Studies. Proceedings of the 6th European Conference of Iranian Studies, held in Vienna, 18–22 September 2007*, eds. Maria Macuch, Dieter Weber and Desmond Durkin-Meisterernst (Wiesbaden: Harrassowitz Verlag, 2010), pp. 133–48.

–, "Der dastwar, 'auctor', im sasanidischen Zivilprozess," in *Archäologische Mitteilungen aus Iran* 21 (1988), pp. 177–88.

–, "Die Zeitehe im sasanidischen Recht–ein Vorläufer der šīᶜitischen mutᶜa-Ehe in Iran?," in *Archäologische Mitteilungen aus Iran* 18 (1985), pp. 187–203.

–, "Inzest im vorislamischen Iran," in *Archäologische Mitteilungen aus Iran* 24 (1991), pp. 141–54.

–, "The Hērbedestān as a Legal Source: A Section on the Inheritance of a Convert to Zoroastrianism," in *Bulletin of the Asia Institute*, New Series 19, Iranian and Zoroastrian Studies in Honor of Prods Oktor Skjærvø (2005), pp. 91–102.

–, "Familie. III. Iran, Sāsānidenperiode," in *Der Neue Pauly: Enzyklopädie der Antike*, vol. 4 (Stuttgart 1998), pp. 407–8.

–, "Frau. E. Iran, Sāsānidenperiode," in *Der Neue Pauly: Enzyklopädie der Antike*, vol. 4 (Stuttgart 1998), pp. 633–34.

–, "Barda and Barda-Dāri. ii. In the Sasanian Period," in *Encyclopædia Iranica*, vol. 3, pp. 763–66.

–, "Inheritance. i. Sasanian Period," in *Encyclopædia Iranica*, vol. 13, pp. 125–31.

–, "Judicial and Legal Systems. iii. Sasanian Legal System," in *Encyclopædia Iranica*, vol. 15, pp. 181–96.

–, "Mādayān ī Hazār Dādestān," in *Encyclopædia Iranica*.

–, "Ein mittelpersischer terminus technicus im syrischen Rechtskodex des Īšōᶜbōḫt und im sasanidischen Rechtsbuch," in *Hkmwt bnth byth: Studia semitica necnon iranica Rudolpho Macuch septuagenario ab amicis et discipulis dedicate*, eds. Maria Macuch, Christa Müller-Kessler and Bert. G. Fragner, (Wiesbaden: Otto Harrassowitz, 1989), pp. 149–60.

–, "Herrschaftskonsolidierung und sasanidisches Familienrecht: zum Verhältnis von Kirche und Staat unter den Sasaniden," in *Iran und Turfan. Beiträge Berliner Wissenschaftler. Werner Sundermann zum 60. Geburtstag gewidmet*, eds. Chr. Reck and P. Zieme (Iranica, 2, Wiesbaden 1995), pp. 149–67.

–, "Die sasanidische Stiftung 'für die Seele'–Vorbild für den islamischen waqf?," in *Iranian and Indo-European Studies. Memorial Volume of Otakar Klíma*, ed. P. Vavroušek (Praha 1994), pp. 163–80.

–, "The Pahlavi Model Marriage Contract in the Light of Sasanian Family Law," in *Iranian Languages and Texts from Iran and Turan. Ronald E. Emmerick Memorial Volume*, eds. Maria Macuch, Mauro Maggi and Werner Sundermann (Iranica, 13, Wiesbaden: Harrassowitz Verlag, 2007), pp. 183–204.

–, "Die sasanidische fromme Stiftung und der islamische waqf. Eine Gegenüberstellung," in *Islamische Stiftungen zwischen juristischer Norm und sozialer Praxis*, eds A. Meier, J. Pahlitzsch and L. Reinfandt (Berlin 2009), pp. 19–38.

–, "Substance and Fruit in the Sasanian Law of Property and the Babylonian Talmud," in *Proceedings of the Conference on "Talmudic Archeology," University College London, June 22–24, 2009* (Leiden: Brill, 2015), pp. 245–59.

–, "The Function of Temporary Marriage in the Context of Sasanian Family Law," in *Proceedings of the Fifth Conference of the Societas Iranologica Europaea held in Ravenna, October 6–11, 2003, vol.* I: *Ancient and Middle Iranian Studies*, eds. A. Panaino and A. Piras (Milano 2006), pp. 585–97.

–, "Zoroastrian Principles and the Structure of Kinship in Sasanian Iran," in *Religious Themes and Texts of pre-Islamic Iran and Central Asia. Studies in Honour of Professor Gherardo Gnoli on the Occasion of his 65th Birthday on 6 December 2002*, eds. Carlo G. Cereti, Mauro Maggi and Elio Provasi (Beiträge zur Iranistik, 24, Wiesbaden: Dr. Ludwig Reichert Verlag, 2003), pp. 231–45.

–, "The adwadād Offence in Zoroastrian Law," in *Shoshannat Yaakov. Jewish and Iranian Studies in Honor of Yaakov Elman*, eds. Shai Secunda and Steven Fine (The Brill Reference Library of Judaism, 35, Leiden and Boston, MA 2012), pp. 247–69.

–, "Law in Pre-Modern Zoroastrianism," in *The Wiley Blackwell Companion to Zoroastrianism*, eds. Michael Strausberg Yuhan S.-D. Vevaina, (Chichester: Wiley Blackwell, 2015), pp. 289–98.

–, "Sasanidische Institutionen in frühislamischer Zeit (Zusammenfassung)," in *Transition Periods in Iranian History: Actes du Symposium de Fribourg-en-Brisgau (22–24 Mai 1985)* (Studia Irania, 5, Leuven 1987), pp. 177–9.

Manekshaw, Sarosh J.H. and Pallan R. Ichaporia, *Proceedings of the Second North American Gatha Conference* (Houston, TX: Federation of Zoroastrian Associations of North America, 1996).

de Ménasce, R. P., "L'Église Mazdéenne dans l'Empire Sassanide," in *Cahiers d'Histoire Mondiale* 2/1 (1954), pp. 554–65.

Payne, Richard E., *A State of Mixture: Christians, Zoroastrians, and Iranian Political Culture in Late Antiquity* (Transformation of the Classical Heritage, 56, Oakland: University of California Press, 2015).

–, "Sex, Death, and Aristocratic Empire: Iranian Jurisprudence in Late Antiquity," in *Comparative Studies in Society and History* 58/2 (2016), pp. 519–49.

–, "East Syrian Bishops, Elite Households, and Iranian Law after the Muslim Conquest," in *Iranian Studies* 48/1 (2015), pp. 5–32.

–, "The Archaeology of Sasanian Politics," in *Journal of Ancient History* 2/2 (2014), pp. 80–92.

Pedersen, Claus V. and Fereydun Vahman, *Religious Texts in Iranian Languages* (Copenhagen: Det Kongelige Danske Videnskabernes Selskab, 2007).

Pigulevskaya, Nina V., "Die Sammlung der Syrischen Rechtsurkunden des Ischobocht und der Matikan," in *Akten des Vierundzwanzigsten Internationalen Orientalisten-Kongresses. München 28. August bis 4. September 1957*, ed. Herbert Franke (Wiesbaden: Franz Steiner, 1959), pp. 219–21.

Rezakhani, Khodadad, "Mazdakism, Manichaeism and Zoroastrianism: In Search of Orthodoxy and Heterodoxy in Late Antique Iran," in *Iranian Studies* 48/1, pp. 55–70.

Rose, Jenny, *Zoroastrianism. An Introduction* (London and New York, NY: I.B. Tauris, 2011).

Schelsky, Helmut, *Soziologie der Sexualität. Über die Beziehungen zwischen Geschlecht, Moral und Gesellschaft* (Hamburg: Rowohlt Taschenbuch Verlag, 1955).

Schippmann, Klaus, *Grundzüge der Geschichte des Sasanidischen Reiches* (Darmstadt: Wissenschaftliche Buchgesellschaft, 1990).

Secunda, Shai, "Talmudic Text and Iranian Context: On the Development of Two Talmudic Narratives," in *AJS Review* 33/1 (2009), pp. 45–69.

Shaked, Shaul, *Dualism in Transformation. Varieties of Religion in Sasanian Iran* (London: School of Oriental and African Studies, 1994).

–, "Eschatology i. In Zoroastrianism and Zoroastrian Influence," in *Encyclopedia Iranica* (1998).

–, "Religion in the late Sasanian Period: Eran, Aneran, and other Religious Designations," in *The Sasanian Era. The Idea of Iran*, vol. III, eds. Vesta S. Curtis and Sarah Stewart (London: I.B. Tauris, 2008), pp. 103–17.

–, "Islam," in *The Wiley Blackwell Companion to Zoroastrianism*, eds. Michael Strausberg Yuhan S.-D. Vevaina, (Chichester: Wiley Blackwell, 2015), pp. 491–8.

Sheffield, Daniel J., "The Wizirgerd ī Dēnīg and the Evil Spirit: Questions of Authenticity in Post-Classical Zoroastrianism," in *Bulletin of the Asia Institute* 19 (2009), pp. 181–9.

–, "Miracles in the Age of Mixed Iron: Sacred Narratives of Zarathustra in Islamic Iran and the Notion of Syncretism in Zoroastrianism." Unpublished manuscript, 2012, pp. 34–83.

Skjærvø, Prods O., "The Achaemenids and the Avesta," in *Birth of the Persian Empire*, eds. Vesta S. Curtis and Sarah Stewart (London and New York, NY: I.B. Tauris, 2005), pp. 52–84.

–, "Zarathustra: First Poet-Sacrificer," in *Paitimāna. Essays in Iranian, Indo-European, and Indian Studies in Honor of Hanns-Peter Schmidt*, ed. Siamak Adhami (Costa Mesa, CA: Mazda Publishers, 2003), pp. 157–94.

–, "The Literature of the Most Ancient Iranians," in *Proceedings of the Second North American Gatha Conference*, eds. Sarosh J.H. Manekshaw and Pallan R. Ichaporia (Houston, TX: Federation of Zoroastrian Associations of North America, 1996), pp. 221–35.

–, "The Avestan Yasna: Ritual and Myth," in *Religious Texts in Iranian Languages*, eds. Claus V. Pedersen and Fereydun Vahman (Copenhagen: Det Kongelige Danske Videnskabernes Selskab, 2007), pp. 57–84.

–, *The Spirit of Zoroastrianism* (New Haven, CT and London: Yale University Press, 2012).

Strausberg, Michael and Yuhan S.-D. Vevaina (eds.), *The Wiley Blackwell Companion to Zoroastrianism* (Chichester: Wiley Blackwell, 2015).

Vevaina, Yuhan S.-D., "Hubris and Himmelfahrt. The Narrative Logic of Kay Us' Ascent to Heaven in Pahlavi Literature," in *Ancient and Middle Iranian Studies: Proceedings of the 6th European Conference of Iranian Studies*, eds. Maria Macuch, Dieter Weber and Desmond Durkin-Meisterernst (Iranica, 19, Wiesbaden: Harrassowitz Verlag, 2010), pp. 231–43.

–, "'Enumerating the Dēn': Textual Taxonomies, Cosmological Deixis, And Numerological Speculations in Zoroastrianism," in *History of Religions* 50, pp. 111–43.

Williams, Alan, "Zoroastrians and Christians in Sasanian Iran," in *Bulletin of the John Rylands University of Manchester* 78/3 (1996), pp. 37–53.

–, "Zoroastrianism and the Body," in *Religion and the Body*, ed. Sarah Coakley (Cambridge: Cambridge University Press, 1997), pp. 155–66.

Yarshater, Ehsan (ed.), *The Cambridge History of Iran*, vol. 3 (1,2): *The Seleucid, Parthian and Sasanian Periods* (Cambridge: Cambridge University Press, 2008).

Young, William G., *Patriarch, Shah and Caliph* (Rawalpindi: Christian Study Centre, 1974).

B. East Syrian law

Primary sources

Ishoᶜbokht, *Syrische Rechtsbücher*, vol. III/1, *Corpus juris des persischen Erzbischofs Jesubocht*, ed. and tr. Eduard Sachau (Berlin: Verlag von Georg Reimer, 1914).

Mar Aba, *Syrische Rechtsbücher*, vol. III/3, *Eherecht des Patriarchen Mâr Abhâ*, ed. and tr. Eduard Sachau (Berlin: Verlag von Georg Reimer, 1914).

Synodicon Orientale ou Recueil de Synodes Nestoriens, ed. and tr. Jean B. Chabot (Paris: Imprimerie Nationale, 1902).

The New Oxford Annotated Bible. New Revised Standard Version with the Apocrypha. An Ecumenical Study Bible, eds. Michael D. Coogan, Marc Z. Brettler, Carol A. Newsom, and Pheme Perkins (Oxford: Oxford University Press, 2010).

Secondary literature

Aptowitzer, Victor, *Die Syrischen Rechtsbücher und das mosaisch-talmudische* Recht (Wien: Alfred Hölder, 1909).

–, "Die Rechtsbücher der syrischen Patriarchen und ihre Quellen," in *Wiener Zeitschrift für die Kunde des Morgenlandes* 24 (1910), pp. 180–224.

Aoun, Marc, "Jésubokt, Métropolitain et Juriste de l'Église d'Orient (Nestorienne). Auteur au VIIIe Siècle du Premier Traité Systématique de Droit Séculier," in *Tijdschrift voor Rechtsgeschiedenis* 73/1 (2005), pp. 81–92.

Baum, Wilhelm, "Shirin, christl. Großkönigin v. Persien († 628)," in *Bio-Bibliographisches Kirchenlexikon* 19 (2001).

Baum, Wilhelm and Dietmar W. Winkler, *The Church of the East. A Concise History* (London and New York, NY: RoutledgeCurzon, 2003).

Baumstark, Anton, *Geschichte der Syrischen Literatur mit Ausschluß der Christlich- Palästinensischen Texte* (Bonn: A. Marcus und E. Webers Verlag Dr. jur. Albert Ahn, 1922), pp. 215–6.

Börm, Henning and Josef Wiesehöfer (eds.), *Commutatio et Contention. Studies in the Late Roman, Sasanian, and Early Islamic Near East. In Memory of Zeev Rubin* (Reihe Geschichte, 3, Düsseldorf: Wellem Verlag, 2010).

Braun, Oscar, "Ein Beitrag zur Geschichte der persischen Gotteslehre," in *Zeitschrift der Deutschen Morgenländischen Gesellschaft* 57/3 (1903), pp. 562–5.

Brinner, William M. and Stephen D. Ricks (eds.), *Studies in Islamic and Judaic Traditions II, Papers Presented at the Institute for Islamic-Judaic Studies, Center for Judaic Studies, University of Denver* (Atlanta, GA: Scholars Press, 1986).

Brock, Sebastian P., "A Martyr at the Sasanian Court under Vahran II: Candida," in *Analecta Bollandiana* 96 (1978), pp. 167–81.

–, *A Brief Outline of Syriac Literature* (Kottayam: St. Ephrem Ecumenical Research Institute, 1997).

–, "Christians in the Sasanian Empire: A Case of Divided Loyalties," in *Religion and National Identity*, ed. Stuart Mews (Studies in Church History, 18, Oxford: Basil Blackwell, 1982), pp. 1–19.

Brown, Peter, *The Rise of Western Christendom. Triumph and Diversity, A.D. 200–1000* (Oxford: Wiley-Blackwell, 2013).

Bruns, Peter und Heinz Otto Luthe (eds.), *Sonderdruck auf Orientalia Christiana. Festschrift für Hubert Kaufhold zum 70. Geburtstag* (Wiesbaden: Harrassowitz Verlag, 2013).

Bruns, Peter, "Bischofswahl und Bischofsernennung im Synodicon Orientale," in *Episcopal Elections in Late Antiquity*, eds. Johan Leemans, Peter Van Nuffelen, Shawn W. J. Keough and Carla Nicolaye (Berlin and Boston, MA: Walter de Gruyter, 2011).

Camplani, Alberto and G. Filoramo (eds.), *Foundations of Power and Conflicts of Authority in Late-Antique Monasticism. Proceedings of the International Seminar. Turin, December 2–4, 2004* (Leuven, Paris and Dudley, MA: Uitgeverij Peeters en Deptartement Oosterse Studies, 2006).

Camplani, Alberto, "The Revival of Persian Monasticism (Sixth to Seventh Centuries): Church Structures, Theological Academy, and Reformed Monks," in *Foundations of Power and Conflicts of Authority in Late-Antique Monasticism. Proceedings of the International Seminar. Turin, December 2–4, 2004*, eds. A. Camplani and G. Filoramo (Leuven: Uitgeverij Peeters en Dept. Oosterse Studies, 2006), pp. 277–95.

Cereti, Carlo G. (ed.), *Iranian Identity in the Course of History*, (Rome, 2010).

Debié, Muriel, "Devenir Chrétien Dans l'Iran Sassanide: La Conversion à la Lumière des Récits Haiographiques," in *Le Problème de la Christianisation du Monde Antique. Actes du Colloque Organisé à l'Université de Paris Ouest, les 26, 27 et 28 Mai 2008*, eds. S. Destephen, H. Inglebert and B. Dumézil (Paris: Picard, 2010), pp. 329–58.

Destephen, S., Inglebert, H. and B. Dumézil (eds.), *Le Problème de la Christianisation du Monde Antique. Actes du Colloque Organisé à l'Université de Paris Ouest, les 26, 27 et 28 Mai 2008*, (Paris: Picard, 2010), pp. 329–58.

Duval, Rubens, *La Littérature Syriaque, Des Origines jusqu'a la Fin de cette Littérature après la Conquête par les Arabes aux XIIIe Siècle, Étude Historique des Différents Genres; La Littérature Religieuse et Ecclésiastique, l'Historiographie, la Philosophie, la Philologie, les Sciences et les Traductions, Suivie de Notices Biographiques sur les Écrivains avec un Index Bibliographique et Général, Troisième Édition, Revue et Augmenté* (Amsterdam: Philo Press), 1970.

Erhart, Victoria, "The Development of Syriac Christian Canon Law in the Sasanian Empire," in *Law, Society, and Authority in Late Antiquity*, ed. Ralph W. Mathisen (Oxford: Oxford University Press, 2001), pp. 115–29.

Gyselen, Rika (ed.), *Contribution à l'Histoire et la Géographie Historique de l'Empire Sassanide*, ed. Rika Gyselen (Res Orientales, 16, Bures-sur-Yvette: Groupe pour l'Étude de la Civilisation du Moyen-Orient, 2004).

Hartmann, Wilfried and Kenneth Pennington (eds.), *The History of Byzantine and Eastern Canon Law to 1500* (Washington, DC: The Catholic University of America Press, 2012).

Herman, Geoffrey (ed.), *Jews, Christians and Zoroastrians: Religious Dynamics in a Sasanian Context* (Piscataway, NJ: Gorgias Press, 2014).

Hess, Hamilton, *The Early Development of Canon Law and the Council of Serdica* (Oxford Early Christian Studies, Oxford: Oxford University Press, 2002).

Hoyland, Robert G., *Seeing Islam as Others Saw It: A Survey and Evaluation of Christian, Jewish and Zoroastrian Writings on Early Islam* (Studies in Late Antiquity and Early Islam, 13, Princeton, NJ: Darwin Press, 1997).

Hunter, Erica C.D., "Aramaic-Speaking Communities of Sasanid Mesopotamia," in *ARAM* 7 (1995), pp. 319–35.

Hutter, Manfred, "Mār Abā and the Impact of Zoroastrianism on Christianity in the 6th Century," in *Religious Themes and Texts of Pre-Islamic Iran and Central Asia. Studies in Honour of Professor Gherardo Gnoli on the Occasion of his 65th Birthday on 6th December 2002*, eds. Carlo G. Gereti, Mauro Maggi and Elio Provasi (Wiesbaden: Dr. Ludwig Reichert Verlag, 2003), pp. 167–73.

Jamali, Nima, "Book VI of Īšōᶜ-Bokht's Corpus Juris and the Emergence of Procedural Laws in the Church of the East," in *Journal of the Canadian Society for Syriac Studies* 17 (2017), 37–47.

Jugie, Martin, *Nestorius et la Controverse Nestorienne* (Paris: Gabriel Beauchesne, 1912).

Jullien, Christelle, "Contribution des Actes des Martyrs Perses á la Géographie Historique et á l'Administration de l'Empire Sassanide," in *Contribution à l'Histoire et la Géographie Historique de l'Empire Sassanide,* ed. Rika Gyselen (Res Orientales, 16, Bures-sur-Yvette: Groupe pour l'Étude de la Civilisation du Moyen-Orient, 2004), pp. 141–67.

–, "Peines et Supplices dans les Actes des Martyrs Persans et Droit Sassanide: Nouvelles Prospections," in *Studia Iranica* 33 (2004), pp. 243–69.

Kaufhold, Hubert, "Der Richter in den syrischen Rechtsquellen. Zum Einfluß islamischen Rechts auf die christlich-orientalische Rechtsliteratur," in *Oriens Christianus* 68 (1984), pp. 91–113.

–, "Sources of Canon Law in the Eastern Churches," in *The History of Byzantine and Eastern Canon Law to 1500,* eds. Wilfried Hartmann and Kenneth Pennington (Washington, DC: The Catholic University of America Press, 2012), pp. 215–342.

Kiperwasser, Reuven and Serge Ruzer, "To Convert a Persian and Teach Him the Holy Scriptures: A Zoroastrian Proselyte in Rabbinic and Syriac Christian Narratives," in *Jews, Christians and Zoroastrians: Religious Dynamics in a Sasanian Context*, ed. Geoffrey Herman (Piscataway, NJ: Gorgias Press, 2014), pp. 91–127.

Kozah, Mario et al. (eds.), *The Syriac Writers of Qatar in the Seventh Century* (Piscataway, NJ: Gorgias Press, 2014).

–, *An Anthology of Syriac Writers from Qatar in the Seventh Century* (Piscataway, NJ: Gorgias Press, 2015).

Leemans, Johan, Van Nuffelen, Peter, Keough, Shawn W. J. and Carla Nicolaye (eds.), *Episcopal Elections in Late Antiquity* (Berlin and Boston, MA: Walter de Gruyter, 2011).

Mathisen, Ralph W. (ed.), *Law, Society, and Authority in Late Antiquity* (Oxford: Oxford University Press, 2001).

McGuckin, John A., *St. Cyril of Alexandria. The Christological Controversy. Its History, Theology, and Texts* (Leiden, New York, NY, and Köln: E.J. Brill, 1994).

de Menasce, Jean-Pierre, "Some Pahlavi Words in the Original and in the Syriac Translation of Išōbōxt's Corpus Iuris," in *Dr. J. M. Unvala Memorial Volume*, Jamshedji Maneckji Unvala (Bombay: Kanga, 1964), pp. 6–11.

Mews, Stuart (ed.), *Religion and National Identity* (Studies in Church History, 18, Oxford: Basil Blackwell, 1982), pp. 1–19.

Nau, François, "Une ordonnance de Mar Aba, patriarche nestorien, relative aux emprêchements de mariage," in *Le Canoniste Contemporain* 23 (1900), pp. 20–27.

Panaino, Antonio C.D., "The Zoroastrian Incestuous Unions in Christian Sources and Canonical Laws: Their (Distorted) Aetiology and Some Other Problems," in *Cahiers de Studia Iranica* 36 (2008), pp. 69–87.

–, "The 'Persian' Identity in Religious Controversies. Again on the Case of the 'Divided Loyalty' in Sasanian Iran," in *Iranian Identity in the Course of History*, ed. Carlo G. Cereti (Rome, 2010), pp. 227–39.

Payne, Richard E., "Avoiding Ethnicity: Uses of the Ancient Past in Late Sasanian Northern Mesopotamia," in *Visions of Community in the Post-Roman World. The West, Byzantium and the Islamic World, 300–1100*, eds. Walter Pohl, Clemens Gantner and Richard Payne (Farnham: Ashgate, 2012), pp. 205–21.

Penn, Michael Philip, *When Christians First Met Muslims, A Sourcebook of the Earliest Syriac Writings on Islam* (Oakland, CA: University of California Press, 2015).

Pigulevskaya, Nina V., "Die Sammlung der Syrischen Rechtsurkunden des Ischobocht und der Matikan," in *Akten des vierundzwanzigsten Internationalen Orientalisten-Kongresses. München 28. August bis 4. September 1957*, ed. Herbert Franke (Wiesbaden: Franz Steiner, 1959), pp. 219–21.

Pohl, Walter, Gantner, Clemens and Richard Payne (eds.), *Visions of Community in the Post-Roman World. The West, Byzantium and the Islamic World, 300–1100* (Farnham: Ashgate, 2012).

Rancillac, Philippe, "Des Origines du Droit Musulman à la Risala d'al-Shafiʿi," in *Mélanges de l'Institut Dominicain d'Études Orientales du Caire* 13 (1977), pp. 147–69.

Rehatsek, Edward, "Christianity in the Persian Dominions, from its Beginning till the Fall of the Sasanian Dynasty," in *Journal of the Bombay Branch of the Royal Asiatic Society* 13 (1878), pp. 18–108.

Selb, Walter, *Orientalisches Kirchenrecht*, vol. 1: *Die Geschichte des Kirchenrechts der Nestorianer (von den Anfängen bis zur Mongolenzeit)* (Wien: Verlag der Österreichischen Akademie der Wissenschaften, 1981).

Simonsohn, Uriel I., *A Common Justice. The Legal Allegiances of Christians and Jews under Early Islam* (Philadelphia, PA: University of Pennsylvania Press, 2011).

–, "Communal Boundaries Reconsidered: Jews and Christians Appealing to Muslim Authorities in the Medieval Near East," in *Jewish Studies Quarterly* 14 (2007), pp. 328–63.

–, "The Christians Whose Force is Hard: Non-Ecclesiastical Judicial Authorities in the Early Islamic Period," in *Journal of the Economic and Social History of the Orient* 53/4 (2010), pp. 579–620.

–, "'Halting Between Two Opinions': Conversion and Apostasy in Early Islam," in *Medieval Encounters* 19 (2013), pp. 342–70.

Van Rompay, L., "Isho'bokht of Rev Ardashir," in *Gorgias Encyclopedic Dictionary of the Syriac Heritage*, eds. Sebastian Brock et al. (Piscataway, NJ: Gorgias Press, 2011), p. 216.

Walker, Joel T., "Ascetic Literacy: Books and Readers in East-Syrian Monastic Tradition," in *Commutatio et Contention. Studies in the Late Roman, Sasanian, and Early Islamic Near East. In Memory of Zeev Rubin*, eds. Henning Börm and Josef Wiesehöfer (Reihe Geschichte, 3, Düsseldorf: Wellem Verlag, 2010), pp. 307–45.

–, "Against the Eternity of the Stars: Disputation and Christian Philosophy in Late Sasanian Mesopotamia," in *Convegno Internazionale. La Persia e Bisanzio (Roma, 14–18 Ottobre 2002)*, eds. Antonio Carile et al. (Rome 2004), pp. 509–37.

Weitz, Lev E., "Syriac Christians in the Medieval Islamic World: Law, Family, and Society" (PhD diss., Princeton University, 2013), accessed July 2, 2017, http://arks.princeton.edu/ark:/88435/dsp01ng451h571.

Widengren, Geo, "The Nestorian Church in Sasanian and Early Post-Sasanian Iran," in *Incontro di Religioni in Asia tra il III e il X Secolo d.C.*, ed. Lionello Lanciotti (Firenze: Leo S. Olschki Editore, 1984), pp. 1–30.

Winkler, Dietmar W., "Zur Rezeption ‚Ökumenischer Konzilien' am Beispiel der persischen und armenischen Kirche," in *Sonderdruck auf Orientalia Christiana. Festschrift für Hubert Kaufhold zum 70. Geburtstag*, eds. Peter Bruns und Heinz Otto Luthe (Wiesbaden: Harrassowitz Verlag, 2013), pp. 615–36.

C. Early Islamic law

Primary sources

al-Balādhūrī, Abū al-Ḥasan Aḥmad b. Yaḥyā b. Jābir, *Futūḥ al-Buldān* (Bayrūt: Dār al-Kutub al-ʿIlmīya, 1971).

al-Shāfiʿī, Muḥammad b. Idrīs, *Al-Shāfiʿī's Risāla, Treatise on the Foundations of Islamic Jurisprudence*, tr. Majid Khadduri (The Islamic Texts Society [1961?]).

al-Shāfiʿī, Muḥammad b. Idrīs, *The Epistle on Legal Theory. Muḥammad ibn Idrīs al-Shāfiʿī*, ed. and tr. J.E. Lowry (New York, NY and London: New York University Press, 2013).

al-Tanūkhī, Saḥnūn b. Saʿīd, *al-Mudawwana al-Kubrā*, ed. Aḥmad ʿAbdal-Salām, 5 vols. (Beirut: Dār al-Kutub al-ʿIlmīya, 1994).

The Qur'an, tr. Tarif Khalidi (London: Penguin Classics, 2008).

Secondary literature

Abū Ṭālib, Ṣūfī Ḥasan, *Bayna al-Sharīʿa al-Islāmīya wa-l-Qānūn al-Rūmānī* (al-Qāhira: Maktabat Nahḍat Miṣr).

Adham, Muṣṭafā Munīr, *Riḥlat al-Imām al-Shāfiʿī ilā Miṣr* (Miṣr: Maṭbaʿat Amīn ʿAbd al-Raḥmān, 1930).

Al-Azmeh, Aziz (ed.), *Islamic Law, Social and Historical Contexts* (London and New York, NY: Routledge, 1988).

Ali, Kecia, *Marriage and Slavery in Early Islam* (Cambridge, MA and London: Harvard University Press, 2010).

Bergsträßer, G., "Anfänge und Charakter des Juristischen Denkens im Islam," in *Der Islam* 14 (1925), pp. 76–81.

Bernards, Monique and John Nawas, *Patronate and Patronage in early and classical Islam* (Leiden and Boston, MA: Brill, 2005).

Borrut, Antoine, *Entre Mémoire at Pouvoir. L'Espace Syrien Sous les Derniers Omeyyades et les Premiers Abbasides (v. 72–193/692–809)* (Leiden and Boston, MA: Brill, 2011).

– and Fred M. Donner (eds.), *Christians and Others in the Umayyad State* (Chicago, IL: The Oriental Institute of the University of Chicago, 2016).

Brinner, William M. and Stephen D. Ricks (eds.), *Studies in Islamic and Judaic Traditions II, Papers Presented at the Institute for Islamic-Judaic Studies, Center for Judaic Studies, University of Denver* (Atlanta, GA: Scholars Press, 1986).

Calder, Norman, "History and Nostalgia: Reflections on John Wansbrough's 'The Sectarian Milieu,'" in *Method & Theory in the Study of Religion* 9/1 (1997), pp. 47–73.

Chaumont, Éric, “Al-Shāfiʿī,” in *EI*², eds. P. Bearman et al.

Crone, Patricia and Martin Hinds, *God’s Caliph. Religious Authority in the First Centuries of Islam* (Cambridge: Cambridge University Press, 1986).

Crone, Patricia, *Roman, Provincial and Islamic Law, The Origins of the Islamic Patronate* (Cambridge: Cambridge University Press, 1987).

–, *Slaves on Horses. The Evolution of the Islamic Polity* (Cambridge: Cambridge University Press, 1980).

von Denffer, Dietrich, “Mutʿa–Ehe oder Prostitution? Beitrag zur Untersuchung des šiʿitischen Islam,” in *Zeitschrift der Deutschen Morgenländischen Gesellschaft* 128/2 (1978), pp. 299–325.

Dutton, Yasin, *The Origins of Islamic Law: The Qur’an, the Muwattaʿ and Madinan ʿAmal* (Richmond Surrey: Curzon, 1999).

El Shamsy, Ahmed, “From tradition to law: The origins and early development of the Shāfi'ī school of law in ninth-century Egypt” (PhD diss., Harvard University, 2009), accessed August 19, 2017, https://search-proquest-com.ezproxy.cul.columbia.edu/docview/304889761?accountid=10226.

–, *The Canonization of Islamic Law. A Social and Intellectual History*, Cambridge: Cambridge University Press, 2013.

Fitzgerald, S.V., “The Alleged Debt of Islamic to Roman Law,” in *The Law Quarterly Review* 67 (1951), pp. 81–102.

Goldziher, Ignaz, *Introduction to Islamic Theology and Law* (Princeton, NJ: Princeton University Press, 1981 [1910]).

Hallaq, Wael B., *An Introduction to Islamic Law* (Cambridge: Cambridge University Press, 2009).

–, *Restating Orientalism. A Critique of Modern Knowledge* (New York, NY: Columbia University Press, 2018).

–, *The Origins and Evolution of Islamic Law* (Cambridge: Cambridge University Press, 2004).

Hourani, George F., “Islamic and Non-Islamic Origins of Muʿtazilite Ethical Rationalism,” in *International Journal of Middle East Studies* 7/1 (1976), pp. 59–87.

Hoyland, Robert G., *In God’s Path. The Arab Conquests and the Creation of an Islamic Empire* (Oxford: Oxford University Press, 2015).

Jokisch, Benjamin, *Islamic Imperial Law, Harun-Al-Rashid’s Codification Project* (Berlin and New York, NY: Walter de Gruyter, 2007).

Lewis, Bernard, *Race and Slavery in the Middle East. An Historical Enquiry* (New York, NY and Oxford: Oxford University Press, 1990).

Lodi, Zaka’ur Rahman Khan, “A Study of the Status of the Married Woman in Roman Law, English Common Law, Church Law and Islamic Law,” in *The Islamic Review & Arab Affairs* 58/10–1 (1970), pp. 26–9.

Lowry, J.E., "The Legal Hermeneutics of al-Shāfiʿī and Ibn Qutayba: A Reconsideration," in *Islamic Law and Society* 11/1 (2004), pp. 1–41.

Margoliouth, David S., "The Sense of the Title Khalīfah," in *A Volume of Oriental Studies. Presented to Edward G. Browne, M.A., M.B., F.B.A., F.R.C.P. Sir Thomas Adams's Professor of Arabic in the University of Cambridge on his 60th Birthday (7 February 1922)*, eds. T. W. Arnold and Reynold A. Nicholsen (Cambridge: Cambridge University Press, 1922), pp. 322–8.

Mitter, Ulrike, "Origins and Development of the Islamic Patronate," in *Patronate and Patronage in early and classical Islam*, eds. Monique Bernards and John Nawas (Leiden and Boston, MA: Brill, 2005), 70-133.

Mundy, Martha, "The Family, Inheritance, and Islam: A Re-Examination of the Sociology of Farāʾiḍ Law," in *Islamic Law, Social and Historical Contexts*, ed. Aziz Al-Azmeh (London and New York, NY: Routledge, 1988), pp. 1–123.

Oßwald, Rainer, *Das islamische Sklavenrecht* (40, Mitteilungen zur Sozial- und Kulturgeschichte der islamischen Welt, Würzburg: Ergon Verlag, 2017).

Paret, Rudi, "Ḫalīfat Allāh–Vicarius Dei. Ein differenzierender Vergleich," in *Mélanges d'Islamologie. Volume dédié à la Mémoire de Armand Abel par ses collègues, ses élèves et ses amis*, ed. Salmon Pierre Salmon (Leiden: E. J. Brill, 1974), pp. 224–32.

Pipes, Daniel, "Mawlas: Freed Slaves and Converts in Early Islam," in *Slavery and Abolition* 1/2 (1980), pp. 132–77.

Rabb, Intisar A, *Doubt in Islamic Law. A History of Legal Maxims, Interpretation and Islamic Criminal Law* (New York, NY: Cambridge University Press, 2015).

Rohe, Matthias, *Islamic Law in Past and Present* (Leiden: Brill, 2015).

Sachedina, Abdulaziz, "Early Muslim Traditionists and Their Familiarity with Jewish Sources," in *Studies in Islamic and Judaic Traditions II, Papers Presented at the Institute for Islamic-Judaic Studies, Center for Judaic Studies, University of Denver*, eds. William M. Brinner and Stephen D. Ricks (Atlanta, GA: Scholars Press, 1986), pp. 49–59.

Savant, Sarah Bowen, *The New Muslims of Post-Conquest Iran, Tradition, Memory, and Conversion* (Cambridge: Cambridge University Press, 2013).

Schacht, Joseph, *An Introduction to Islamic Law* (Oxford: Clarendon Press, 1964).

–, "Foreign Elements in Ancient Islamic Law," in *Journal of Comparative Legislation and International Law* 32/3-4 (1950), pp. 9–17.

–, *The Origins of Muhammadan Jurisprudence* (Oxford: Clarendon Press, 1950).

Schneider, Irene, *Kinderverkauf und Schuldknechtschaft. Untersuchungen zur frühen Phase des islamischen Rechts* (Stuttgart: Steiner, 1999).
Urban, Elizabeth,"The early Islamic mawālī: a window onto processes of identity construction and social change" (PhD diss., University of Chicago, 2012), accessed August 18, 2017, https://search.proquest.com/docview/1027764937? accountid= 8555.
Watt, W. Montgomery, "God's Caliph. Qur'ānic Interpretations and Umayyad Claims," in *Iran and Islam. In Memory of the late Vladimir Minorsky*, ed. C.E. Bosworth (Edinburgh: Edinburgh University Press, 1971), pp. 565–74.
Wegner, Judith Romney, "Islamic and Talmudic Jurisprudence: The Four Roots of Islamic Law and Their Talmudic Counterparts," in *The American Journal of Legal History* 26/1 (1982), pp. 25–71.
Wüstenfeld, Ferdinand, *Der Imâm el-Schâfi'í seine Schüler und Anhänger bis zum J. 300 d. H.* (Göttingen: Dieterich'sche Verlags-Buchhandlung, 1890).

Index